The Complete Book of Business and Legal Forms

Lynne Ann Frasier

Sourcebooks Inc.
Naperville, Illinois

Published by: **Sourcebooks, Inc.**
P.O. Box 372, Naperville, Illinois 60566
(630) 961-3900
FAX: 630-961-2168

This publication is designed to provide accurate and authoritative information in regard to the subject matter covered. It is sold with the understanding that the publisher is not engaged in rendering legal, accounting, or other professional service. If legal advice or other expert assistance is required, the services of a competent professional person should be sought.

From a Declaration of Principles Jointly Adopted by a Committee of the American Bar Association and a Committee of Publishers and Associations

Library of Congress Cataloging-in-Publication Data

Frasier, Lynne Ann,
The complete book of business & legal forms / by Lynne Ann Frasier.
p. cm. -- (Small business sourcebooks)
ISBN 1-57071-112-7 (pbk.)
1. Commercial law--United States--Forms. 2. Small business--law and legislation--United States--Forms. 3. Forms (Law)--United States. I. Title. II. Series.
KF886.F73 1996
346.73 ' 07 ' 0269--dc20
[347.30670269] 96-33709
CIP

Printed and bound in the United States of America.

Paperback — 10 9 8 7 6 5 4 3

Contents

Section II: Business Letters  169

Introduction

The Complete Book of Business and Legal Forms offers you, the entrepreneur or company manager, useful action letters, complete legal agreements, and the most sought-after government forms used in business today, as well as tips for using these essential letters, agreements, and forms.

Following this Introduction is the *Legal Audit Questionnaire* which is designed to make you aware of legal issues and risks. By answering these questions, you will be in a better position to adopt safer, more productive, and more beneficial ways of conducting your business. You can answer the questions in the Legal Audit section and skip to the back of the book to review your answers in Section IV, or you can jump right into the first section.

Section I begins with *Questions Designed to Make You a Better Entrepreneur*. These nine situational questions are guaranteed to make you twist and turn as you answer difficult multiple choice questions designed to test your current entrepreneurial ability. After you answer these questions, you will see how easy it is to turn a good deal into a bad one and will be eager to dive into the form-by-form descriptions which follow this quiz.

The form-by-form descriptions of the agreements in Section I will tell you what they mean, how they may apply to you and your business, and when to use them.

Following these descriptions, Section I offers *Tips for Drafting, Negotiating, and Entering Into Agreements*. These tips are designed to make you "think like a lawyer." As a result, your agreements will better reflect your intentions and you should make better deals.

Finally, the heart of Section I is the collection of the most important legal agreements for today's business world. While each agreement will differ in its purpose and specific contents, most will contain many of the same clauses, called "boilerplate."

Boilerplate is commonly called the "small print" and sometimes is presented in the color gray or on the back of the document. Too many times, it is the boilerplate that puts the owner out of business. With the explanations presented in Section I, you will understand the effect of boilerplate, and will therefore know how to use it to your advantage.

Section I continues with the most popular legal forms and agreements common to any successful business. The agreements presented in this section are encompassing and indispensable. They are clear, concise, and straightforward, and have been carefully drafted by a business attorney who handles these matters on a day-to-day basis. All of the agreements and forms have proven effective at helping businesses of all types and sizes.

The first group of agreements will help you set up or purchase a business. The next group deals with documents needed to maintain confidentiality of business affairs and trade secrets. Following that, Section I presents essential employment documents vital to the success of any business with employees. It continues with a variety of business relationship agreements, like consulting, independent contracting, and specially commissioned agreements. Finally, Section I offers examples of promissory notes and ends with forms to help you protect your intellectual property.

The entrepreneur or manager who cannot afford to hire an attorney to draft an agreement from scratch can benefit from these forms and agreements. Consult the Table of Contents to locate a form or agreement that would be useful in a particular situation and adapt it to your situation at hand. To be savvy and thorough, take the finished product to an attorney for a quick review to ensure the document is in compliance with applicable laws.

Many entrepreneurs and company managers sign preprinted forms because of the legitimacy of print—they think that the printed word is set in concrete. They do not realize that they can add, amend, or cross out the preprinted form. As a result, they end up with an onerous situation which may lead them straight into bankruptcy.

The agreements in Section I are designed to provide you with the tools necessary to avoid or reduce the chances of ending up in a bad deal.

Section II will save you time, money, and often most importantly, headaches. By using the letters in this section, you will not have to spend countless hours trying to find the right words to express your thoughts. Instead, you will be able to send off, in less than five minutes, an effective letter that will help you get what you intended.

In addition, Section II includes *Tips for Letter Writing*. These tips are designed to help you get your desired results and increase your chances of success. Then Section II shows examples of crisp, clear, and concise business letters designed to help you get the best results for handling the most difficult business challenges facing entrepreneurs and business managers today.

These letters are carefully drafted and have been proven in the real world. They increase your chances of obtaining better outcomes in what are often touchy situations. Without them, you risk spending too much time producing a result which could hurt rather than help your business.

Most of the letters presented in Section II involve matters affecting every business owner or manager at one time or another. For example, every entrepreneur will sooner or later need to collect some payment due the company. Section II has three letters for making such requests. The first is a friendly reminder, the second is a general statement of collection, and the third shows how to get tough when you need to.

Many times, sending a simple letter like the ones presented here will resolve the matter entirely. For this reason, Section II will assist you not only in saving costs and retaining a greater profit for your business, but also in allowing you to focus your time and attention on more positive aspects of the business—like making sales and adding to the bottom line to keep your company prosperous.

Business letters are important. Unfortunately, such letters are often drafted in a hurry and some never get out at all. The business owner who ignores writing such a letter invites a bigger problem later on.

With the models of letters presented in Section II, you don't have to take such risks. All you have to do is consult the Table of Contents to locate a letter that would be useful in your particular situation and adapt it to your circumstances.

Section III comprises the most widely-used and important governmental forms that a business owner or manager will ever need. It includes forms in every area from intellectual property to the most popular and necessary business transaction forms.

Once again, Section III will help you handle the occasionally maddening realities of dealing with the government with *Tips for Obtaining and Preparing Government Forms*. Follow these tips and you will enhance your chances of success in dealing with government agencies. Those who do not follow these tips will do so at their peril.

Section III includes forms for the four most common types of U.S. copyright registration and both federal and state trademark registration. These registrations are often critical for any business which plans on staying around for awhile.

It also includes business transaction forms like a form for obtaining a "dba" to conduct business under a different name, followed by a form to obtain the federal employer identification number—which is the number generally needed to open a bank account in the business name. The business owner who uses the forms presented in this section could save hundreds and even thousands of dollars in attorney's fees.

Section IV offers answers to the Legal Audit Questionnaire. You will be able to analyze whether your business records are in order and in compliance with regulatory requirements as well as whether your business policies, procedures, and practices might expose your company to legal risks and future litigation and challenges.

The Appendix lists telephone numbers of 50 state agencies, plus the District of Columbia, which handle incorporation and state trademarks.

By following the templates of business letters, agreements, and forms in *The Complete Book of Business and Legal Forms*, you will be able to save time, eliminate confusion, and avoid unnecessary costs in managing your business.

The advantages of owning or managing a successful business are plentiful. *The Complete Book of Business and Legal Forms* is intended to be useful to the reader who wants to save time and costs in running his or her business, as well as those interested in reducing risks of litigation and penalties.

Whether you are well-versed in governmental or legal affairs or have limited knowledge in these areas, you will find *The Complete Book of Legal and Business Forms* helpful.

However, keep in mind that this book, as with any form book, must be used as a guideline. It is not intended to render legal, accounting, or other professional advice. If legal advice or other expert assistance is required, you should seek the services of competent professionals.

Although much care has been taken to ensure the accuracy and adaptability of the materials in this book, the author assumes no liability to any party for loss or damage caused by errors or omissions contained in this book whether such errors or omissions are the result of negligence or otherwise. Additionally, the author and publisher make no warranty that the suggestions and forms are suitable for all business circumstances.

However, this book has been carefully prepared and the legal documents contained in it—when used properly—provide the business owner, manager, or start-up entrepreneur with the most up-to-date legal document guidelines necessary to running a successful business.

Dedication

To my husband, Roland, and my furry and feathery kids, Napa, Sonoma, Misty, and Casper.

Acknowledgments

Special thanks to Dominique Raccah, my publisher, Todd Stocke, my editor, and Renee Calomino, my publicist, who have added so much of the mortar and substance to this book and my career as an author.

Thanks to Roland Frasier, III, my husband and partner in life and in law, for encouraging me to write and for standing by me in all of my endeavours.

Thanks also to my family, Tony and Marlene Maraschiello, Debbie and Frank James, Jane Maraschiello, Juanita Freasier, and Roland Freasier, Jr. for reading the endless drafts of material I present to them.

Lastly, thanks to Davida Jeppson, for copying, faxing, proofreading, and doing all the extraordinary things to help bring this book to the bookshelves.

I appreciate all of you and know that it takes a winning team to succeed in any business.

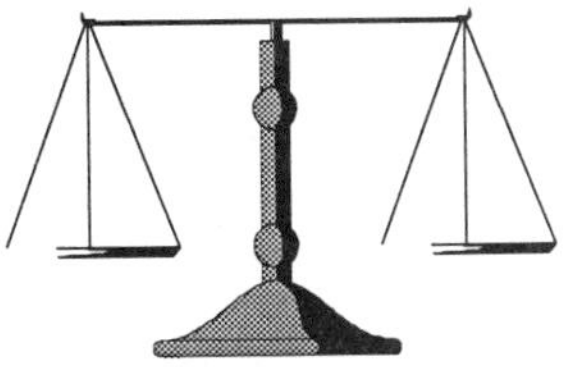

Legal Audit Preventative Maintenance Program

What is a legal audit? A legal audit is preventative law. It is a review of your business designed to reduce the risk of a crisis. If performed carefully and accurately, the legal audit will provide the following information:

1. A determination of whether your business records are in proper order and generally in compliance with applicable regulatory requirements.

2. A review of your business structure to identify tax strategies and asset protection opportunities which may have been overlooked in the past.

3. A determination of whether tangible and intangible business assets are properly protected against casualty and misappropriation.

4. A way to identify current policies, procedures, and practices which might expose your business to legal risks and future litigation and penalties.

Why should you conduct a legal audit for your company? A legal audit is designed to make you aware of legal issues and risks. Once aware, you are in a better position to adopt safer, more productive, and more beneficial ways of conducting your business. An audit will save you time, headaches, and money by reducing the likelihood of litigation caused by implementing poorly conceived ideas.

The time you spend on the audit will be time spent on determining how to acquire a new business, how to develop better services and products, how to protect what has been developed, and how to expand the affairs of the business rather than fight fires caused by haphazard implementation and operation.

What can you expect from a legal audit? Among others, the following problems may be exposed during your legal audit:

1. Marketing practices that hinder your business, such as product liability exposure, poorly drafted or infringing advertising materials, or violations of consumer protection laws.

2. Employment practices that violate EEOC, labor, environmental, or safety regulations.

3. Potential loss of copyright, trademark, or patent rights because of the lack of registration with the proper government agency.

4. Inappropriate business structuring which causes a loss in business revenue.

5. Lack of or inadequate insurance to cover essential activities of running a successful business.

6. Director and insider exposure to state and federal securities violations due to lack of proper instruction.

7. Poorly drafted agreements and documents which can hinder more than help your business.

8. Potential exposure because of noncompliance with regulatory agencies.

9. Inappropriate documentation and record keeping.

10. Needless payment of hundreds or thousands of dollars which could have been avoided had the proper procedures been in place.

How does the legal audit work? The legal audit is not a test. You cannot pass or fail. You can only learn more about the way you are conducting business. Simply start on the next page with the first category. Start with whichever entity applies to your situation and answer the questions in that category. Continue answering the questions until you have answered all 98 questions in the 7 essential categories. After you have finished the questionnaire, turn to the back of the book and compare your answers, or continue with the forms, letters, and documents in the book, saving your comparisons until the end.

What should you do after you complete the legal audit questionnaire? Review your answers and begin working on the areas most lacking in your business. This will immediately reduce your company's exposure. Once you get the challenging areas on track, reducing the company's risks of exposure, pay attention to all your business affairs and handle them appropriately. If you do, you could save thousands of dollars by avoiding future fines, litigation costs, and damage awards. If you do not maintain good business practices, you will undoubtedly encounter a breakdown of your system and sooner or later will end up in litigation or paying needless penalties. Do not allow this to happen to you. More business losses could have been prevented had the business owner only taken the time to institute a procedure such as the legal audit.

LEGAL AUDIT QUESTIONNAIRE

A. Form of Business

1. Sole Proprietorship

a. Has the company applied for a Business License? Yes ________ No __________
b. Has the company obtained a Resale Permit? Yes ________ No __________
c. Has the company filed a Fictitious Name Statement in the county where the business is located? Yes ________ No __________
d. Has the company obtained a Federal Employer Identification Number (FEIN)? Yes ________ No __________

2. Partnership

a. Has the partnership recorded a Notice of Partnership in the county where the partnership is located? Yes ________ No __________
b. Have the partners signed a written Partnership Agreement? Yes ________ No __________
c. Has the partnership applied for a Business License? Yes ________ No __________
d. Has the partnership obtained a Resale Permit? Yes ________ No __________
e. Has the partnership obtained its Federal Employer Identification Number (FEIN)? Yes ________ No __________
f. Has the partnership filed a Fictitious Business Name Statement in the county where the partnership is located? Yes ________ No __________

3. Corporation

a. Is a copy of the Articles of Incorporation in the corporate minute book? Yes ________ No __________
b. Have you checked into the benefits of electing Subchapter S status? Yes ________ No __________
c. Is a copy of the corporate bylaws in the corporate minute book? Yes ________ No __________
d. Are copies of the incorporating documents in the corporate minute book? Yes ________ No __________
e. Are the original shares certificates in the corporate minute book or in a safe place? Yes ________ No __________
f. Have all shareholders signed a Shareholders' Agreement? Yes ________ No __________
g. Are the corporate annual minutes prepared each year? Yes ________ No __________
h. Are the corporate annual statements filed with the applicable state agency each year? Yes ________ No __________
i. Has the corporation obtained its Federal Employer Identification Number (FEIN)? Yes ________ No __________

j. Has the corporation applied for a Business License? Yes _______ No _________
k. Has the corporation obtained a Resale Permit? Yes _______ No _________
l. Has the corporation filed a Fictitious Business Name Statement in the county where the business is located? Yes _______ No _________
m. If the corporation is doing business in a different state than where incorporated, has it filed for Foreign Registration in the state where it is doing business? Yes _______ No _________

4. Prior Business Entities

a. Is the business a continuation of a previous business? Yes _______ No _________

B. Employment Considerations

1. Written Agreements, Handbooks, and Manuals

a. Does the company use written employment agreements? Yes _______ No _________
b. Are at-will employees informed of their at-will status in a written agreement? Yes _______ No _________
c. Does the company have a written employee handbook? Yes _______ No _________
d. If so, are the terms of the handbook followed consistently on a day-to-day basis? Yes _______ No _________
e. Are employees required to sign a statement acknowledging that they received the handbook? Yes _______ No _________
f. Does the company have a written policies and procedures manual? Yes _______ No _________
g. If so, are the terms of the policies and procedures manual followed day-by-day? Yes _______ No _________
h. Are employees required to sign a statement acknowledging that they received the manual and agree to its terms? Yes _______ No _________
i. Are employees with access to company trade secrets or confidential information required to sign Confidentiality Agreements? Yes _______ No _________
j. Does the company have agreements with employees regarding the ownership of ideas and inventions developed by them in the course of their employment? Yes _______ No _________
k. Does the company have agreements restricting employees from working for competitors after leaving the company? Yes _______ No _________

2. Equal Employment Opportunity

a. Does the company have pending EEO-type complaints? Yes _______ No _________
b. Does the company use standard forms and procedures for interviewing, hiring, and firing? Yes _______ No _________

c. If yes, have the forms and written policies been reviewed by legal counsel? Yes _______ No _________
d. Does the company prepare and keep on file written employee performance reviews? Yes _______ No _________
e. Does the company prepare and consistently use written employee warnings? Yes _______ No _________
f. If yes, have such documents and policies been reviewed by legal counsel? Yes _______ No _________

3. Labor Regulations

a. Is the company working within the Fair Labor Standards Act provisions for equal pay and hours? Yes _______ No _________
b. Is the company operating in compliance with the Americans w/ Disabilities Act and corresponding state law? Yes _______ No _________
c. Is the company operating in compliance with the Family Leave Act and corresponding state law? Yes _______ No _________
d. Do company pension plans comply with the Internal Revenue Service and ERISA? Yes _______ No _________
e. Does the company have any outstanding workers' compensation claims? Yes _______ No _________

4. Employee vs. Independent Contractor

a. Does the company use the services of independent contractors for consulting services or supplemental labor? Yes _______ No _________
b. If so, are agreements with contractors in writing? Yes _______ No _________
c. If the company hires independent contractors, has it checked the Internal Revenue Service factors to make sure they will not be misclassified as employees by the IRS? Yes _______ No _________

C. Goods and Distribution

1. Pricing and General Distribution

a. Does the company sell from a price list? Yes _______ No _________
b. Does the company sell through distributors or independent sales representatives? Yes _______ No _________
c. Does the company have written distribution or sales representative agreements with these individuals? Yes _______ No _________
d. Does the company have agreements for international distribution? Yes _______ No _________
e. Have both the domestic and international agreements been reviewed by legal counsel? Yes _______ No _________

2. Product Safety and Warranties

a. Is someone at the company familiar with product safety and government standards in your industry? Yes _______ No _________
b. Does the company have written policies and procedures for personnel to voice product safety concerns? Yes _______ No _________
c. Has the company received any product safety complaints or notices from personnel? Yes _______ No _________
d. Does the company offer consumer product warranties? Yes _______ No _________

3. Confidentiality

a. Has the company taken steps to assure confidentiality of new products while they are being developed? Yes _______ No _________
b. Have procedures and agreements regarding trade secrets been reviewed by legal counsel? Yes _______ No _________

4. Copyright, Trademark, Patent, and Trade Secret Protection

a. Have copyright registrations been obtained for company-owned works of authorship? Yes _______ No _________
b. Have trademark registrations been obtained for company names and marks? Yes _______ No _________
c. Have patents been obtained for company-owned inventions, design works, and discoveries? Yes _______ No _________
d. Has a trade secret program been put into effect? Yes _______ No _________
e. Have intellectual property and trade secret issues been reviewed by legal counsel? Yes _______ No _________

5. Advertising and Media

a. Have company advertising and copy graphics been reviewed with legal counsel? Yes _______ No _________
b. Do company advertisements, marketing brochures, products, etc., prominently display registration indication marks for trademarked ™ and copyrighted © materials? Yes _______ No _________
c. Are calls from the media regarding the company or company products promptly relayed to legal counsel? Yes _______ No _________
d. Does the company have a written policy for employees to follow when contacted by members of the press? Yes _______ No _________

D. Contracts and Leases

1. Goods

a. Does the company use written purchase orders? Yes ______ No ______
b. Does the company use written sales invoices? Yes ______ No ______
c. Does the company use written bills of lading? Yes ______ No ______
d. Does the company use written receipts? Yes ______ No ______

2. Relationships

a. Does the company use written Sales Agreements? Yes ______ No ______
b. Does the company use written License Agreements? Yes ______ No ______
c. Does the company use written Royalty Agreements? Yes ______ No ______
d. Does the company use written Distribution Agreements? Yes ______ No ______
e. Does the company use written Employment, Consultant, and Contractor Agreements? Yes ______ No ______
f. Does the company use written Work Made for Hire Agreements? Yes ______ No ______
g. Does the company use written Non-Competition and Confidentiality Agreements? Yes ______ No ______
h. Have all written agreements been reviewed by legal counsel? Yes ______ No ______

3. Equipment and Property Leases

a. Is the company a party to any lease of the premises? Yes ______ No ______
b. Is the company a party to any equipment lease? Yes ______ No ______
c. Is the company a party to any vehicle lease? Yes ______ No ______
d. Are the company owners required to sign any personal guarantees in any leasing situation? Yes ______ No ______

E. Regulatory Compliance

1. Occupational Safety and Health Act (OSHA)

a. Is the company in compliance with OSHA and the applicable state safety requirements? Yes ______ No ______

2. Environmental Protection Act (EPA)

a. Has the company considered any potential EPA-type or other hazardous materials problems? Yes ______ No ______

b. If yes, have all such matters been reviewed by legal counsel? Yes _______ No _________

3. Permits/Zoning

a. Are the company premises and location in compliance with zoning regulations? Yes _______ No _________
b. Have permits to operate your business been obtained? Yes _______ No _________

F. Insurance and Pension

1. Insurance Concerns

a. Has the company obtained general liability insurance? Yes _______ No _________
b. Are company automobiles adequately covered by a company automobile policy? Yes _______ No _________
c. Has the company obtained sufficient workers' compensation insurance? Yes _______ No _________
d. Has the company obtained adequate product liability insurance? Yes _______ No _________
e. Do company owners and key individuals have adequate health insurance? Yes _______ No _________
f. Do company owners have a Buy/Sell Agreement? Yes _______ No _________
g. Does the company have key man or director's insurance for key employees? Yes _______ No _________
h. Do company owners and key individuals have adequate disability insurance? Yes _______ No _________
i. If a license is required, has sufficient professional negligence insurance been obtained? Yes _______ No _________
j. Has the company considered business interruption insurance? Yes _______ No _________
k. Has the company considered an umbrella policy? Yes _______ No _________

2. Pension Concerns

a. Do company owners have an IRA, KEOGH account, 401(k), or other retirement plan? Yes _______ No _________
b. Do company owners have an ISOP/ESOP/ISOT or other stock ownership plan? Yes _______ No _________
c. Do company owners have a deferred compensation plan? Yes _______ No _________

G. Financial and Security Matters

1. Financial Concerns

a. Does the company own any assets which are subject to a security interest? Yes ______ No ________
b. Has the company recorded UCC statements to protect its ownership in assets? Yes ______ No ________
c. Does the company have pending collection matters? Yes ______ No ________
d. Are all company financial transactions recorded on corporate books in accordance with generally accepted accounting principles? Yes ______ No ________

2. Securities Concerns

a. Has the company stock been issued in compliance with securities laws or exemptions? Yes ______ No ________
b. Have company securities transactions been reviewed by legal counsel experienced in securities laws? Yes ______ No ________

H. Miscellaneous

1. Record Keeping

a. Does the company have a written records retention policy? Yes ______ No ________
b. If yes, are records maintained by the company in accordance with the policy? Yes ______ No ________
c. Are company records in storage kept in an orderly fashion to permit retrieval or destruction in accordance with the records retention policy? Yes ______ No ________

2. Litigation

a. Has the company received any threats of lawsuits? Yes ______ No ________
b. Is the company currently involved in litigation? Yes ______ No ________

Section I

Legal Agreements

Questions Designed to Make You a Better Entrepreneur (bet you'll miss at least one!)

1. If you are party to a contract and are later sued under that contract and ultimately win the case, will your attorney's fees be paid by the other party?

A. Yes, if you had an attorney's fees clause in your contract specifying that the winner gets his or her attorney's fees paid.

B. Yes, if statutory law requires that the winner be paid.

C. Yes, if A or B are true.

D. No, each party will have to pay his or her own attorney's fees.

2. If you accept two consecutive late payments from a party who owes you money under a contract, do you lose your right to future payments being made on time?

A. Yes, by accepting two consecutive late payments, you forego your rights to have future payments made on time.

B. Yes, unless you have a clause in your agreement stating that you are not waiving your rights to future payments being made on time.

C. No, but if you accept the third consecutive late payment, you will lose your right to future payments being made on time.

D. Yes, unless you write the party a demand letter stating that you will not accept any more late payments.

3. If you are merely selling T-shirts on the street corner, do you need a business license?

A. Yes, but only when your profits equal your expenses.

B. No, because you are a street vendor.

C. Yes, because you are a street vendor.

D. No, if you are only pursuing a hobby.

4. If you contribute $7,500 for a 75% interest in a partnership and your partner contributes nothing but his sweat and tears for his 25%, and you do not have a written partnership agreement, will you receive 75% of the profits?

A. No, the profits will be split on a 50/50 basis.

B. Yes, and your partner will receive 25% of the profits.

C. No, the profits will be split on a 50/50 basis after you recoup your $7,500 investment.

D. Yes, after you recoup your $7,500 investment, you will receive 75% of the profits.

5. If you operate under the corporate structure and the corporation is sued, but does not have sufficient funds to pay the claim, could you lose your personal assets, such as your home?

A. Yes, but only if you did not keep your personal and corporate accounts separate.

B. Yes, but only if you did not keep your corporate records up to date.

C. No, unless you did not keep your personal and corporate accounts separate or you did not keep your corporate records up to date.

D. No, because of the limited liability advantage of operating as a corporation.

6. If you and your best friend are shareholders of a corporation and your best friend dies, will you be in business with your friend's heirs?

A. Yes, and the heirs will have an equal right to manage the corporation with you.

B. Yes, unless you had a written shareholder agreement with buy/sell provisions to provide for a buyout or transfer of shares upon the death of a shareholder.

C. No, but the business will be appraised as of the date of death and you will have to pay the heirs the value of the late shareholder's ownership interest.

D. No, but the heirs could force you into a dissolution of the corporation.

7. If there are three directors in a corporation and one shows up for a director's meeting and one calls in for that meeting via the telephone, will the corporation be bound to the resolutions that the two directors discussed and approved?

A. No, unless the director who showed up in person had a proxy from the absent director.

B. No, a meeting can be conducted only if at least two directors are present in person.

C. Yes, if the corporate bylaws allow for a director to be present via the telephone.

D. No, all directors must be present in person or by proxy in order to bind the corporation.

8. If you purchase a business, can you be hit with hidden liabilities after the sale?

A. Yes, if you purchased the business by purchasing stock.

B. Yes, if you purchased the business by purchasing the assets.

C. Yes, if either A or B are true.

D. No, if you included an indemnity provision in the agreement.

9. If you hire a software programmer to create a software program for your business, is the business the owner of the finished product?

A. Yes, if the programmer is an employee acting within the scope of his or her employment relationship.

B. Yes, if the programmer is an independent contractor and the parties have signed a written agreement stating that the business is the owner.

C. No, the business is a joint owner with the programmer.

D. Yes, if either A or B are true.

Answers

1. If you are party to a contract and are later sued under that contract and ultimately win the case, will your attorney's fees be paid by the other party?

The correct answer is C. There are two possible ways to get your attorney's fees paid if you are sued under a contract and ultimately win the case: 1) if you had an attorney's fees clause in your contract specifying that the winner gets his or her attorney's fees paid, or 2) if statutory law requires that the winner be paid. Look at the "Attorney's Fees" clause in the Boilerplate Clauses of Section I (page 20).

2. If you accept two consecutive late payments from a party who owes you money under a contract, do you lose your right to future payments being made on time?

The correct answer is B. Unless you have a waiver clause in your agreement, an argument can be made that you have acquiesced to the late payments and have thereby waived your rights to have future payments made on time. Look at the "Non-Waiver" clause in the Boilerplate Clauses of Section I (pages 22-23).

3. If you are merely selling T-shirts on the street corner, do you need a business license?

The correct answer is C. You are conducting business and therefore must obtain a business license. Check your local city or county agency to obtain such a license. If you operate without a license, you may incur a penalty.

4. If you contribute $7,500 for a 75% interest in a partnership and your partner contributes nothing but his sweat and tears for his 25%, and you do not have a written partnership agreement, will you receive 75% of the profits?

The correct answer is A. State law governs partnerships, but generally, each state law provides that if two people have joined together to make a profit they are operating as a partnership. If there is no written partnership agreement, most state laws will provide that the parties split profits on a 50/50 basis, regardless of their investment. See the forms on Partnerships in Section I (pages 24-35) for details.

5. If you operate under the corporate structure and the corporation is sued, but does not have sufficient funds to pay the claim, could you lose your personal assets, such as your home?

The correct answer is C. The general rule is that a corporation is a separate entity from its owners and, therefore, the owners will not be liable if the corporation cannot pay a claim. However, if the owners of the corporation do not keep their personal and corporate accounts separate or keep corporate records up to date and follow other corporate formalities, the owners could be personally liable for corporate debts because the corporation will be regarded as the alter ego of its owners. This is known as "piercing the corporate veil." Other times when the corporate veil can be pierced include situations where fraud or criminal activities are involved or if the corporation is undercapitalized. See the section on Corporations in Section I (pages 36-70).

6. If you and your best friend are shareholders of a corporation and your best friend dies, will you be in business with your friend's heirs?

The correct answer is B. Unless you had a written shareholder's agreement with buy/sell provisions to provide for a buyout or transfer of shares upon the death of a shareholder, you could very well end up in business with the heirs of the late shareholder. See the Shareholders' Agreement in Section I (pages 55-66).

7. If there are three directors in a corporation and one shows up for a director's meeting and one calls in for that meeting via the telephone, will the corporation be bound to the resolutions that the two directors discussed and approved?

The correct answer is C. Directors may be present in person or via the telephone if the corporate bylaws permit such meetings. Proxies are used for shareholder meetings, not director's meetings. See the Corporate Bylaws in Section I (pages 37-48).

8. If you purchase a business, can you be hit with hidden liabilities after the sale?

The best answer is C, because it includes A and B. If you purchased the business by purchasing the stock, you acquire the assets and liabilities of the business. This is not always the case when you purchase just the assets, but sometimes it could happen. See the Sale of Stock and Sale of Assets forms in Section I (pages 71-79).

9. If you hire a software programmer to create a software program for your business, is the business the owner of the finished product?

The correct answer is D. If the programmer is an employee acting within the scope of his or her employment relationship or if the programmer is an independent contractor and the parties have signed a written agreement stating that the business is the owner, then the business owns the program. See the Confidentiality Agreement and Invention Assignment forms in Section I (pages 86-91).

For more quizzes and thorough explanations of these and other challenging legal issues, see my other small business resource book, *The Small Business Legal Guide: The Critical Legal Matters Affecting Your Business*, available at your local bookstore, or call Sourcebooks at (708) 961-3900.

Important!

All of the forms, examples, and agreements in this section must meet with current federal and state laws. Do not just copy the examples listed verbatim until you have checked your state laws to ensure compliance. Instead, prepare your own forms using the examples in this section, and obtain legal counsel to review them.

Form 1. Boilerplate Clauses. Last year, millions of people signed contracts. This year, many will lose thousands of dollars litigating over those very contracts. Why? For some it is because they did not read the "boilerplate." Many of these people will sign on the dotted line and turn their signed deals into sour deals. Do not let this happen to you. Review each of the following "boilerplate" clauses for possible addition to every agreement in which you are a party.

• **Additional Documents.** Use this clause if you believe a party may need to sign additional documents or instruments or perform additional acts in the future to carry out the terms of your agreement. It states that the parties will agree to act in good faith in facilitating such obligations.

• **Arbitration.** Use this clause if you want to settle your claim in front of an arbitrator rather than go to court. Whether or not to include an arbitration clause in your agreements is a personal decision. Proponents use them because they believe the process is less expensive and faster than bringing their case in a court of law. Opponents argue against them because they believe that the arbitration process is as lengthy as litigation, some arbitrators are not qualified, and most of the time, the case is split down the middle with each party paying half, even when it is clear one party is not at fault.

• **Assignment.** Use this clause to allow or prevent one or both parties from assigning their rights and/or duties under the agreement.

• **Attorney's Fees.** Use this clause to request that your attorney's fees be paid by the other party in the event a dispute arises between the parties. However, make sure that your language specifies what the attorney's fees should include, because if the clause is too vague, it might not cover fees that you intended or it might cover more than what you intended.

• **Authority.** Use this clause to show that the parties represent and warrant that they possess the full and complete authority and authorization to enter into the agreement. This clause is especially helpful if one party is not a natural person [e.g., a partnership or corporation]; then the signatory for that party must show his or her authority and authorization before signing the agreement.

• **Binding Effect.** Use this clause to show

that the parties intend to bind themselves, each other, and their respective successors and heirs to the terms of the agreement.

• **Construction.** Use this clause to show that in the event of a dispute, the terms of the agreement shall be interpreted according to their fair meaning and shall not be construed against a party because the agreement was drafted by that party.

• **Entire Agreement.** Use this clause to show that the agreement is the final expression of the parties' contract. If you include this clause, it serves to supersede all prior oral and written agreements or statements by or among the parties, so make sure that every term discussed and desired is in the agreement. Many individuals have signed a contract believing that the written word includes the verbal representations made by the other party, but found out that the two were quite different. Therefore, if a party verbally says one thing, but the written contract says another, get him or her to put it in writing. If he will not, then beware—you are probably not going to get what you bargained for.

• **Exhibits.** Use this clause if you will have any attachments or exhibits to your agreement. Its purpose is to treat the agreements and any attached documents as one document.

• **Force Majeure.** Use this clause if you will conduct business overseas or to protect yourself from acts of God, war, riot, fire, strikes, or other causes beyond your control which may render performance impossible.

• **Governing Law.** Use this clause to state the laws of the state or jurisdiction which will govern the terms of the agreement.

• **Indemnification.** Use this clause to ensure that one or both parties indemnify the other if a party incurs or suffers an injury or damages as a result of the other party's breach, covenant, or warranty under the agreement.

• **Jurisdiction.** Use this clause to state the jurisdiction that you are willing to be bound to in the event of a dispute or breach of the agreement. If you are located in California but signed a contract with a jurisdictional clause in New York, you should be prepared to travel to New York, because by the terms of the contract you consented to its jurisdiction.

• **Modification.** Use this clause to require a writing to amend or modify an agreement.

• **No Authority to Bind.** Use this clause to show that nothing in the agreement is to be construed to constitute either party as a partner, employee, or joint venturer (whatever the case may be) of the other, nor that either shall have the authority to bind the other.

• **Non-Waiver.** Use this clause to show that you are not waiving your rights to future payments or to payments being made on time just because you allow the other party to forego a payment, or if you accept a late payment.

• **Notices.** Use this clause to provide the addresses where each party can be served or provided documents.

• **Severability.** Use this clause to require the balance of an agreement to remain in full force if one provision of the agreement is held invalid for any reason.

Partnerships

When two or more people join together to make a profit, a general partnership is formed. No legal filing is necessary to form a general partnership. However, it is a good idea to have a written partnership agreement, because without one, state law prevails and the agreement created by your state may not be what you had in mind. General partnerships are governed by uniform partnership laws, so make sure to check with your state laws for details. The following agreements are frequently used in partnership situations. Use them as a template and tailor them to meet your needs.

Form 2. General Partnership Agreement. Use the General Partnership Agreement as a guideline when forming your Partnership Agreement. If the partnership will own real property, contact your county recorder to determine if the partnership can record a written notice of such real property ownership.

Form 3. Partnership Dissolution and Winding Up. Use the Partnership Dissolution Agreement in this section as a guideline when dissolving your partnership and tailor it to meet your needs. Also, make sure to review your state laws to determine if you must notify the partnership's creditors of the dissolution and/or file a notice of dissolution with the county recorder where the business of the partnership is being conducted.

Form 4. Transfer Partnership Assets to Corporation. Use the Transfer of Assets Agreement in this section as a guideline when you want to change business entities and transfer the assets of your partnership to a corporation. To complete the transfer, you may need to prepare bills of sales, transfer deeds, titles, etc., and furthermore, the transfer may need to comply with bulk sales laws. If you are unsure of whether you need to perform such tasks, it is best to check with an attorney in your area. Note: you can also tailor the transfer form presented in this section to transfer assets from a proprietorship to a corporation.

Corporations

A corporation is a separate legal entity, apart from its owners. The owners are called shareholders, because they hold shares of stock in the corporation. The shareholders elect directors who are responsible for managing the affairs of the corporation. If more than one director is elected, the corporation has a board of directors. The directors oversee operations of the corporation and either elect or appoint officers to carry out the day to day functions. The officers usually comprise a president, secretary, and treasurer, and sometimes one or more vice presidents. Of course, in many small corporations, one person may hold all of the above positions. Use the documents in this section if you are operating as a corporation and tailor them to fit your corporate needs.

Form 5. Articles of Incorporation. The corporation is created when the Articles of Incorporation are filed with the office of the Secretary of State or similar state agency. The

Articles of Incorporation is a legal document which lists essential information about the corporation. As shown in the form in this section, the Articles typically include the corporate name, purpose, number of shares authorized, name and address of the initial corporate agent, and the principal place of business. The Articles for each state are similar to the Articles presented in this section. However, some states do not use forms, but rather hand out instructions for filing; but again, the information requested is typically the same as presented in this section. States which do not use forms are as follows: Arizona, Georgia, Idaho, Iowa, Kentucky, Nebraska, New Hampshire, New York, South Carolina, Texas, and Utah. Check the Appendix or look up the telephone number of the agency in your state to inquire about incorporating there.

Form 6. Corporate Bylaws. Although the Bylaws are somewhat lengthy and complicated, it is important that they be carefully prepared and read, as they provide guidance in handling the corporation's affairs. Use the bylaws presented in this section as a guideline for preparing the bylaws for your corporation.

Form 7. Minutes of First Meeting of Board of Directors. The Minutes of the First Meeting of the Board of Directors contains resolutions regarding actions required to be taken by the board of directors in connection with the formation of the corporation. Use the Minutes of First Meeting of Board of Directors presented in this section as a guideline for preparing the Minutes for your First Directors' Meeting.

Form 8. Shareholders' Agreement. Use the Shareholders' Agreement presented in this section to provide a buyout or transfer of shares upon dissolution or death of a shareholder. However, before finalizing such an agreement, discuss it with your accountant or tax attorney because the buy/sell provisions in any Shareholders' Agreement have tax and estate planning consequences.

Form 9. Written Consent of Shareholders. Shareholders must conduct annual meetings. However, note that this form is titled "Written Consent in Lieu of Annual Shareholders' Meeting." You can prepare written consents in lieu of holding annual meetings if your corporate bylaws authorizes such action. Whether you hold formal meetings or take action by using the written consents, you can use the form presented in this section as a guideline because the information presented and the action taken is the same—the only difference is one requires holding a meeting and the other does not.

Form 10. Written Consent of Directors. Generally, under the laws of every state, the directors are also required to conduct annual meetings. These meetings and their proper documentation are important for many reasons, including protecting shareholders from personal liability as a result of piercing the corporate veil and protecting corporate directors, officers, and shareholders from personal liability to past, present, and future creditors and tax agencies. Use the Written Consent in this section as a guideline in preparing your own Director written consent or annual meeting minutes.

Purchase/Sale of a Business

The term "caveat emptor" (buyer beware) truly applies when purchasing a business. As many unfortunate purchasers can attest, the process of negotiating and completing the purchase of a business is difficult enough without being haunted afterwards by undisclosed or unknown debts.

A purchaser new to the entrepreneurial world, as well as a veteran, should at least follow these procedures to help ward off such unpleasant surprises: 1) determine the seller's motivation for selling (i.e., is the seller's real motivation for selling his health, retirement, or an out-of-state move, or is it really a cover for obsolete products, an expiring lease, problems with creditors, or the inability to expand); 2) get industry statistics and historical data from the Chamber of Commerce and trade associations to find out statistics about industry averages; and 3) look at the financial condition of the company. Do a spreadsheet analysis of the company's last five years financial statements and federal tax returns. Check for any patterns or peaks and make adjustments on your spreadsheet and determine the true worth of the business.

The most common ways to purchase a business are to purchase the assets or purchase the stock. The following agreements will offer the intricacies of each.

Form 11. Sale of Stock Agreement. A sale of stock occurs when the entire business is sold, including all the assets and liabilities, the latter meaning current as well as future liabilities. The sale of stock is an easier way of acquiring a business, if the seller has a small number of stockholders. It avoids detailed paperwork and it is not essential to physically transfer the assets and rights of the seller.

A disadvantage to the seller with this type of sale is when the purchaser has the right to offset payments due to the seller if a loss occurs or unexpected liabilities from past operations come up. The purchaser's disadvantage with the sale of stock arrangement is that hidden liabilities may be forced on him after the sale. (A savvy purchaser would obtain legal assurances that the corporation is in the same condition as represented and warranted by the seller. Furthermore, the purchaser would include an indemnity provision in the agreement in case the situation ends up otherwise.) Use the Sale of Stock agreement in this section as a guideline in preparing your own Sale of Stock Agreement.

Form 12. Sale of Assets Agreement. A sale of assets is the most common form of selling a business; however, it is more complicated than the sale of stock because it requires transferring deeds, assigning leases and contracts, preparing individual bills of sale for assets being transferred, and sometimes, complying with bulk transfer laws. Nevertheless, the advantage of the sale of assets is that since only assets are sold and not the entire business, the purchaser will be responsible only for the debts and liabilities which he specifically assumes. (Except, by law, certain liabilities will be the responsibility of the purchaser, even if he did not expressly assume them.)

Several types of assets are typically involved in the sale, including: 1) Real Estate, including land, improvements, and fixtures; 2) Equipment, including machinery, office equipment, computer hardware and software, automobiles, trucks; 3) Furniture, including a desk, chair, reception room furniture, art, plants, etc.; 4) Records, including tax records, financial records, customer lists, supplier lists, bank accounts, bank lists, mailing lists, contracts, leases, files, clients, etc.; and 5) Intellectual

Property, including goodwill, patents, copyrights, trade names, trademarks, covenants not to compete. Use the Sale of Assets Agreement presented in this section as a guideline in preparing your own Sale of Assets agreement.

Form 13. Bill of Sale and Assignment. Use the Bill of Sale and Assignment presented in this section as a guideline in preparing your own Bill of Sale and Assignment to physically transfer personal assets which are part of an asset sale.

Confidentiality Agreements and Forms

Confidentiality Agreements are used to prevent disclosure of trade secrets and confidential information by current and former employees, licensees, vendors, suppliers, consultants, independent contractors, agents, etc. Many of these agreements contain restrictive clauses that are enforceable in order to protect the business from misappropriation or abuse of confidential information. However, poorly drafted agreements may hinder the company's rights. Therefore, it is essential that each person planning to use Confidentiality Agreements have them reviewed by legal counsel before instituting their use. The agreements presented in this section are typically used in the context that they are presented.

Form 14. Confidentiality for Evaluating the Sale of a Business. Use the Confidentiality Agreement presented in this section as a guideline for preparing your Confidentiality Agreement when you need to allow others to look at your books, records, etc., when selling your business.

Form 15. Confidentiality for Allowing Potential Business Associates Access to Confidential Information. Use the Confidentiality Agreement presented in this section as a guideline for preparing a Confidentiality Agreement before allowing a potential business associate access to your confidential information for the purpose of determining whether to enter into a business relationship with you.

Form 16. Employee Confidentiality and Invention Assignment Agreement. Use the Confidentiality and Invention Assignment presented in this section as a guideline for preparing such an agreement for employment situations where employees are hired to create intellectual property for your company's use and ownership. If your employees are clerical or do not have access to any trade secrets or confidential information, instead of using this agreement, all you need to do is to include a confidentiality clause in your employment agreements. (See Form 22, Simple At-Will Employment Agreement below.)

Form 17. Non-Disclosure—Non-Competition—Non-Circumvention. Use the Non-Disclosure—Non-Competition—Non-Circumvention Agreement presented in this section as a guideline for preparing your agreement for use with vendors, suppliers, and others to discourage their disclosure of your trade secrets and confidential information, to discourage them from circumventing your contracts with third parties, and to discourage them from competing with your business unlawfully.

Form 18. Confidentiality Legend. Use the Confidentiality Legend presented in this section as a guideline for preparing a Confidentiality Legend when handing out confidential documents to others. Make sure to consecutively number the documents and keep a list of the individuals who were provided the documents.

Employment Forms and Agreements

As a result of numerous decisions, rulings, and interpretations, federal and state labor laws are constantly changing. With such constant activity, the beginning entrepreneur, as well as the veteran, will find it difficult to keep abreast of current trends. However, it is essential to do so.

While it is not the purpose of this section to offer complete forms and agreements which are in compliance with all federal and state labor laws (which may overlap), the forms and agreements presented in this section are essential to the success of any business. Use them as guidelines in preparing your own forms and agreements and make sure that all written documents are consistent, carefully drafted, reviewed by management and labor counsel, and distributed to the supervisors before implemented.

Form 19. Employment Application. Use the Employment Application presented in this section as a guideline for preparing your Employment Application for use in screening potential employees. By using an application like the one shown in this section, you may gain more insight about a prospective employee than had you only reviewed the applicant's resume. The application will often comprise questions not always disclosed on resumes.

Form 20. Interview Questions. Use a written list of questions like the ones presented in this section when interviewing prospective employees. By using written questions, you reduce the risks of potential liability for discrimination or wrongful termination litigation later on. After implementing such procedures, make sure everyone involved in the interview process uses only the approved written material when interviewing. This practice will reduce your company's risk of the above mentioned lawsuits.

Form 21. Offer Letter. Some employers like to send an Employment Offer Letter to the prospective employee, offering him or her a position with the company. If you prefer using an offer letter, use the one presented in this section as a guideline and prepare yours to fit your company needs. Make sure it complies with discrimination laws and does not negate the at-will nature of the employment relationship, if that is the relationship the company desires.

Form 22. At-Will Employment Agreement (Simple). Use the Employment Agreement presented in this section as a guideline for preparing your Employment Agreement where the employment relationship will be a simple one. If you desire an at-will relationship, where the employee can leave the relationship at any time or you can terminate him or her at any time without cause, include the at-will language as shown in the agreement presented in this section.

Form 23. Employment Agreement with Stock Options (Complex). Use the Employment Agreement presented in this section as a guideline for preparing your Employment Agreement when hiring managers or those who will have stock options. Make sure to indicate whether the agreement is for a certain term or is at-will.

Form 24. Employee Handbook. To reduce the potential of liability, it is recommended that all employers prepare and use an Employee Handbook. Use the Handbook presented in this section as a guideline for preparing your Employee Handbook. As with any written document, your handbook should be carefully drafted and reviewed by management, then submitted to experienced labor counsel for review. The employer who fails to submit the handbook to labor counsel because he or she wants to save costs may want to rethink his or her strategy, because the potential liability for outdated or ambiguous language can far outweigh the costs of a labor law review. Once the handbook is completed, it should be distributed to management and supervisors, who should be trained regarding the terms prior to the date that the policies will be implemented.

Form 25. Employee Performance Evaluation. Use the Employee Performance Evaluation presented in this section as a guideline for preparing your Performance Evaluations if you plan to keep written evaluations for all of your employees. If you institute such a policy and implement such a form, make sure to do so in a consistent manner. Otherwise, the evaluation could work against the company in the event of a lawsuit.

Form 26. Employee Warning Notice. Use the Warning Notice presented in this section as a guideline for preparing your Warning Notices for situations where you believe the written notice is necessary to help the employee improve in the work environment. If you incorporate such procedures, make sure that you use these notices on a consistent basis. Showing preference for some employees over others will harm the company should a disgruntled employee take action.

Form 27. Sexual Harassment Complaint Form. Use the Sexual Harassment Complaint Form presented in this section as a guideline for preparing your Complaint Form to help reduce the company's liability in the event an employee comes forward with a sexual harassment claim. Inform all employees that such a form exists and can be picked up in personnel or your human resources department. Make sure that all employees know that there will be no retaliation for filing the complaint with personnel or human resources.

Form 28. Exit Letter. Some employers like to send an exiting employee an Exit Letter like the one shown in this section. One reason for doing so is to remind the employee not to use or disclose the company's trade secrets. Another reason is to remind the employee to return company material. Use the Exit Letter presented in this section as a guideline for preparing your Employment Exit Letter.

Business Relationship Agreements

Whether you are an entrepreneur contracting with an independent contractor, a consultant, or a partner, you need to be aware of what you are signing before you put yourself (and your company) at risk. The agreements in this section offer some tips to take with you to your next business relationship bargaining table.

Form 29. Agency Agreement. Use the Agency Agreement presented in this section as a guideline for preparing your Agency Agreement. Make sure to state the details of your relationship (e.g., whether you want the relationship to be exclusive or non-exclusive, or if the relationship will involve working in a specific territory or worldwide, etc.). The agreement presented in this section is for the exclusive right to sell and distribute company goods. Tailor it to meet your company's needs.

Form 30. Consulting Agreement. Use the Consulting Agreement presented in this section as a guideline for preparing your Consulting Agreement when hiring consultants to assist in operating your business. For example, if you have purchased a business and want the seller to consult with your company's business affairs for a certain term, use this type of an agreement.

Form 31. Specially Commissioned Work Agreement. Use the Specially Commissioned Work Agreement presented in this section as a guideline for preparing your agreement where your company will hire an independent contractor to perform services for the company when you want the company to keep copyright ownership of the results of the constructor's services. For example, if you hire an artist to draw a company logo or if you hire a software programmer to complete a company program, draft this type of an agreement to retain copyright ownership of the logo or program.

Form 32. Independent Contractor Agreement. Use the Independent Contractor Agreement presented in this section as a guideline for preparing your Contractor Agreement when hiring contractors. Written agreements are helpful in warding off attacks of alleged employee status from the IRS or similar state taxing authority. Look at Form SS-8 in Section III, Government Forms, to review the 20 factors the IRS uses to determine if a relationship looks more like an independent contractor than an employee.

Form 33. Distribution Agreement. Use the Distribution Agreement in this section as a guideline in preparing your Distribution Agreement when you will use distributors to sell your goods. The agreement presented in this section is for a wholesale distributor. Tailor it to meet your needs.

Form 34. Purchase Order Terms and Conditions. Use the Purchase Order Terms presented in this section to retain copyright ownership when you will sell materials that contain such copyrighted works.

Promissory Notes and Security Agreements

Promissory notes are used when a borrower promises to pay the holder of the note a certain amount of money. The promissory notes in this section are designed to assist the entrepreneur and company manager with simple transactions.

Form 35. Promissory Demand Note. Use the Promissory Note presented in this section as a guideline in preparing your own note when the note will be payable in full on demand.

Form 36. Promissory Note with Installment Payments. Use the Promissory Note with Installment Payments as a guideline in preparing your own note when the note will be payable in monthly installments.

Form 37. Promissory Note with Security Agreement. Use the Promissory Note with Security Agreement as a guideline in preparing your own note when the note is to be secured by collateral.

Intellectual Property Agreements

Intellectual Property is a body of law encompassing copyrights, trademarks, patents, and sometimes trade names and trade secrets. The agreements in this section are designed to assign the rights from one party to another. Intellectual property is more fully discussed in the Government Forms section where copyright, trademark, and patent forms are presented and explained.

Form 38. Copyright Assignment. Use the Copyright Assignment presented in this section as a guideline in preparing your own Copyright Assignment when you need to transfer copyright rights from one party to a subsequent party.

Form 39. Trademark Assignment. Use the Trademark Assignment presented in this section as a guideline in preparing your own Trademark Assignment when you need to transfer trademark rights from one party to a subsequent party.

Form 40. Patent Assignment. Use the Patent Assignment presented in this section as a guideline in preparing your own Patent Assignment when you need to transfer patent rights from one party to a subsequent party.

TIPS FOR DRAFTING, NEGOTIATING, AND ENTERING INTO AGREEMENTS

TIP #1
Integrity matters

The agreement that you enter into is only as good as the people behind it. Deal with ethical people and you will increase your chances of a successful relationship and reduce your chances of litigation 100 times over.

TIP #2
Be dollar wise without being penny foolish

Use any form agreement, whether it is in *The Complete Book of Business and Legal Forms* or otherwise, as a guideline in tailoring your own agreements. Do not just copy a form agreement and use it verbatim unless it applies to your situation verbatim. Once you have drafted an agreement to meet your situation at hand, decide whether it is necessary to have it reviewed by legal counsel. After all, it is a legal document, and a quick review at minimal cost to ensure compliance with applicable laws is well worth its weight in gold.

TIP #3
Sweat the small stuff

Many people do not read the boilerplate—i.e., the small print of the contract that may be written in gray or on the back of the contract. Do not be one of them. The standard boilerplate clauses in an agreement are every bit as legal as the particular terms at hand. Signing an agreement without reading the boilerplate could very well turn your signed deal into a sour deal. Make sure that you agree with *all* of the terms of the agreement before you sign on the dotted line.

TIP #4
The power of print

Many people believe that the printed word cannot be questioned and challenged. This is not so. You can and should amend, add, delete, or change the printed word when it is advantageous to do so. You may not get all of your desired changes, but such bargaining will get you closer to what you desire. If you are savvy, you will also use the power of print to your advantage when it is beneficial to do so.

TIP #5
It is wiser to choose what to draft than draft what you choose

Once you have signed an agreement, you will need to abide by its terms Therefore, make sure that the agreement is carefully drafted and says what you intend it to mean. Otherwise, you may end up having to abide by terms not to your liking—or terms which could put you in litigation.

TIP #6
Care, but not that much

One of the cardinal rules in negotiating is not to negotiate for yourself. This is because people tend to care too much in personal negotiation situations. Whether you negotiate for yourself or not is your decision. Just make sure in all of your negotiations that the other side knows you *want* but don't *need* the deal.

TIP #7
Stick to your goals

In contract negotiations, separate the issues from the people. Keep reminding yourself of the issues and the goals you are trying to accomplish and never lose sight of why you are in negotiations. Your effort and courage to enter into negotiations are not enough without purpose and direction.

TIP #8
Timing is everything

If possible, negotiate when the other side is happy and when you are in a good mood. Never enter into an agreement when you are tired. The results may not be what you had in mind.

TIP #9
Beware of the 11th hour

Most contract negotiations happen as close to the deadline as possible, so be patient and wait for the 11th hour. As you approach a deadline, understand that a power shift may occur and you may find yourself in a better (or worse) bargaining position. Be prepared and act accordingly.

Additional Documents and Acts. Each Party agrees to execute, acknowledge, and deliver such additional documents and instruments and to perform such additional acts as may be necessary or appropriate to effectuate, carry out, and perform all of the terms, provisions, and conditions of this Agreement and the transactions contemplated hereby, and each Party agrees to act in good faith and fair dealing in facilitating, maintaining, and carrying out the duties and obligations of this Agreement.

Arbitration. Any controversy or claim arising out of this Agreement, the interpretation of any of the provisions hereof, or the action, inaction, or breach of any Party hereunder shall be settled by arbitration in [*city, state*]. Any award or decision obtained from any such arbitration proceeding shall be final and binding on the Parties, and judgment upon any award thus obtained may be entered in any court having jurisdiction thereof. There shall be one arbitrator, mutually agreeable to the Parties, or if the Parties cannot agree on an arbitrator, then an arbitrator shall be appointed by a court of competent jurisdiction. The losing Party shall pay all the expenses of the arbitration. No action at law or in equity based upon any claim arising out of or related to this Agreement shall be instituted in any court by any Party except: (a) an action to compel arbitration pursuant to this Agreement, or (b) an action to enforce an award obtained in an arbitration proceeding in accordance with this Agreement.

Assignment. Either Party's interest in this Agreement shall not be sold, assigned, pledged, encumbered, or transferred by that Party without the written consent of the other Party. In the event of an assignment of one Party's interest by operation of law, or in the event there shall be filed by or against that party in any court pursuant to any statute either of the United States or any state, a petition in bankruptcy, insolvency, or for reorganization, or for the appointment of a receiver or trustee of all or a portion of that Party's property, or if that party makes an assignment for the benefit of creditors, or petitions for or enters into an arrangement, then in any such event, the other Party may, at its option terminate this Agreement and shall have all remedies available. [*Note: this clause can be reversed so one or both parties have the right to assign.*]

Attorney's Fees. In the event that any dispute between the Parties should result in litigation or arbitration, the prevailing Party in such dispute shall be entitled to recover from the other Party all reasonable fees, costs, and expenses of enforcing any right of the prevailing Party, including, without limitation, reasonable attorney's fees, expert witness fees, and expenses. Attorney's fees and costs include costs for such items for any appeals. This paragraph shall remain independent from any judgment entered to enforce its terms, shall not merge therewith, and shall entitle the prevailing Party to attorney's fees and costs incurred in connection with post-judgment collection and enforcement efforts.

Authority. The Parties hereto represent and warrant that they possess the full and complete authority to covenant and agree as provided in this Agreement and, if applicable, to release other Parties as provided herein. If any Party hereto is not a natural person, the signatory for any such non-natural person represents and warrants that he or she possesses the authority and has been authorized by the entity to enter into this Agreement on the entity's behalf, whether by resolution, or upon the instruction by an authorized officer, or as authorized in the bylaws of the entity on whose behalf the signatory is executing this Agreement. No Party to this Agreement will be required to determine the authority of the individual signing this Agreement to make any commitment or undertaking on behalf of such entity.

Binding Effect. This Agreement will be binding upon and inure to the benefit of the Parties, and their respective heirs, successors, and assigns. Nothing expressed or implied in this Agreement is intended, nor shall be construed, to confer upon or give any person, partnership, or corporation, other than the Parties, their heirs, successors, and assigns, any benefits, rights, or remedies under or by reason of this Agreement, nor shall anything in this Agreement relieve or discharge the obligation or liability of any third person to any Party to this Agreement, nor shall any provision give any third person any right of subrogation or action over or against any Party to this Agreement, except to the extent of any contrary provision herein contained.

Construction. In the event of a dispute hereunder, this Agreement shall be interpreted in accordance with its fair meaning and shall not be interpreted for or against any Party hereto on the ground that such party drafted or caused to be drafted this Agreement or any part hereof, nor shall any presumption or burden of proof or persuasion be implied by virtue of the fact that this Agreement may have been prepared by or at the request of a particular Party or his or her counsel.

Entire Agreement. This Agreement and any Exhibits attached hereto or mentioned herein reflect the final expression of the Parties' agreement and contain a complete and exclusive statement of the terms of that agreement, which such terms supersede all prior oral and written agreements or statements by and among the Parties. There are no other agreements, representations, or warranties not set forth herein. No representation, statement, condition, or warranty not contained in this Agreement or its attached Exhibits will be binding on the Parties or have any force or effect whatsoever.

Exhibits. All Exhibits attached hereto or mentioned herein in this Agreement are incorporated by reference for all purposes and shall be treated as if set forth herein.

Force Majeure. Any Party shall be released from its obligations under this Agreement in the event that an act of God, war, riot, fire, strike, or other labor dispute, epidemic, or other causes beyond the control of that Party, render performance by that Party impossible.

Governing Law. The Parties to this Agreement agree that all questions respecting the negotiation, execution, construction, interpretation, or enforcement of this Agreement, or the rights, obligations, and liabilities of the parties hereto, shall be determined in accordance with the applicable provisions of the laws of the state of [*state*].

Indemnification. Each party shall indemnify the other against any and all claims, demands, losses, costs, obligations, and liabilities that the Party may incur or suffer as a result of the other Party's breach of any agreement, covenant, or warranty in this Agreement.

Jurisdiction. Each Party hereby consents to the exclusive jurisdiction of the state of [*state*] whether such action be for arbitration or litigation, or otherwise. Each Party further agrees that personal jurisdiction over him or her may be effected by service of process by registered or certified mail addressed as provided in the Notice section of this Agreement, and that when so made shall be as if served upon him or her personally within the state of [*state*].

Modification. The provisions of this Agreement may be waived, altered, amended, modified, or repealed, in whole or in part, only by the written consent of all Parties to this Agreement.

No Authority to Bind. Nothing contained in the Agreement shall be construed to constitute either Party as a partner, employee, joint venture, or agent of the other Party, nor shall either Party have any authority to bind the other in any respect, it being intended that each shall remain an independent and responsible for his/hers/its own actions. Furthermore, each Party shall not use the name or credit of the other Party in any manner whatsoever, nor incur any obligation in the other Party's name.

Non-Waiver. The failure of any Party to insist upon the prompt and punctual performance of any term or condition in this Agreement, or the failure of any Party to exercise any right or remedy under the terms of this Agreement on any one or more occasions shall not constitute a waiver of that or any other term, condition, right, or remedy on that or any subsequent occasion, unless otherwise expressly provided for herein.

Notices. Any notice or other document to be given or to be served upon any Party hereto in connection with this Agreement must be in writing (which may include facsimile) and will be deemed to have been given and received when delivered to the address specified in this Agreement; and if none is specified, to the last known address by the Party to receive the notice. Any Party may, at any time by giving five (5) days prior written notice to the other Parties, designate any other address in substitution of the foregoing address to which such notice will be given.

Severability. If any provision of this Agreement or the application of such provision to any person or circumstance shall be held invalid for any reason, the remainder of this Agreement or the application of such provision to persons or circumstances other than those to which it is held invalid shall be unaffected by such holding. If the invalidation of any such provision materially alters the Agreement of the Parties, then the Parties shall immediately adopt new provisions to replace those which were declared invalid.

GENERAL PARTNERSHIP AGREEMENT

This Agreement is entered into on this [*date*], by and between [*name*], whose business address is [*address*], and [*name*], whose business address is [*address*] (hereinafter referred to as "Partners").

Recitals

WHEREAS, the Partners wish to associate to form a general Partnership for the purpose of [*state purpose of partnership, e.g., conducting sales, operating a sports equipment store, etc.*], and for any other businesses agreed upon by the Partners;

NOW THEREFORE, in consideration of the mutual covenants, agreements, representations, and warranties, the receipt and sufficiency of which is hereby acknowledged, the Parties hereby agree as follows:

Agreement

1. **Recitals Part of Agreement.** Recitals are a material part of this Agreement.

2. **Partnership Name.** The Partnership name shall be [*name*].

3. **Term.** The term of this Agreement shall begin on the date of this Agreement, and shall continue for a period of [*years*], unless dissolved by agreement of the Partners or terminated sooner pursuant to the provisions of this Agreement.

4. **Place of Business.** The Partnership's principal place of business shall be [*address*]. The Partnership may maintain other places of businesses as agreed upon by the Partners.

5. **Initial Capital.** The Partnership's initial capital shall be $[*amount*]. The Partnership shall open and maintain a Partnership bank account at such banking institutions as the Partners agree.

6. Profits and Losses. The Partners shall share in Partnership net profits and net losses as follows: [*state how profits and losses will be distributed*]. The term "net profits" shall include all income remaining after payment of ordinary and necessary business operating expenses and authorized Partnership draws.

7. Books of Account. Partnership books shall be open for inspection and copying by the Partners at any time.

8. Fiscal Year. The Partnership's fiscal year shall end on [*December 31 or other date*] of each year.

9. Accountings. Complete accountings of the Partnership affairs at the close of business on the last days of March, June, September, and December of each year shall be rendered to each Partner within [60] days after the close of each such month. At the time of each accounting, the profits of the Partnership shall be retained by the Partnership for Partnership purposes, unless both of the Partners agree that the Partnership profits shall be distributed to the Partners as provided in this Partnership Agreement.

10. Time Devoted to Partnership Activities. Each Partner shall devote such time as is necessary for carrying on the Partnership business.

11. Management and Authority. Each Partner shall [*have equal right in management decisions of the Partnership or specify the Partners' rights to manage*]. Each Partner shall have the right and authority to bind the Partnership in making contracts and incurring obligation in the Partnership name or on its credit for sums less than $[*amount*]. Any Partnership obligation in excess of $[*amount stated previously*] shall require the signatures of both Partners. Any obligation incurred in violation of this provision shall be charged to and collected from the Partner who incurred the obligation.

12. Partner's Salaries. [*No Partner shall be entitled to a salary, or state salary requirements of the Partners.*]

13. Withdrawal of Partner. Upon [60] days written notice of intent to the other Partner, either Partner may withdraw from the Partnership.

14. Dissolution. On dissolution of the Partnership, the Partnership affairs shall be wound up, the Partnership assets liquidated, its debts paid, and the surplus divided among the Partners according to their participation percentages described in this Agreement.

[*Add boilerplate clauses as needed*]

AGREEMENT FOR DISSOLUTION AND WINDING UP OF PARTNERSHIP

This Dissolution Agreement is made on [*date*] between [*partnership name*] (hereinafter referred to as the "Partnership"), a partnership formed under a partnership agreement dated [*date*], with principal offices at [*address*], and [*partner.1*] and [*partner.2*], its general partners (hereinafter referred to as the "Partners"), to provide for the dissolution and orderly winding up of the partnership business.

1. Dissolution. By agreement of the Partners, the Partnership shall be dissolved effective [*date and time*] (the "Date of Dissolution"), and the Partners agree that the Partnership shall be wound up and liquidated.

2. Appointment of Liquidating Partner. [*Partner.1*] shall be the liquidating partner (hereinafter referred to as the "Liquidating Partner") and shall have exclusive rights and responsibilities for winding up the partnership business. After the Date of Dissolution, no other partner shall have authority to act on behalf of or bind the Partnership or participate in its management or control for purposes of winding up its business or otherwise.

3. Powers of Liquidating Partner. The Liquidating Partner shall have authority to wind up the partnership business, including full power and authority to:

(a) Sell, transfer, hypothecate, pledge, or otherwise encumber or dispose of all the partnership's assets, in whole or piecemeal, including but not limited to its goodwill and its name, for cash or a cash equivalent at a price and on terms that the liquidating partner shall determine necessary or appropriate to accomplish an orderly and timely liquidation of the partnership at the best price and on the best terms available.

(b) Represent and act on behalf of the Partnership in all matters affecting it during the winding-up period, including the power to engage professional and technical services of others (including without limitations, accountants, attorneys, appraisers, brokers, auctioneers) and to institute and defend any legal proceedings that may be pending or brought by or against the Partnership.

(c) Prepare, execute, file, record, and publish on behalf of the Partners and the Partnership any agreements, documents, or instruments connected with the dissolution and winding up of the business and affairs of the Partnership.

(d) Pay or otherwise settle or discharge all of the debts, liabilities, and other obligations of the Partnership.

(e) Distribute any Partnership assets, including the proceeds of any sale of assets remaining after payment of debts, liabilities, and other obligations to Partners in proportion to their respective interests.

(f) Take all other action necessary, appropriate, or incidental to the foregoing powers or to the performance of the duties of the Liquidating Partner under this agreement.

4. Duties of Liquidating Partner. The Liquidating Partner shall use his or her best efforts to complete liquidation of the partnership within [90] days from the date of this agreement (the "Termination Date"). On the Termination Date, the Liquidating Partner shall have the authority and the duty to execute any deeds, bills of sale, or other conveyance by and for the Partnership that shall be necessary or appropriate to evidence or effect the transfer of the remaining assets to the Partners according to the plan. The Liquidating Partner shall also have the following duties:

(a) Report to the other Partners the actions taken toward liquidation of the partnership business, including specific reports on the disposition of any Partnership assets and the proceeds of the disposition;

(b) Notify each of the Partnership's known creditors (including suppliers with unpaid accounts) of the Partnership's dissolution and the lack of authority of non-liquidating Partners;

(c) Prepare, file, publish, and record in a timely manner all appropriate agreements, documents, and instruments, including federal and state tax returns, to reflect the dissolution and termination of the Partnership and the cessation of the use of its name; obtain any necessary or desirable permits or other authorizations; to the extent required by law, cancel any existing authorizations, licenses, or permits; and resolve or dispose of other matters related to the dissolution in a manner required by law or consistent with the purposes of this agreement.

In the performance of these duties, the Liquidating Partner shall act diligently, honestly, and in good faith and shall account to the Partnership for any benefit or profits derived from transactions connected with the liquidation.

5. Indemnification of Liquidating Partner. The Partners, jointly and severally, shall indemnify and hold harmless the Liquidating Partner from all losses, claims, expenses, damages, liabilities, or obligations of any kind (including legal fees and expenses) arising from or connected with the winding up and liquidation of the Partnership and the performance of his duties under this agreement, except for losses, claims, expenses, damages, liabilities, or obligations (including legal fees and expenses) arising from or connected with the Liquidating Partner's breach of his obligations under this agreement or willful misconduct, or of his other obligations as a Partner.

6. Distributions. Proceeds from the disposition of Partnership assets shall be applied first to the satisfaction of its debts and liabilities. Proceeds and assets, if any, remaining after payment of creditors shall be distributed as follows:

(a) Cash proceeds distributed to the Partners on the basis of their respective interests.

(b) Particular assets: [*i.e. company trade name, telephone number, contracts in the name of the partnership, accounts receivable, inventory, equipment, furniture, etc.*] to [*specify who receives particular assets*].

7. Indebtedness of Partners. Each Partner who is indebted to the Partnership shall pay on demand of the Liquidating Partner all debts or other obligations that he or she owes to the Partnership. However, the Liquidating Partner shall not make such a demand if the obligation is not otherwise due, unless the Liquidating Partner determines that the amount owed by the Partner is required for the payment of creditors (including Partners) or other liabilities or to satisfy the interest of other Partners. Debts or other obligations owed by any partner to the Partnership shall not be canceled or extinguished by the transfer of any assets (other than cash payment in full) to or from the Partner unless otherwise agreed in writing by all the Partners; these debts shall be taken into account in the final settlement among the Partners.

8. Substitution of Liquidating Partner. If the Partnership has not been wound up by the Termination date, or if the Liquidating Partner has died or withdrawn from the Partnership or has materially breached the provisions of this agreement, this agreement shall continue in effect, but the withdrawing or breaching Liquidating Partner shall have no further authority to bind the Partnership or to act as agent of the other Partners. The Partners holding a majority interest of the Partnership shall have the right to designate by written consent a substitute Liquidating Partner.

9. Contribution If Partnership Assets Are Insufficient. If the Partnership assets are insufficient to satisfy its debts and obligations (including but not limited to expenses of liquidation, reasonable provisions for reserves for contingent liabilities, and debts to Partners for money or property loaned or services rendered to the Partnership), each Partner shall make contributions to the Partnership in proportion to his or her respective share of Partnership losses, as stated in the Partnership Agreement. If any Partner fails to contribute that Partner's share, the other Partners shall contribute pro rata, based on their respective interests, to make up the deficiency, and shall be indemnified by the defaulting partner for all amounts so contributed, with interest at the maximum rate of interest allowed by law on the unpaid balance and all costs and expenses of collection, including reasonable attorney's fees. Any Partner, including the Liquidating Partner, shall have the right to demand, at any time after the Partner who is so demanding has contributed the amount representing his or her share of the deficiency, that the other Partners pay their share of the deficiency to the Liquidating Partner.

10. Release of Claims. Each Partner hereby releases each of the other Partners and the Partnership from all known claims arising under the Partnership agreement, except as stated elsewhere in this agreement.

11. Mutual Representations and Warranties. Each Partner represents and warrants to each of the other Partners that, except as stated in the Partnership books, incorporated by reference in this dissolution agreement: (a) the Partner has not incurred any obligation or liability on behalf of or as apparent agent of the Partnership or the other Partners, or for which the Partner or any other Partner may be charged, or for which the Partner intends to claim refund or reimbursement from the Partnership; and (b) the Partner has not received, discharged, or transferred any credit, monies, property, or other assets of the Partnership. These representations and warranties shall survive the final termination of the Partnership.

12. Power of Attorney to Liquidating Partner. Each Partner, being fully informed and aware that this grant of authority is a special power of attorney coupled with an interest and is thus irrevocable, hereby constitutes and appoints the Liquidating Partner as that Partner's attorney-in-fact, in his or her name and for his or her use and benefit to prepare, execute, acknowledge, verify, file, record, and publish:

(a) All agreements, certificates, and other instruments and documents amending the Partnership Agreement that may be appropriate to reflect: (i) a change of the name or location of the principal place of business of the Partnership; (ii) a change of the name or address of a Partner; (iii) the disposal of a Partner's interest in the Partnership in any manner permitted by this dissolution agreement or the Partnership Agreement; (iv) a person's withdrawing from or becoming an additional Partner of the Partnership; (v) a change in or amendment to any provisions of the Partnership Agreement required by the dissolution agreement; (vi) the exercise by any person of any right or rights in the Partnership Agreement or in this dissolution agreement; or (vii) distributions that may constitute a return of capital, to which distributions the undersigned hereby consents;

(b) All other agreements, notices, instruments, and documents required or appropriate to effect the continuation, dissolution, liquidation, or termination of the Partnership, pursuant to the terms of this agreement, under the applicable partnership laws of the state or jurisdiction in which the Partnership is doing business, or the rules and regulations of any governmental agency in regard to the activities, business, name of the Partnership, or changes affecting the membership of the Partnership. Each of these agreements, certificates, notices, instruments, and documents shall be in such form as the attorney-in-fact here appointed and the counsel for the Partnership both shall deem appropriate, and may be executed by the attorney-in-fact by listing all of the Partners on whose behalf the agreement, certificate, notice, instrument, or document is being executed, with his or her single signature as attorney-in-fact acting for all of them. Each Partner further authorizes the attorney-in-fact to take any further action that the attorney-in-fact shall consider necessary or advisable in connection with any of the foregoing, giving the attorney-in-fact full power and authority to do and perform every act or thing requisite or advisable to be done in this matter as fully as the Partner could do if acting in person, and ratifies and confirms all that the attorney-in-fact shall lawfully do or cause to be done under this provision.

The foregoing grant of authority and power of attorney shall survive the executing Partner's death, insanity, disability, incapacity, or delivery of an assignment of the whole or any portion of his or her interest in the Partnership, subject to the limitations set forth in this agreement.

[*Add boilerplate clauses as needed*]

Consent of Spouse

In consideration of the execution of the foregoing agreement by the other Partners in [*partnership*], I, [*name of spouse*], spouse of [*specify partner.1 or partner.2*], a Partner, do hereby join with my spouse in executing this agreement and agree to be bound by its terms in lieu of any marital rights to which I might otherwise be entitled.

Dated: ______________________________

By:__________________________________

[*Spouse of partner.1 or partner.2*]

AGREEMENT TO TRANSFER ASSETS TO CORPORATION

This Agreement is made this [*date*], between [*partner.1*], [*partner.2*], general partners of a Partnership doing business under the name [*partnership name*] (hereinafter referred to as the "Partnership"), located at [*address*], and [*corporation name*], a [*state, e.g., California*] Corporation (hereinafter referred to as the "Corporation"), located at [*address*].

Recitals

WHEREAS, Partnership owns and desires to sell all of the assets of the above business on the terms and conditions herein set forth; and

WHEREAS, Corporation desires to purchase the assets of the business listed in Exhibit A, and is willing to assume all obligations and liabilities of Partnership of these assets, on the terms and conditions herein set forth.

NOW THEREFORE IN CONSIDERATION of the mutual covenants, agreements, representations, and warranties, and in exchange for good and valuable consideration, the receipt and sufficiency of which is hereby acknowledged, the parties hereby agree as follows:

Agreement

1. Recitals. The Recitals are a material part of this Agreement.

2. Sale of Assets. On the terms and conditions set forth herein, the Partnership shall sell, transfer, and deliver to the Corporation and the Corporation shall purchase, at the close of business on [*date*], all of the assets of the above business, as listed in Exhibit A, including the trade, business, name, goods, and other intangible assets of the business, subject to all liens, claims, and encumbrances and to changes occurring therein in the ordinary course of business between the date of the balance sheet, listed as Exhibit B, and the close of business on the date of transfer, except for: [*list exceptions*].

3. Consideration. As consideration for the sale and transfer, the Corporation agrees to: (a) assume all debts and liabilities of the Partnership referred to on the balance sheet, together with those resulting from changes occurring in the ordinary course of business from the date of the balance sheet and the close of business on the date of transfer; and (b) issue and deliver, at the close of business on the date of transfer, fully paid and non-assessable shares of the Corporation's Common Stock to the persons and in the amounts as follows:

Names	Number of Shares
______________________________	__________________
______________________________	__________________

4. Instruments of Transfer. The Partnership agrees to execute and deliver to Corporation such instruments of transfer and other documents as may be required to transfer title to Corporation and in order to fully carry out the obligations of Partnership as herein set forth.

5. Partnership's Representations and Warranties. Exhibit B as the balance sheet of the Partnership, fairly represents the financial position of the Partnership at said date in accordance with generally accepted accounting principles.

6. Exhibits Incorporated by Reference. All exhibits referred to herein are incorporated by reference and are so incorporated for all purposes.

[*Add boilerplate clauses as needed*]

ARTICLES OF INCORPORATION
OF
[*CORPORATION*]

ARTICLE I - NAME. The name of this corporation is [*name*], Inc.

ARTICLE II - PURPOSE. The purpose of the corporation is to engage in any lawful act or activity for which a corporation may be organized under the corporate laws of [*state*] other than the banking business, the trust company business, or the practice of a profession permitted to be incorporated by the [*state*] law.

ARTICLE III - INITIAL AGENT FOR SERVICE. The name and address in this state of this corporation's initial agent for the service of process is: [*name, street address, city, state, zip*].

ARTICLE IV - CORPORATE SHARES. This corporation is authorized to issue [*only one class*] of shares, which shall be designated "common" shares. The total number of such shares authorized to be issued is [*1,000,000*] shares.

Dated: ____________________

____
Incorporator

ACKNOWLEDGMENT

I hereby declare that I am the person who executed the foregoing Articles of Incorporation, which execution is my act and deed, on this [*date*], at [*location*], [*state*]. I declare under penalty of perjury that the foregoing is true and correct.

____
Incorporator

BYLAWS OF [*CORPORATION*]

Article I: Shareholders

Section 1.1. *Annual Meetings.* An annual meeting of shareholders shall be held for the election of directors at such date, time, and place, either within or without the state of [*state*], as may be designated by resolution of the Board of Directors from time to time. Any other proper business may be transacted at the annual meeting.

Section 1.2. *Special Meetings.* Special meetings of shareholders for any purpose or purposes may be called at any time by the Board of Directors, or by a committee of the Board of Directors which has been duly designated by the Board of Directors and whose powers and authority, as expressly provided in a resolution of the Board of Directors, include the power to call such meetings, but such special meetings may not be called by any other person or persons.

Section 1.3. *Notice of Meetings.* Whenever shareholders are required or permitted to take any action at a meeting, a written notice of the meeting shall be given which shall state the place, date, and hour of the meeting, and, in the case of a special meeting, the purpose or purposes for which the meeting is called. Unless otherwise provided by law, the Articles of Incorporation, or these Bylaws, the written notice of any meeting shall be given not less than ten (10) nor more than sixty (60) days before the date of the meeting to each stockholder entitled to vote at such meeting. If mailed, such notice shall be deemed to be given when deposited in the mail, postage prepaid, directed to the stockholder at his or her address as it appears on the records of the corporation.

Section 1.4. *Adjournments.* Any meeting of shareholders, annual or special, may adjourn from time to time to reconvene at the same or some other place, and notice need not be given of any such adjourned meeting if the time and place thereof are announced at the meeting at which the adjournment is taken. At the adjourned meeting, the corporation may transact any business which might have been transacted at the original meeting. If the adjournment is for more than thirty (30) days, or if after the adjournment a new record date is fixed for the adjourned meeting, a notice of the adjourned meeting shall be given to each stockholder of record entitled to vote at the meeting.

Section 1.5. *Quorum.* Except as otherwise provided by law, the Articles of Incorporation, or these Bylaws, at each meeting of shareholders the presence in person or by proxy of the holders of shares of stock having a majority of the votes which could be cast by the holders of all outstanding shares of stock entitled to vote at the meeting shall be necessary and sufficient to constitute a quorum. In the absence of a quorum, the shareholders so present may, by majority vote, adjourn the meeting from time to time in the manner provided in Section 1.4 of these bylaws until a quorum shall attend. Shares of its own stock belonging to the corporation or to another corporation, if a majority of the shares entitled to vote in the election of directors of such other corporation is held, directly or indirectly, by the corporation, shall neither be entitled to vote nor be counted for quorum purposes; provided, however, that the foregoing shall not limit the right of the corporation to vote stock, including but not limited to its own stock, held by it in a fiduciary capacity.

Section 1.6. *Organization.* Meetings of shareholders shall be presided over by the Chairman of the Board, if any, or in his absence by the Vice Chairman of the Board, if any, or in his or her absence by the President, or in his or her absence by a Vice President, or in the absence of the foregoing persons by a chairman designated by the Board of Directors, or in the absence of such designation by a chairman chosen at the meeting. The Secretary shall act as secretary of the meeting, but in his or her absence the chairman of the meeting may appoint any person to act as secretary of the meeting.

Section 1.7. *Voting; Proxies.* Except as otherwise provided by the Articles of Incorporation, each shareholder entitled to vote at any meeting of shareholders shall be entitled to one vote for each share of stock held by him or her which has voting power upon the matter in question. Each shareholder entitled to vote at a meeting of shareholders may authorize another person or persons to act for him or her by proxy, but no such proxy shall be voted or acted upon after three (3) years from its date, unless the proxy provides for a longer period. A duly executed proxy shall be irrevocable if it states that it is irrevocable and if, and only as long as, it is coupled with an interest sufficient in law to support an irrevocable power. A shareholder may revoke any proxy which is not irrevocable by attending the meeting and voting in person or by filing an instrument in writing revoking the proxy or another duly executed proxy bearing a later date with the Secretary of the corporation. Voting at meetings of shareholders need not be by written ballot and need not be conducted by inspectors of election unless so determined by the holders of shares of stock having a majority of the votes which could be cast by the holders of all outstanding shares of stock entitled to vote thereon which are present in person or by proxy at such meeting. At all meetings of shareholders for the election of directors, a plurality of the votes cast shall be sufficient to elect. All other elections and questions shall, unless otherwise provided by law, the Articles of Incorporation, or these Bylaws, be decided by the vote of the holders of shares of stock having a majority of the votes which could be cast by the holders of all shares of stock entitled to vote thereon which are present in person or represented by proxy at the meeting.

Section 1.8. *Fixing Date for Determination of Shareholders of Record.* In order that the corporation may determine the shareholders entitled to notice of or to vote at any meeting of shareholders or any adjournment thereof, or to express consent to corporate action in writing without a meeting, or entitled to receive payment of any dividend or other distribution or allotment of any rights, or entitled to exercise any rights in respect of any change, conversion, or exchange of stock or for the purpose of any other lawful action, the Board of Directors may fix a record date, which record date shall not precede the date upon which the resolution fixing the record date is adopted by the Board of Directors and which record date: (1) in the case of determination of shareholders entitled to vote at any meeting of shareholders or adjournment thereof, shall, unless otherwise required by law, not be more than sixty (60) nor less than ten (10) days before the date of such meeting; (2) in the case of determination of shareholders entitled to express consent to corporate action in writing without a meeting, shall not be more than ten (10) days from the date upon which the resolution fixing the record date is adopted by the Board of Directors; and (3) in the case of any other action, shall not be more than sixty (60) days prior to such other action. If no record date is fixed: (1) the record date for determining shareholders entitled to notice of or to vote at a meeting of shareholders shall be at the close of business on the day next preceding the day on which notice is given, or, if notice is waived, at the close of business on the day next preceding the day on which the meeting is held; (2) the record date for determining shareholders entitled to express consent to corporate action in writing without a meeting when no prior action of the Board of Directors is required by law, shall be the first date on which a signed written consent setting forth the action taken or proposed to be taken is delivered to the corporation in accordance with applicable law, or, if prior action by the Board of Directors is required by law, shall be at the close of business on the day on which the Board of Directors adopts the resolution taking such prior action; and (3) the record date for determining shareholders for any other purpose shall be at the close of business on the day on which the Board of Directors adopts the resolution relating thereto. A determination of shareholders of record entitled to notice of or to vote at a meeting of shareholders shall apply to any adjournment of the meeting; provided, however, that the Board of Directors may fix a new record date for the adjourned meeting.

Section 1.9. *List of Shareholders Entitled to Vote.* The Secretary shall prepare and make, at least ten (10) days before every meeting of shareholders, a complete list of the shareholders entitled to vote at the meeting, arranged in alphabetical order, and showing the address of each stockholder and the number of shares registered in the name of each stockholder. Such list shall be open to the examination of any stockholder, for any purpose germane to the meeting, during ordinary business hours, for a period of at least ten (10) days prior to the meeting, either at a place within the city where the meeting is to be held, which place shall be specified in the notice of the meeting, or, if not so specified, at the place where the meeting is to be held. The list shall also be produced and kept at the time and place of the meeting during the whole time thereof and may be inspected by any stockholder who is present. Upon the willful neglect or refusal of the directors to produce such a list at any meeting for the election of directors, they shall be ineligible for election to any office at such meeting. The stock ledger shall be the only evidence as to who are the shareholders entitled to examine the stock ledger, the list of shareholders or the books of the corporation, or to vote in person or by proxy at any meeting of shareholders.

Section 1.10. *Action by Consent of Shareholders.* Unless otherwise restricted by the Articles of Incorporation, any action required or permitted to be taken at any annual or special meeting of the shareholders may be taken without a meeting, without prior notice and without a vote, if a consent in writing, setting forth the action so taken, shall be signed by the holders of outstanding stock having not less than the minimum number of votes that would be necessary to authorize or take such action at a meeting at which all shares entitled to vote thereon were present and voted. Prompt notice of the taking of the corporate action without a meeting by less than unanimous written consent shall be given to those shareholders who have not consented in writing.

Article II: Board of Directors

Section 2.1. *Number; Qualifications.* The Board of Directors shall consist of one or more members, the number thereof to be determined from time to time by resolution of the Board of Directors. Directors need not be shareholders.

Section 2.2. *Election; Resignation; Removal; Vacancies.* The Board of Directors shall initially consist of the persons [*named as directors in the Articles of Incorporation or named as directors in the First Meeting of Directors*], and each director so elected shall hold office until the first annual meeting of shareholders or until his or her successor is elected and qualified. At the first annual meeting of shareholders and at each annual meeting thereafter, the shareholders shall elect directors each of whom shall hold office for a term of one year or until his successor is elected and qualified. Any director may resign at any time upon written notice to the corporation. Any newly created directorship or any vacancy occurring in the Board of Directors for any cause may be filled by a majority of the remaining members of the Board of Directors, although such majority is less than a quorum, or by a plurality of the votes cast at a meeting of shareholders, and each director so elected shall hold office until the expiration of the tern of office of the director whom he or she has replaced or until his or her successor is elected and qualified.

Section 2.3. *Regular Meetings.* Regular meetings of the Board of Directors may be held at such places within or without the state of [*state*] and at such times as the Board of Directors may from time to time determine, and if so determined, notices thereof need not be given.

Section 2.4. *Special Meetings.* Special meetings of the Board of Directors may be held at any time or place within or without the state of [*state*] whenever called by the President, any Vice President, the Secretary, or by any member of the Board of Directors. Notice of a special meeting of the Board of Directors shall be given by the person or persons calling the meeting at least twenty-four (24) hours before the special meeting.

Section 2.5. *Telephonic Meetings Permitted.* Members of the Board of Directors, or any committee designated by the Board of Directors, may participate in a meeting thereof by means of conference telephone or similar communications equipment by means of which all persons participating in the meeting can hear each other, and participation in a meeting pursuant to this bylaw shall constitute presence in person at such meeting.

Section 2.6. *Quorum; Vote Required for Action.* At all meetings of the Board of Directors, a majority of the whole Board of Directors shall constitute a quorum for the transaction of business. Except in cases in which the Articles of Incorporation or these Bylaws otherwise provide, the vote of a majority of the directors present at a meeting at which a quorum is present shall be the act of the Board of Directors.

Section 2.7. *Organization.* Meetings of the Board of Directors shall be presided over by the Chairman of the Board, if any, or in his absence by the Vice Chairman of the Board, if any, or in his absence by the President, or in their absence by a chairman chosen at the meeting. The Secretary shall act as secretary of the meeting, but in his absence the chairman of the meeting may appoint any person to act as secretary of the meeting.

Section 2.8. *Informal Action by Directors.* Unless otherwise restricted by the Articles of Incorporation or these Bylaws, any action required or permitted to be taken at any meeting of the Board of Directors, or of any committee thereof, may be taken without a meeting if all members of the Board of Directors or such committee, as the case may be, consent thereto in writing, and the writing or writings are filed with the minutes of proceedings of the Board of Directors or such committee.

Article III: Officers

Section 3.1. *Executive Officers; Election; Qualifications; Term of Office; Resignation; Removal; Vacancies.* The Board of Directors shall elect a President, Treasurer and Secretary, and it may, if it so determines, choose a Chairman of the Board and a Vice Chairman of the Board from among its members. The Board of Directors may also choose one or more Vice Presidents, one or more Assistant Secretaries, and one or more Assistant Treasurers. Each such officer shall hold office until the first meeting of the Board of Directors after the annual meeting of shareholders next succeeding his election, and until his successor is elected and qualified or until his earlier resignation or removal. Any officer may resign at any time upon written notice to the corporation. The Board of Directors may remove any officer with or without cause at any time, but such removal shall be without prejudice to the contractual rights of such officer, if any, with the corporation. Any number of offices may be held by the same person. Any vacancy occurring in any office of the corporation by death, resignation, removal, or otherwise may be filled for the unexpired portion of the term by the Board of Directors at any regular or special meeting.

Section 3.2. *Powers and Duties of Executive Officers.* The officers of the corporation shall have such powers and duties in the management of the corporation as may be prescribed by the Board of Directors and, to the extent not so provided, as generally pertain to their respective offices, subject to the control of the Board of Directors. The Board of Directors may require any officer, agent, or employee to give security for the faithful performance of his duties.

Article IV: Stock

Section 4.1. *Certificates.* Every holder of stock shall be entitled to have a certificate signed by or in the name of the corporation by the Chairman or Vice Chairman of the Board of Directors, if any, or the President or a Vice President and by the Treasurer or an Assistant Treasurer, or the Secretary or an Assistant Secretary, of the corporation, certifying the number of shares owned by him in the corporation. Any of or all the signatures on the certificate may be a facsimile. In case any officer, transfer agent, or registrar who has signed or whose facsimile signature has been placed upon a certificate shall have ceased to be such officer, transfer agent, or registrar before such certificate is issued, it may be issued by the corporation with the same effect as if he were such officer, transfer agent, or registrar at the date of issue.

Section 4.2. *Lost, Stolen, or Destroyed Stock Certificates; Issuance of New Certificates.* The corporation may issue a new certificate of stock in the place of any certificate theretofore issued by it, alleged to have been lost, stolen, or destroyed, and the corporation may require the owner of the lost, stolen, or destroyed certificate, or his legal representative, to give the corporation a bond sufficient to indemnify it against any claim that may be made against it any account of the alleged loss, theft, or destruction of any such certificate or the issuance of such new certificate.

Article V: Indemnification

Section 5.1. *Right to Indemnification.* The corporation shall indemnify and hold harmless, to the fullest extent permitted by applicable law as it presently exists or may hereafter be amended, any person who was or is made or is threatened to be made a party or is otherwise involved in any action, suit, or proceeding, whether civil, criminal, administrative, or investigative (a proceeding) by reason of the fact that he, or a person for whom he is the legal representative, is or was a director, officer, employee, or agent of the corporation or is or was serving at the request of the corporation as a director, officer, employee, or agent of another corporation or of a partnership, joint venture, trust, enterprise, or non-profit entity, including service with respect to employee benefit plans, against all liability and loss suffered and expenses reasonably incurred by such person. The corporation shall be required to indemnify a person in connection with a proceeding initiated by such person only if the proceeding was authorized by the Board of Directors of the corporation.

Section 5.2. *Prepayment of Expenses.* The corporation shall pay the expenses incurred in defending any proceeding in advance of its final disposition, provided, however, that the payment of expenses incurred by a director or officer in advance of the final disposition of the proceeding shall be made only upon receipt of an undertaking by the director or officer to repay all amounts advanced if it should be ultimately determined that the director or officer is not entitled to be indemnified under this Article or otherwise.

Section 5.3. *Claims.* If a claim for indemnification or payment of expenses under this Article is not paid in full within sixty (60) days after a written claim therefor has been received by the corporation, the claimant may file suit to recover the unpaid amount of such claim and, if successful in whole or in part, shall be entitled to be paid the expense of prosecuting such claim. In any such action, the corporation shall have the burden of proving that the claimant was not entitled to the requested indemnification or payment of expenses under applicable law.

Section 5.4. *Non-Exclusivity of Rights.* The rights conferred on any person by this Article shall not be exclusive of any other rights which such person may have or hereafter acquire under any statute, provision of the Articles of Incorporation, these Bylaws, agreement, vote of shareholders, disinterested directors, or otherwise.

Section 5.5. *Other Indemnification.* The corporation's obligation, if any, to indemnify any person who was or is serving at its request as a director, officer, employee, or agent of another corporation, partnership, joint venture, trust, enterprise, or non-profit entity shall be reduced by any amount such person may collect as indemnification from such other corporation, partnership, joint venture, trust, enterprise, or non-profit enterprise.

Section 5.6. *Amendment or Repeal.* Any repeal or modification of the foregoing provisions of this Article shall not adversely affect any right or protection hereunder of any person in respect of any act or omission occurring prior to the time of such repeal or modification.

Article VI: Miscellaneous

Section 6.1. *Fiscal Year.* The fiscal year of the corporation shall be determined by resolution of the Board of Directors.

Section 6.2. *Seal.* The corporate seal shall have the name of the corporation inscribed thereon and shall be in such form as may be approved from time to time by the Directors.

Section 6.3. *Waiver of Notice of Meetings of Shareholders and Directors.* Any written waiver of notice, signed by the person entitled to notice, whether before or after the time stated therein, shall be deemed equivalent to notice. Attendance of a person at a meeting shall constitute a waiver of notice of such meeting, except when the person attends a meeting for the express purpose of objecting, at the beginning of the meeting, to the transaction of any business because the meeting is not lawfully called or convened. Neither the business to be transacted at, nor the purpose of any regular or special meeting of the shareholders, directors, or members of a committee of directors need be specified in any written waiver of notice.

Section 6.4. *Interested Directors; Quorum.* No contract or transaction between the corporation and one or more of its directors or officers, or between the corporation and any other corporation, partnership, association, or other organization in which one or more of its directors or officers are directors or officers, or have a financial interest, shall be void or voidable solely for this reason, or solely because the director or officer is present at or participates in the meeting of the Board of Directors or committee thereof which authorizes the contract or transaction, or solely because his or their votes are counted for such purpose, if: (1) the material facts as to his relationship or interest and as to the contract or transaction are disclosed or are known to the Board of Directors or the committee, and the Board of Directors or committee in good faith authorizes the contract or transaction by the affirmative votes of a majority of the disinterested directors, even though the disinterested directors be less than a quorum; or (2) the material facts as to his relationship or interest and as to the contract or transaction are disclosed or are known to the shareholders entitled to vote thereon, and the contract or transaction is specifically approved in good faith by vote of the shareholders; or (3) the contract or transaction is fair as to the corporation as of the time it is authorized, approved, or ratified, by the Board of Directors, a committee thereof, or the shareholders. Common or interested directors may be counted in determining the presence of a quorum at a meeting of the Board of Directors or of a committee which authorizes the contract or transaction.

Section 6.5. *Amendment of Bylaws.* These Bylaws may be altered or repealed, and new Bylaws made, by the Board of Directors, but the shareholders may make additional Bylaws and may alter and repeal any Bylaws whether adopted by them or otherwise.

Certificate of Secretary

I, the undersigned, do hereby certify as follows: I am the present duly elected and acting Secretary of the above named corporation, under the laws of the state of [*state*]; and the foregoing Bylaws constitute the original Bylaws of said corporation as duly adopted by the directors on [*date*].

WITNESS WHEREOF, I have subscribed my name and affixed the seal of this Corporation on [*date*].

____

Secretary

MINUTES OF FIRST MEETING OF BOARD OF DIRECTORS

The First Meeting of the Board of Directors of [*corporation*] was held on the date, time, and at the place set forth in the written Waiver of Notice signed by the directors, fixing such time and place, and prefixed to the Minutes of this meeting.

Directors Present; Officers of the Meeting. The following directors were present:

____

____

The meeting was called to order by [*name*]. It was moved, seconded, and unanimously carried that [*name*] act as Temporary Chairman, and that [*name*] act as Temporary Secretary.

Waiver of Notice. The Chairman announced that the meeting was held pursuant to written Waiver of Notice thereof and Consent thereto signed by all of the Directors of the Corporation; said Waiver and Consent was presented to the meeting and upon motion duly made, seconded, and unanimously carried was made a part of the records of the meeting and now precedes the Minutes of this meeting in the Minute Book of this corporation.

Articles Filed. The Chairman announced that the corporation was incorporated on [*date*], the date on which the [*Articles of Incorporation, or sometimes known as Certificate of Incorporation*] were filed by the Secretary of State. The Chairman presented a certified copy of the [*Articles or Certificate*] and directed the Secretary to insert it in the corporation's minute book.

Approval or Appointment of Agent for Service of Process. The Chairman informed the Board that the corporation is required by statute to designate an agent for service of process in the state of [*state*], and that [*name*] had been designated as that agent in the corporation's articles filed with the Secretary of State. After discussion, and on motion duly made, seconded, and unanimously carried, the following resolution was adopted:

> RESOLVED, that [*person or corporation*], a resident of [*state of incorporation*], whose address is [*location*], is approved as this corporation's agent for service of process in [*state*] as required by [*state*] corporate law.

Bylaws. The matter of the adoption of Bylaws for the regulation of the corporation was next considered. The Secretary presented to the meeting a copy of the proposed Bylaws of this corporation. On motion duly made, seconded, and unanimously carried, the following resolutions were adopted:

> RESOLVED, that the Bylaws presented to this meeting and discussed hereto be and the same hereby are adopted as and for the Bylaws of this corporation.

> RESOLVED FURTHER, that the Secretary of this corporation is authorized and directed to execute a certificate of the adoption of those Bylaws and to insert those Bylaws as so certified in the Minute Book of this corporation and to cause a copy of those Bylaws, as they may be amended from time to time, to be kept and maintained at the principal executive office of this corporation, in accordance with [*state*] corporate law.

Election of Officers. The meeting proceeded to the election of a President, Vice President, Secretary, and Chief Financial Officer [*Treasurer*]. The following were duly nominated and elected to the offices indicated after their names:

PRESIDENT	______________________
VICE PRESIDENT	______________________
SECRETARY	______________________
CHIEF FINANCIAL OFFICER	______________________

Each officer so elected, being present, accepted his or her office, and thereafter the President presided at the meeting as Chairman and the Secretary acted as Secretary of the meeting.

Corporate Seal. The Chairman presented to the board for its approval a proposed seal of the corporation. On motion duly made, seconded, and unanimously carried, the following resolution was adopted:

> RESOLVED, that the corporate seal in the form, words, and figures presented at this meeting be and the same hereby is adopted as the seal of this corporation.

Share Certificate. The Chairman then presented to the Board of Directors for its approval a proposed form of share certificate to be used by the corporation for its common shares. On motion duly made, seconded, and unanimously carried, the following resolution was adopted:

> RESOLVED, that the proposed form of common share certificate presented to this meeting is adopted for use by the corporation for its common shares, and the Secretary is instructed to insert a copy of this certificate in the Minute Book following the Minutes of this meeting.

Issuance of Shares Under Securities Exemption. The Chairman stated that the next order of business was to consider the issuance of the corporation's capital stock. He or she advised the Board that in order to qualify for a securities exemption, the following conditions must be met by the corporation:

[*check state law to determine stock exemption requirements*]

Issuance of Shares for Legal Consideration. The Board next discussed the issuance of shares, and on motion duly made, seconded, and unanimously carried, the following resolutions were adopted:

RESOLVED, that the corporation issue and sell a total of [*amount*] shares of its authorized common stock to the following persons, in the number and for the consideration set forth opposite their names, respectively:

Name	Number of shares	Consideration and (if other than cash) Fair Market Value
____________________	______	______________
____________________	______	______________

RESOLVED FURTHER, that the Officers of the corporation be and they hereby are authorized, empowered, and directed to execute all documents and to take all action which they deem necessary or advisable in order for this corporation to issue and sell the above-listed shares to the persons named, in accordance with applicable laws, and that those actions shall include doing all acts that may be necessary under the federal securities laws and the securities laws of the state of incorporation; and doing all acts necessary to expedite these transactions or conform them, or any of them, to the requirements of any applicable law, ruling, or regulation.

RESOLVED FURTHER, that each of the officers of this corporation be and each hereby is authorized and directed to execute all documents and to take any other action necessary or advisable to carry out the purposes of this resolution.

Bank Resolution. The Chief Financial Officer informed the Board that it would be necessary to establish one or more bank checking and savings accounts and to select a depository for the corporation's taxes trust funds. He or she reported that an SS-4 form had been filed with the Internal Revenue Service, applying for an employer identification number for the corporation. [*See SS-4 in Section III, Government Forms, for instructions on filing this form. It is required to open a bank account.*] On motion duly made and seconded, the following resolutions were made and unanimously adopted:

> RESOLVED, that the corporation open an account or accounts with [*bank*] located at [*address*], that the President and Secretary of this corporation are authorized to establish an account or accounts, on terms and conditions as agreed on with the bank.
>
> RESOLVED FURTHER, that until such authority is revoked by sealed notification to said bank of such action by the Board of Directors of this Corporation, that its Officers are [*list officers and titles*], and they are authorized, [*any one acting alone or any two acting jointly for amounts over $________*], to execute checks and other items for and on behalf of this corporation.

Payment of Expenses of Incorporation. The meeting then considered the payment of the expenses of incorporation and organization. The Chief Financial Officer reported on the fees and expenses that had been incurred to date in this connection. On motion duly made, seconded, and unanimously carried, the following resolution was adopted:

> RESOLVED, that the Chief Financial Officer is authorized and directed to pay the expenses of incorporation and organization, and to reimburse the persons advancing funds to the corporation for this purpose, as stated in the Treasurer's report presented to this meeting.

Principal Office Location. After some discussion, the location of the principal office of the corporation for the transaction of business of the corporation was fixed pursuant to the following resolution unanimously adopted, upon motion duly made and seconded:

RESOLVED that the location of the principal office for the transaction of the business of this corporation, until changed by subsequent resolution of the Board shall be as follows: [*address*]

Adjournment. There being no further business to come before the meeting, upon motion duly made, seconded, and unanimously carried, the meeting was adjourned.

____

Temporary Chairman

____

Temporary Secretary

____

Director

____

Director

SHAREHOLDERS' AGREEMENT

This Shareholders' Agreement ("Agreement") is entered into as of the [*date*], by and between [*corporation*] (hereinafter referred to as "Corporation"), [*shareholder.1*] ("Shareholder.1"), [*shareholder.2*] ("Shareholder.2"), and their spouses and heirs, where applicable (hereinafter collectively referred to as "Shareholders" and individually as "Shareholder").

Recitals

WHEREAS, [*shareholder.1*] and [*shareholder.2*] are the owners of [*total number of shares issued*] shares each of the capital stock of [*corporation*], which shares constitute all issued and outstanding shares of Corporation; and

WHEREAS, the Shareholders desire to become parties to and subject their shares of capital stock presently owned or hereafter acquired in Corporation to a Shareholders' Agreement; and

WHEREAS, the Shareholders desire to agree on the scope and description of how the business of Corporation shall be conducted; and

WHEREAS, the Parties believe that it is in the best interests of Corporation that all stock of Corporation, whether owned by Shareholders as of the date of this Agreement or subsequently acquired by Shareholders (the "Shares") be made available for sale to the Corporation and/or the other Shareholder upon occurrence of certain events in order to ensure continuity of management and control of the common stock by other Shareholders;

NOW THEREFORE, in consideration of the mutual covenants, conditions, promises, and agreements herein contained, and in exchange for other good and valuable consideration, the receipt and sufficiency of which is acknowledged, the parties hereby agree as follows:

Agreement

1. Recitals. The Recitals are a material part of this Agreement.

2. Board of Directors/Officers: Unless otherwise agreed in writing, the

Shareholders agree that, for so long as [*shareholder.1*] continues as a key employee of Corporation, [*shareholder.1*] will be elected as the Chairman of the Board of Directors. Additionally, the Parties agree that the following persons will be elected to the following positions:

President	[*Specify*]
Vice President	[*Specify*]
Treasurer	[*Specify*]
Secretary	[*Specify*]

3. Scope and Direction: The parties agree that the Corporation shall operate a [*describe business*], located at [*address*], until otherwise changed.

4. Nature and Amount of Contributions: The nature and amount of the equity contributions of Shareholders are as follows: [*Describe what each shareholder will contribute to the corporation in exchange for his or her stock.*] If any Shareholder fails to make any required contribution including working the necessary hours as required by this Agreement, the non-defaulting party shall have the right to exclude the defaulting party from management and affairs of Corporation.

5. Management of Corporation: The business and affairs of Corporation shall be managed and all corporate powers shall be exercised by or under the direction of the Shareholders (in proportion to their respective ownership interest in Corporation), who shall have the authority to delegate certain tasks to any Director, Officer, or Employee; provided, however, that no Director, Officer, or Employee shall have the authority to do any of the following without the prior written consent of the other Shareholders: (1) issue or sell on behalf of Corporation any additional Shares of its capital stock; (2) sell all or substantially all of Corporation's assets; or (3) cause Corporation to engage in any business other than that in which it is presently engaged or plans to engage.

Each Shareholder agrees to indemnify and hold harmless every other Shareholder and their successors and assigns from and against any claim, loss, damage, liability, or cost (including reasonable attorney's fees) asserted against or incurred by the other Shareholders as a result of exceeding the exercise of corporate powers by each Shareholder; provided, however, that no Shareholder shall be liable for losses incurred as a result of forces beyond his/her reasonable control, including but not limited to extraordinary events or circumstances such as fire, earthquake, other natural disasters, theft, armed robbery, or a drop in market prices for the Corporation's goods and services.

Each party understands and agrees that the Shareholders have the right to manage the affairs of the Corporation as per their percentage of ownership in the Corporation. If the Shareholders cannot agree such that an impasse occurs, then the Parties shall enter into non-binding mediation. If mediation fails, then the Parties agree to enter into binding arbitration, with an arbitrator mutually agreed upon by the parties. If the Parties cannot agree upon an arbitrator, the Parties agree that an independent arbitrator, appointed by any court of competent jurisdiction shall arbitrate the matter and shall be acceptable to the Parties.

6. Income and Disbursments: Subject to the limitations of [*state*] law, operating requirements of the Corporation and/or alternative vote of a majority of shares of the Corporation, all income derived from operation of the business of the Corporation shall be paid in the following manner each month, continuing until paid in full:

A. Rent expenses of the Corporation's business premises;

B. Supplies, equipment, non-principal employee wages, and all other charges, debts, and obligations incurred by the Corporation or on its behalf; and

C. Officers salaries to [*names*] in the amount of $[*amount*] per month, which shall be paid in the event that there are enough profits after the payments provided for above and a reasonable reserve for anticipated operational expenses.

D. Any additional monthly profits shall be retained by the Corporation, unless the Shareholders agree and the Corporation can legally pay out a dividend to the Shareholders, then such profits shall be paid to the Shareholders in proportion to their ownership of the stock of the Corporation.

7. Restriction on Transfer of Shares

A. DEFINITIONS

1) Ownership Percentage. For purposes of this Agreement, a Shareholder's "Ownership Percentage" shall equal the ratio of the number of Shares held by such Shareholder at the time such right or option is to be exercised to the number of Shares owned by all Shareholders who elect to exercise such right or option.

2) Purchase Price. The "Purchase Price" of Shares purchased pursuant to this Agreement shall be computed in accordance with the provisions of Paragraph 10A of this Agreement and shall be paid to the Shareholder in accordance with the provisions of Paragraph 10B of this Agreement.

3) Triggering Event. Any condition occurring as specified in Paragraph 7B(2).

4) Offer Notice. Written notice of Triggering Event as more particularly specified in Paragraph 7B(3).

5) Exercise Notice. The Shareholder's and/or Corporation's written notice of exercising his/her/its rights to purchase shares as more particularly described in Paragraph 7B(5).

B. RESTRICTIONS ON TRANSFER OF SHARES [*This section should be discussed with your tax attorney or accountant.*]

1) Restrictions on Transfer of Shares. Except as otherwise provided in this Agreement, no Shareholder or Shareholder's heirs, executors, administrators, or permitted assigns, shall sell, assign, mortgage, pledge, or otherwise transfer or encumber any Shares or any right or interest in them; and any such assignment, mortgage, pledge, or other transfer or encumbrance of such Shares in violation of this Agreement shall be null and void.

2) Events Triggering Option to Purchase Shares. Notwithstanding Paragraph 1 of this section, the following events shall trigger an option to purchase Shares:

a) If a Shareholder dies while owning any Shares;

b) Except as otherwise permitted herein, if a Shareholder attempts to assign, mortgage, pledge, or transfer or otherwise encumber any shares;

c) If a Shareholder engages in any conduct with respect to Corporation which is adjudicated as fraudulent, willful misconduct, or gross negligence ("improper conduct");

d) In the event a Shareholder is adjudicated a bankrupt (voluntary or involuntary) or makes an assignment for the benefit of his/her creditors;

e) In the event a Shareholder is physically or mentally incapacitated for more than six (6) months as shown by his/her inability to participate in the business of Corporation;

f) In the event a Shareholder is divorced or legally separated from such Shareholder's spouse and such spouse becomes the owner of or entitled to any interest in the Shares of Corporation incident to such divorce.

g) In the event one or more Shareholders shall enter into an agreement to sell to a third party a majority of the issued and outstanding Shares of Corporation.

3) Notice of Triggering Event. Upon the occurrence of any Triggering Event, the Shareholder triggering the event or his or her estate shall provide written notice ("Offer Notice") to the Corporation, and other Shareholders, of such Triggering Event. The Offer Notice shall be communicated to the Corporation, and other Shareholders by mailing such Offer Notice by registered or certified mail to the persons listed herein. Such Offer Notice shall be sent to all Shareholders and Corporation on the same date and shall be exercisable for the persons listed herein for forty-five days (45) days from the date that the Offer Notice is sent.

4) Option to Purchase. Upon the occurrence of any Triggering Event, then [*shareholder.1*] so long as he or she is a Shareholder, and [*shareholder.2*] so long as he or she is a Shareholder, shall have an equal right to purchase such Shares (in proportion to their respective ownership interests in Corporation). If there are remaining Shares, the Corporation, next, and any

remaining Shareholders (in proportion to their respective ownership interests in Corporation), last, shall have the option, to purchase any Shares for which a prior option holder does not exercise his/hers/its option hereunder.

5) Exercise of Notice. Any Shareholder or the Corporation shall exercise his/her/its option under this Section by giving written notice of such exercise ("Exercise Notice") and the number of Shares to be purchased to the Shareholder or his/her estate involved in the Triggering Event at any time prior to forty-five (45) days after the Offer Notice of the Triggering Event was first provided to the Shareholders and the Corporation. It is understood that the forty-five (45) day option period shall begin on the same date for all shareholders and the Corporation, which shall be the first date that any Shareholder or the Corporation receives notice of the Triggering Event.

[*Shareholder.1*] and [*shareholder.2*] shall have the option (in proportion to their ownership interests) to purchase the shares first, Corporation has the option to purchase second, and any other Shareholders have the option to purchase any remaining shares third. If the Exercise Notices of [*shareholder.1*] and [*shareholder.2*] reflect more shares are available for purchase by the Corporation, then the Corporation's Exercise Notice shall be implemented. If notice of the Exercise Notice from the Corporation reflects more shares are available for purchase by any other remaining Shareholders, then any such remaining Shareholder shall have be entitled to purchase the available shares in proportion to the percentage of the Corporation's Shares he/she/it holds bears to the number of the Corporation's shares held by all Shareholders electing to purchase.

In the event this option is not exercised as to all the shares owned by the selling Shareholder, such selling Shareholder or Shareholder's successor in interest will no longer be obligated to sell to any Shareholder or the Corporation those Shares that each Shareholder and the Corporation fails to accept or elects not to purchase, provided that any subsequent sale of such Shares shall not be on terms more favorable to the transferee than the terms and conditions stipulated in the Offer Notice.

6) Obligations of Transferees. Each Transferee or any subse-

quent transferee of Shares in Corporation, and their spouses, shall hold the shares or interest in the shares subject to all provisions of this Agreement and shall make no further transfers except as provided in this Agreement. Transfer of the Shares shall not be entered on the books of Corporation until an amended copy of this Agreement or an addendum to the Agreement has been executed by the prospective transferee. Failure or refusal to sign such an amended copy of this Agreement shall not relieve any transferee from any obligations under this obligation.

7) Sale of a Majority of Shares. In the event that one or more Shareholders shall enter into an Agreement to sell to a third party a majority of the issued and outstanding stock of Corporation, selling Shareholders shall give the other Shareholders written notice of such Agreement and Shareholder's receiving any such notice shall have the right to require that their shares be included in a proportional amount with the noticing Shareholder's shares to sell at the same price per Share and on the same terms as applicable to the shares of the noticing Shareholders.

8. Insurance Policies

A. Insurance Policies. Any Shareholder and/or the Corporation are authorized to take out insurance policies on the life of any Shareholder. All insurance policies taken out shall be evaluated at least once per year to ensure that the fluctuation of the market value of the stock is regularly updated.

1) Ownership Rights in Insurance Policies. The person taking out such policies shall be the sole owner thereof and such policies shall constitute such owner's sole and absolute property.

2) Submission to Physical Examinations. The Shareholders shall submit, from time to time, but in no event may any one person be required to submit to more than one such examination per year, to any physical examinations as may be required by the insurance carrier for any life insurance policy which may be taken out by the other Shareholders and/or the Corporation on the life of any Shareholder.

B. Excess Proceeds. In the event any insurance proceeds on the life of a Shareholder payable to the Corporation or the other Shareholders exceed the amount necessary to accomplish their purchases of Shares under this Agreement, such excess may be retained by the recipient thereof for its or their sole ownership and benefit.

C. Exhibit "A". Each such policy taken out for the purposes of this Agreement, whether existing or additional policies hereafter acquired for the same purposes, shall be listed and described in Exhibit "A" to this Agreement.

9. Spouse Subject to Agreement

A. Spouse Subject to Agreement. Spouses of each married Shareholder hereby join in the execution of this Agreement to indicate such spouses' agreement to be bound by the terms hereof and to evidence that such spouses' community interest, if any, in and to any of Shares of the Corporation now or hereafter registered in the name of such Shareholder is covered by and embraced within the terms and provisions of this Agreement in all respects. The purchase of shares of a Shareholder pursuant to this Agreement shall include the shares of the Corporation or any interest therein owned by the spouse of such Shareholder.

B. Transfers to Shareholder. Any other provision of this Agreement to the contrary notwithstanding, the transfer by the spouse of a Shareholder to or for the benefit of such Shareholder of all or part of such spouse's community interest, if any, in shares of the Corporation effected by means of sale, gift, testamentary bequest, divorce, legal separation, under the laws of intestate succession, or otherwise shall not create any right of the other Shareholders or of the Corporation to purchase such interest in the shares of Corporation from such spouse or such spouse's estate, unless otherwise provided for herein.

C. Divorce or Legal Separation of Spouse. In the event a Shareholder is divorced or legally separated from such spouse and such spouse or such spouse's estate becomes the owner of or entitled to any interest in the Shares of Corporation incident to such divorce or legal separation, then the Shareholder shall have the option to purchase all or any part of the interest of such spouse in the shares of Corporation, and the remaining Shareholders and the Corporation shall in that order of priority have the next option to purchase the interest of such spouse for which Shareholder does not exercise his or her option hereunder.

All Shareholders and the Corporation shall exercise their options by giving written notice in the form of Exercise Notice in accordance with this Agreement.

10. Purchase Price: Installment Payments [*This section should be discussed with your accountant or tax attorney.*]

A. Valuation of Shares by Appraisal. The purchase price to be paid for the shares subject to this Agreement shall be determined by an appraisal of the fair market value of the shares to be purchased, performed by a qualified appraiser mutually agreed upon by the Parties in interest, or if the Parties cannot so agree, then an independent appraiser shall be appointed by a court of competent jurisdiction to perform such appraisal. The fair market value shall be determined as of the date of the Triggering Event.

B. Payment of Purchase Price. At the option of the purchaser of any Shares, the full amount of the Purchase Price determined under Paragraph 10A may be paid immediately in cash to the seller of such Shares, or such full amount may be paid ten percent (10%) in cash on the Triggering Event date and the remaining aggregate balance amount paid in [*x*] equal annual installments bearing interest at ten percent (10%) per annum, or the highest rate of interest allowed by law, whichever is lower. The first such installment of the purchase price shall be due and payable one year from the Triggering Event. The deferred portion of the purchase price for any Shares purchased under this Agreement shall be represented by a promissory note executed by any purchasing Shareholders.

C. Continuing Right to Purchase in Certain Circumstances. If, at the time the Corporation is required to make payment of the Purchase Price for any shares upon the exercise of any option to purchase the shares described in these Sections, and it cannot legally do so under applicable state law because its capital or surplus is insufficient for such purpose, then the Corporation shall purchase as many shares as it can lawfully purchase. Payment for the shares so purchased shall be made and its value as determined under Paragraph 10A hereof, and in the manner prescribed in Paragraph 10B. If, and to the extent that, under applicable state law, the Corporation is not able to purchase the shares of Shareholder at such time because of an insufficiency of capital or surplus, then subject to availability and prior sale, the Corporation shall continue to have the right to purchase the shares it could not lawfully purchase, which right may be exercised at such time and to the extent that the capital or surplus of Corporation becomes sufficient therefor.

D. Purchase Price for Tax Purposes. It is understood that the Purchase Price, as set forth above, shall be the value of the purchased Shares for all tax purposes. In the event such value is later increased by any federal or state taxing authority, any tax liability resulting from such increase shall be borne by the selling Shareholder of his or her executor, administrator, or personal representative, as the case may be.

11. Miscellaneous Provisions

A. Inscription on Shares Certificate. Upon the execution of this Agreement, the certificate or certificates of shares subject hereto shall be surrendered to Corporation and inscribed as follows: "This certificate is transferable only upon compliance with the provisions of a Shareholders' Agreement made as of [*date*], by and among [*shareholder.1*, *shareholder.2*], a copy of which is on file in the office of the secretary of the corporation."

After inscription, the certificates shall be returned to the Shareholder and the Shareholder shall, subject to the terms of this Agreement, be entitled to exercise all rights of ownership of such shares. Any shares of common stock of the Corporation acquired and/or sold by any Shareholder will be subject to all the terms and conditions of this Agreement, and will be tendered by such Shareholder for proper legend inscription in accordance with the provisions of this Agreement. Any subsequent shares purchased or sold by any Shareholder will in all respects be covered by this Agreement.

B. Administrative Approvals. The Corporation agrees to apply for, and use its best efforts to obtain, all governmental and administrative approvals required in connection with the purchase and sale of the shares under this Agreement. The Shareholders agree to cooperate in obtaining the approvals and to execute any and all documents that may be required to be executed by them in connection with the approvals. The Corporation shall pay all costs and filing fees in connection with obtaining the approvals. Each Party agrees to perform any further acts and execute and deliver any documents that may be necessary to carry out the provisions of this Agreement.

C. Closings. The closing of any purchase and sale of any shares described herein shall take place at the principal offices of the Corporation within forty-five (45) days after the exercise of any option (Exercise Notice) or right to purchase the shares described herein. At the closing, the seller of such shares shall deliver certificates representing the shares to be sold properly endorsed or accompanied by an appropriate stock power. Unless otherwise agreed in writing among Shareholders, any transfer of shares described herein shall be free and clear of all liens and encumbrances.

D. Shareholder Wills and Trusts. When appropriate, each Shareholder agrees to include in his/her Will and Trust a direction and authorization to his/her executor to comply with the provisions of this Agreement and to sell his/her shares in accordance with this Agreement; however, the failure of any Shareholder to do so shall not affect the validity or enforceability of this Agreement.

E. Termination of the Agreement. This Agreement shall cease and terminate on the occurrence of any of the following acts: (a) cessation of the corporate business or enterprise of Corporation during the lifetime of Shareholders; (b) dissolution or insolvency of Corporation; or (c) mutual agreement of termination between Corporation and Shareholders.

[*Add boilerplate clauses as needed*]

CONSENT OF SPOUSES

The undersigned is the spouse of [*shareholder.1*] and acknowledges that [*she/he*] has read the Shareholder Agreement dated [*date*] (the "Agreement"), by and between [*shareholder.1 and shareholder.2*] (collectively referred to as "Shareholders") and [*corporation*] (the "Corporation"), and clearly understands their provisions. The undersigned is aware that, by the provisions of the Agreement, [*she and her/he and his*] spouse have agreed to sell or transfer all their interest in Corporation, [*including any community property interest*] in accordance with the terms and provisions of the Agreement. The undersigned hereby expressly approves of and agrees to be bound by the provisions of the Agreement in its entirety, including, but not limited to, those provisions relating to the sales and transfers of the interest in Corporation. If the undersigned predeceases [*her/his*] spouse when her spouse owns an interest in Corporation, [*she/he*] hereby agrees not to devise or bequeath whatever [*community*] property interest she may have in Corporation in contravention of the Agreement.

Dated: ______________________

____

[*Name, Spouse of Shareholder.1*]

Note: Use the same consent form if Shareholder.2 is married.

ANNUAL WRITTEN CONSENT
OF SHAREHOLDERS

The undersigned, being the majority of Shareholders of [*corporation*], a [*state*] Corporation, in accordance with [*state*] law and the Bylaws of this Corporation, do hereby consent to the adoption of the following recitals and resolutions:

ELECTION OF DIRECTORS

WHEREAS, the Shareholders have the authority under law and by the Bylaws of this Corporation to elect the Directors;

NOW THEREFORE BE IT RESOLVED, that the following persons are unanimously elected as the Directors to serve at the pleasure of the Shareholders until their successors have been duly elected and qualified:

[*List Directors*]

RESOLVED FURTHER, that the Secretary is directed to file this Written Consent with the minutes of Directors' proceedings.

RATIFICATION AND APPROVAL OF ACTIONS

WHEREAS, the Directors and Officers of the Corporation have taken action between the last meeting or written consent and this written consent; and

WHEREAS, it would be in the best interests of the Corporation to ratify and approve the actions of the Directors and Officers of the Corporation occurring between the last meeting or written consent and this written consent;

RESOLVED, that the Shareholders ratify and approve the actions of the Directors and Officers of the Corporation occurring between the last meeting or written consent and this consent.

Dated: ______________________________

____

[*Shareholder.1*]

____

[*Shareholder.2*]

ANNUAL WRITTEN CONSENT
OF DIRECTORS

The undersigned, being the Board of Directors of [*corporation*], a [*state*] Corporation (the "Corporation"), in accordance with [*state*] law and the Bylaws of this Corporation, do hereby consent to the adoption of the following recitals and resolutions without a meeting and without notice:

ELECTION OF OFFICERS

WHEREAS, the Board of Directors has the authority under law and by the bylaws of this Corporation to elect the officers;

NOW THEREFORE BE IT RESOLVED, that the following persons are unanimously elected to the office indicated opposite their names to serve at the pleasure of the Directors until the next annual meeting and until their successors are duly elected and qualified:

OFFICE	NAME
President	______________________
Vice President	______________________
Secretary	______________________
Treasurer	______________________

RESOLVED FURTHER, that the Secretary is directed to file this Written Consent with the minutes of Directors' proceedings.

RATIFICATION AND APPROVAL OF ACTIONS

WHEREAS, the Directors and Officers of the Corporation have taken action between the last meeting or written consent and this written consent; and

WHEREAS, it would be in the best interests of the Corporation to ratify and approve the actions of the Directors and Officers of the Corporation occurring between the last meeting or written consent and this written consent;

RESOLVED, the Directors ratify and approve the actions of the Directors and Officers of the Corporation occurring between the last meeting or written consent and this written consent.

Dated: ______________________

____

[*Director.1*]

____

[*Director.2*]

SALE OF STOCK
AGREEMENT

This Agreement is made and entered into by and between [*seller*] (hereinafter referred to as "Seller"), and [*buyer*], hereinafter referred to as "Buyer."

Recitals

WHEREAS, Seller is the owner of [*number*] shares of common stock ("stock") of [*corporation*], a [*state of incorporation*] Corporation (hereinafter referred to as "Company"); and

WHEREAS, Seller is willing to sell, and Buyer is willing to purchase Seller's stock in Company upon the terms and conditions hereinafter set forth.

NOW THEREFORE IN CONSIDERATION of the mutual covenants, agreements, representations, and warranties, and in exchange for good and valuable consideration, the receipt and sufficiency of which is hereby acknowledged, the parties hereby agree as follows:

Agreement

1. Recitals. The Recitals are a material part of this Agreement.

2. Purchase of Common Stock. Seller agrees to sell, and Buyer agrees to buy Seller's stock in Company for the sum of [*amount of purchase/sale of business*]. The purchase price shall be paid as follows: [*list terms of purchase, e.g., cash to the Seller at the closing of (amount); and by the execution and delivery to Seller of a promissory note in the amount of (note), bearing interest at (percentage) percent per annum, (date of first payment due) with principal and interest payable in monthly installments, beginning (date of first payment date) and continuing on the first day each month until paid in full.*]

3. Assignment and Transfer. Seller hereby sells and transfers to Buyer his or her [*number*] shares (and any other shares) of common stock in Company. Seller shall execute and deliver to Buyer at the closing, or at any subsequent time as may be demanded by Buyer, such bill of sale, assignment, or other documents evidencing the conveyance of Seller's common stock of the Company to Buyer. At the closing, Seller shall deliver such certificate or certificates evidencing such shares, duly endorsed in blank, to Buyer, naming [*agent*], as his or her agent for transferring said shares on the books and records of the Corporation as herein provided.

4. Warranties of Seller. Seller hereby represents and warrants that he or she is the owner, beneficially and of record, of said [*number*] shares of common stock of Company free and clear of all liens, encumbrances, security agreements, equities, options, claims, charges, and restrictions. Seller further represents that these are the only shares or other interest in the Company which he or she owns. Seller has full power to transfer the common stock without obtaining the consent or approval of any person or entity.

5. Liabilities. Seller warrants and represents that he or she has not knowingly incurred any liabilities in the name of the Company which are obligations of the Company. Seller agrees to indemnify and hold Buyer free and harmless from any liabilities knowingly incurred by Seller in the name of the Company which are not reflected on the books and records of the company on the date of this agreement.

6. Recovery of Litigation or Arbitration Costs. If any legal action is brought for the enforcement of this agreement or because of an alleged dispute, breach, default, or misrepresentation in connection with any of the provisions of this agreement, the successful or prevailing party shall be entitled to recover reasonable attorney's fees and other costs incurred in that action or proceeding in addition to any other relief to which said party may be entitled.

7. Survival of Representations. Except as herein specifically provided, the representations and warranties made by any party hereto, and the obligations of any party to be performed hereunder, shall survive and continue beyond the transfer date of said Company interest.

8. Closing Date. This transaction shall close on [*date*] at [*time*] at [*location*], or any other day prior thereto when all documents herein described have been delivered.

[*Add boilerplate clauses as needed*]

SALE OF ASSETS
AGREEMENT

This Agreement is made this [*date*], between [*corporation*] (hereinafter referred to as "Seller"), having its principal office located at [*address*], and [*purchaser*] (hereinafter referred to as "Buyer"), having its principal office located at [*address*].

Recitals

WHEREAS, Seller owns and operates [*describe business*], and desires to sell to Buyer the purchased assets, as hereinafter defined, subject to the assumed liabilities, as hereinafter defined, on the terms and conditions herein set forth; and WHEREAS, Buyer desires to purchase the same assets, and is willing to assume all obligations and liabilities of Seller of these assets as hereinafter defined, on the terms and conditions herein set forth.

NOW THEREFORE IN CONSIDERATION of the mutual covenants, agreements, representations, and warranties and in exchange for good and valuable consideration, the receipt and sufficiency of which is hereby acknowledged, the parties hereto agree as follows:

Agreement

1. Recitals. The Recitals are a material part of this Agreement.

2. Assets Being Sold and Purchased. Upon the terms and subject to the conditions of this Agreement, at the Closing (as defined in this Agreement), Seller shall sell, transfer, and deliver, or cause to be sold, transferred, and delivered, to Buyer and Buyer shall purchase from Seller all of Seller's right, title, and interest in and to the following assets: [*list assets*]. It is expressly agreed that Seller is not selling, assigning, conveying, or transferring to Buyer any assets, interests, rights, and properties of Seller, other than those specifically conveyed to Buyer pursuant to this section.

3. Purchase Price. On the terms and subject to the conditions herein expressed, in consideration of and in exchange for the purchased assets, Buyer shall pay a purchase price according to the following schedule: [*list purchase price and terms of payment*]. The purchase price shall be allocated among the assets in the following manner: [*list allocation of purchase price for the assets sold*].

4. Assumption of Liabilities. On the terms and subject to the conditions herein expressed, in consideration of and in exchange for the purchased assets, Buyer shall pay the purchase price pursuant to this Agreement and assume the following debts, obligations, and liabilities (hereinafter collectively referred to as "Assumed Liabilities"): (a) All liabilities and obligations which relate to the assets being sold and purchased in accordance with this Agreement; (b) All liabilities and obligations arising from and after the Closing date under the contracts pursuant to the terms thereof; and (c) All liabilities and obligations specifically undertaken by Buyer pursuant to other provisions of this Agreement. Buyer shall not be liable for any obligations or liabilities of Seller of any kind and nature other than those specifically assumed under this section. Buyer will indemnify Seller against any and all liability under the contracts and obligations assumed hereunder, provided that Seller is not in default under any of the contracts or obligations at the date of Closing.

5. Closing/Instruments of Transfer. The completion of the transactions contemplated by this Agreement (hereinafter referred to as the "Closing") shall take place on the Closing date at [*time*]. The Closing shall take place at [*location*]. The Closing date shall be [*date*], provided that the conditions, precedent, and contingencies set forth in accordance with this Agreement are satisfied. At the Closing: (a) Seller shall deliver to Buyer all such bills of sale, contract assignments, consents, or other documents and instruments of sale, assignment, conveyance, and transfer as are appropriate or necessary with the terms of this Agreement and such other documents as Buyer may reasonably request to carry out the purposes of this Agreement; and (b) Buyer shall deliver to Seller the Closing payments in accordance with this Agreement and documents evidencing assumptions by Buyer of the Assumed Liabilities and such other documents as Seller may reasonably request to carry out the purposes of this Agreement.

6. Assignment of Lease and Contract Rights. If any lease or contract assignable to Buyer under this Agreement may not be assigned without the consent of the other party thereto, Seller shall use its best efforts to obtain the consent of the other party to such assignment.

7. Joint Covenants, Representations, and Warranties. Buyer and Seller shall cooperate and use their best efforts to prepare all instruments of transfer or other documents as promptly as practicable; and Buyer and Seller shall act in good faith and fair dealing in facilitating, maintaining, and carrying out the duties and obligations of this Agreement.

8. Seller's Covenants, Representations, and Warranties. Seller represents and warrants as follows: (a) Organization. Seller is [*a corporation*], organized, existing, and in good standing under the laws of the state of [*list state of incorporation*]; [*it is qualified to do business in (state where it's doing business if different than state of incorporation)*]; (b) Authority. The signatory for Seller warrants that he/she possesses the authority and has been authorized by Seller to enter into this Agreement; (c) Financial Statements. Seller has delivered to Buyer copies of its financial statements, as requested by Buyer; (d) Title to Assets. Seller is the owner of and has good and marketable title to all assets, which are to be sold and purchased in accordance with the terms of this Agreement, and free of all restrictions on transfer or assignment and of all encumbrances except: (i) as otherwise disclosed in the financial statements or in this Agreement; (ii) the liens for taxes not yet due and payable; (e) Absence of Default. Seller is not in default in payment of any of its obligations under any agreement or contract for the assets listed in Paragraph 2 of this Agreement; (f) Absence of Pending or Threatened Litigation. To the best of Seller's knowledge, no proceedings, judgments, or liens are now pending or threatened against the assets listed in

Paragraph 2 of this Agreement; and (g) Seller's Expenses and Liabilities. Seller shall pay any applicable tax, other than sales tax, arising out of the transfer of assets. Seller shall be responsible for any expense or tax, other than sales tax, of any kind related to any period before the date of execution of this Agreement.

9. Buyer's Representations and Warranties. Buyer represents and warrants as follows: (a) Organization. Buyer is a [*Sole Proprietorship, Partnership, or Corporation*] and has all requisite power and authority to enter into and perform and carry out this Agreement and the transaction contemplated hereby; (b) Authority. The signatory for Buyer warrants that he/she possesses the authority and has been authorized by Buyer to enter into this Agreement; (c) Books and Records. If applicable, Buyer shall afford Seller, or Seller's representative, access to inspect during regular business hours upon five business days prior written demand, Buyer's records and books of Seller's list of customer accounts on a monthly basis, provided that Seller's investigation and use of same shall be for the sole purpose to ensure payment of Buyer's liabilities to Seller; (d) Financial Statements. Buyer shall deliver to Seller copies of financial statements of Buyer on a quarterly basis throughout any payout periods, all of which have been prepared in accordance with generally accepted accounting principles applied on a consistent basis, including, with respect to each of the Buyer's last fiscal years, a balance sheet and a statement of profit and loss accounts and surplus and quarterly financial statements for the sole purpose to ensure payment of Buyer's liabilities to Seller; and (e) Note. At the date of Closing, Buyer agrees to execute a Note to secure payments as reflected in this Agreement.

10. Contingencies or Conditions to Buyer's Obligations. The obligations of Buyer under this Agreement are subject to fulfillment of the following contingencies or conditions: (a) The instruments and conveyances of transfer executed and delivered by Seller in accordance with this Agreement shall, to the best of Seller's knowledge, be valid in accordance with their terms and shall effectively vest in Buyer good and marketable title to the assets as contemplated by this Agreement, contingent upon the liabilities and obligations assumed by Buyer as provided in this Agreement; (b) All assets and equipment being sold and purchased as listed in this Agreement are in good and operable condition and working order to the best of Seller's knowledge as of the date of Closing; (c) Representations and warranties made by Seller in this Agreement shall be true and accurate in all material respects on the date of Closing; and (d) All proceedings required to be taken by Seller to authorize it to enter into this Agreement have been properly taken.

11. Contingencies or Conditions to Seller's Obligations. All obligations of Seller under this Agreement are subject to fulfillment of the following contingencies or conditions: (a) Representations and warranties made by Buyer in this Agreement shall be true and accurate in all material respects on the date of Closing; (b) Buyer shall have performed and complied in all material respects with all agreements and covenants on Buyer's part required to be performed or complied with on or prior to the Closing date; and (c) All proceedings required to be taken by Buyer to authorize it to enter into this Agreement have been properly taken.

12. Insurance. Buyer shall maintain sufficient insurance on all tangible assets listed in this Agreement and Buyer shall pay all costs associated with such insurance. Buyer agrees to keep the assets in good order and repair and free of all taxes, liens, and encumbrances, other than those existing at the date of Closing.

13. Indemnification. (a) Indemnification of Seller. Buyer shall indemnify and hold Seller harmless against any and all claims, demands, losses, costs, obligations, and liabilities that Seller may incur or suffer as a result of Buyer's: (i) breach of this agreement, and (ii) any inaccuracy or misrepresentation in or breach of any covenant, warranty, representation, or agreement made by Buyer in this Agreement; and (b) Indemnification of Buyer. Seller shall indemnify and hold Buyer harmless against any and all claims, demands, losses, costs, obliga-

hold Buyer harmless against any and all claims, demands, losses, costs, obligations, and liabilities that Buyer may incur or suffer as a result of Seller's: (i) breach of this agreement, and (ii) any inaccuracy or misrepresentation in or breach of any covenant, warranty, representation, or agreement made by Seller in this Agreement.

[Add boilerplate clauses as needed]

[Check your state laws to determine if the sale must comply with bulk transfer laws]

BILL OF SALE AND ASSIGNMENT

Under the Sale of Assets Agreement, dated [*date*], the undersigned [*seller*] ("Seller"), for valuable consideration, receipt of which is hereby acknowledged, does hereby grant, convey, sell, assign, and transfer over to [*buyer*] ("Buyer") an equal undivided interest in the following properties of the corporation:

[*list assets being sold*]

Title to all properties specified as being conveyed and transferred shall become fully and completely conveyed and transferred to the above-named Buyer.

IN WITNESS WHEREOF, Seller has caused this Bill of Sale and Assignment to be executed on [*date*].

[*Seller*]

By: ____________________

State of [*state*]

County of [*county*]

On [*date*], before me, the undersigned, a notary public for the state of [*state*], personally appeared [*seller*] known to me or proved to me on the basis of satisfactory evidence to be the person(s) who executed this instrument on behalf of Seller named herein.

[Seal]

____

Notary Public

CONFIDENTIALITY AGREEMENT

This Agreement is made and entered into on [*date*], by and between [*individual, partnership, corporation*] (hereinafter referred to as "Seller"), whose address is located at [*location*], and [*name*] (hereinafter referred to as "Prospective Purchaser"), an [*individual, partnership, corporation*], whose address is located at [*address*].

Recitals

WHEREAS, Seller offers for sale in whole or in part a [*describe business*] business;
WHEREAS, Prospective Purchaser is interested in investigating Seller's operation for the sole purpose of purchasing, in whole or in part, Seller's business;
WHEREAS, the parties wish to provide for protection of Seller's disclosure of its name, decision to sell its business, trade secrets, and other information of any kind, nature, or description concerning any manners affecting or relating to Seller's business (the "Proprietary Information").
NOW THEREFORE IN CONSIDERATION of the mutual covenants, agreements, representations, and warranties, and in exchange for good and valuable consideration, the receipt and sufficiency of which is hereby acknowledged, the parties hereby agree as follows:

Agreement

1. Recitals Part of Agreement. Recitals are a material part of this Agreement.

2. Grant of Access. Seller will allow Prospective Purchaser to investigate the operations of Seller's business, whose principal business is located at the above address, and at such other locations as seller may have, and will disclose information relating to the operation as reasonably requested by Prospective Purchaser.

2. Use of Information. Prospective Purchaser will use the information relating to operations for the sole purpose of analyzing Prospective Purchaser's benefits and risks of purchasing Seller's business. By his or her initials, [*space for initials*], Prospective Purchaser warrants and expressly agrees that he or she will at no time, in any fashion, form, or manner, either directly or indirectly: a) divulge, disclose, or communicate to Seller's employees, suppliers, customers, people in the trade, or any other third party, person, firm, or corporation associated with Seller, in any manner whatsoever, the Proprietary Information he or she receives from Seller, except: (i) as authorized by Seller in writing; (ii) upon written notice to Seller, to Prospective Purchaser's legal counsel and accountant for the sole purpose of investigating the business opportunity; b) use the Proprietary Information for the purpose of establishing [*describe business*]; or c) otherwise compromise Seller's business by use of Proprietary Information.

3. No Intent to Bind. The Parties acknowledge that by signing this Confidentiality Agreement, that they do not intend to bind Prospective Purchaser or Seller to execute a Purchase/Sale Agreement or to otherwise establish a relationship between the Parties except as set forth herein. Prospective Purchaser may not rely on this Confidentiality Agreement as binding Seller to sell his/her/its business to Prospective Purchaser.

4. Breach. Prospective Purchaser hereby grants to Seller the right to seek an injunction in a court of competent jurisdiction for breach of this Confidentiality Agreement and to receive liquidated damages in the amount of [*state reasonable amount*] dollars upon a finding by a court of law of breach by Prospective Purchaser of this Confidentiality Agreement. In the event that Seller can prove in a court of law that Prospective Purchaser intentionally disclosed any proprietary information of Seller's, Seller shall have the right, in lieu of liquidated damages, to seek actual and punitive damages from Prospective Purchaser. If either party to this Agreement shall employ legal counsel to protect its rights under this Agreement or to enforce any term or provision of this Agreement, then the party prevailing in any such legal action shall have the right to recover from the other party all of its reasonable attorney's fees, costs, and expenses incurred in relation to such claim.

[*Add boilerplate clauses as needed*]

CONFIDENTIALITY AGREEMENT

This Agreement is made and entered into on [*date*], by and between [*name*] (hereinafter referred to as "Disclosing Party"), whose business address is located at [*location*], and [*name*] (hereinafter referred to as "Recipient"), whose business address is located at [*location*].

Recitals

WHEREAS, Disclosing Party has developed certain [*ideas and formats which shall be used as the company logo*] for the Disclosing Party's business ("Confidential Information"); and

WHEREAS, Disclosing Party desires to allow Recipient access to Disclosing Party's Confidential Information for the purpose of determining whether Recipient wants to develop a business relationship with Disclosing Party, on the terms and conditions herein set forth; and

WHEREAS, Recipient desires to evaluate whether it has an interest in such Confidential Information to decide whether it should develop a business relationship with Disclosing Party, on the terms and conditions herein set forth.

NOW THEREFORE IN CONSIDERATION of the mutual covenants, agreements, representations, and warranties, and in exchange for good and valuable consideration, the receipt and sufficiency of which is hereby acknowledged, the parties hereby agree as follows:

Agreement

1. Recitals Part of Agreement. Recitals are a material part of this Agreement.

2. Definitions. Where used in this Agreement, "Confidential Information" or "Information" shall mean any and all tangible and intangible information, that is clearly marked as being confidential which is written or put in other tangible form, or if orally or visually furnished, is identified as being confidential in a writing submitted to the Recipient to be the Confidential Information of the Disclosing Party.

3. Purpose. Recipient will use the Confidential Information for the sole purpose of evaluating whether he/she should develop a business relationship with Disclosing Party.

4. Limitation on Disclosure and Use. Recipient agrees to maintain the Information of Disclosing Party received hereunder in confidence using the same degree of care Recipient uses to protect his/her own Information. Recipient agrees not to divulge, disclose, or communicate to any third party, person, firm, or corporation in any manner whatsoever, the Information Recipient received from Disclosing Party, except: (a) as authorized by Disclosing Party in writing; or (b) upon written notice to Disclosing Party, to Recipient's legal counsel or accountant for the purposes of investigating the business opportunity.

5. No Further Obligation. The Information being disclosed to Recipient pursuant to this Agreement is with the express understanding that neither Disclosing Party nor Recipient will be obligated to enter into any further agreement relating to the Confidential Information, and nothing in this Agreement shall be construed as granting any license to Recipient relating thereto.

6. Ownership of Property. All materials, including, but not limited to [*describe confidential information, e.g., ideas, formats, copyrights, trademarks, service marks, trade names, products, drawings, and designs*] furnished to Recipient by Disclosing Party, shall remain the property of Disclosing Party and shall be returned to Disclosing Party promptly at its request with all copies made thereof.

7. Recipient's Rights. This Agreement shall impose no obligation upon Recipient with respect to any Confidential Information on the Disclosing Party which (a) is now or which subsequently becomes generally known or available; (b) is known to the Recipient at the time of receipt of the same from the Disclosing Party without restrictions on disclosure; (c) is provided by the Disclosing Party to a third party without restriction on disclosure; (d) is subsequently rightfully provided to the Recipient by a third party without restriction on disclosure; or (e) is independently developed by the Recipient provided the person or persons developing same have not had access to the Information of the Disclosing Party.

[*Add boilerplate clauses as needed*]

EMPLOYEE CONFIDENTIALITY AND INVENTION ASSIGNMENT AGREEMENT

This agreement ("Agreement") is entered into on [*date*], between [*name*] (hereinafter referred to as "Company"), located at [*address*], and [*name*] (hereinafter referred to as "Employee").

NOW THEREFORE IN CONSIDERATION of the mutual covenants, agreements, representations, and warranties, and in exchange for good and valuable consideration of Employee's employment, the wages, training, and other benefits of such employment, the receipt and sufficiency of which is hereby acknowledged, Employee hereby acknowledges and agrees with Company as follows:

1. Effective Date. This Agreement shall become effective on the earlier of the first date of Employee's employment with Company or the date that any Confidential Information (as defined herein) was or is first disclosed to Employee, whichever comes first.

2. Confidential Information. Employee acknowledges that Company has and will develop, compile, and own certain copyrightable works of authorship, proprietary techniques, trademarks, service marks, trade secrets, products, inventions, patents, and like information that is essential to the goodwill of the business of Company. Employee further acknowledges that Company is perpetually working on enhancements of its copyrightable works of authorship, proprietary techniques, trademarks, service marks, trade secrets, products, inventions, patents and like information and has access to such copyrightable works of authorship, proprietary techniques, trademarks, service marks, trade secrets, products, inventions, patents, and like information of Company's Customers, Potential Customers, or those persons or entities for whom Company bids to perform, or performs services for.

Employee agrees that said works of authorship, techniques, trademarks, service marks, trade secrets, products, inventions, patents, and like information shall be collectively referred to in this Agreement as "Confidential Information." Confidential Information shall be defined broadly and shall include the following: (a) any idea or invention conceived by Employee during the course of Employee's employment relationship with Company; (b) any information that has commercial value or other utility in the business of Company or its Customers or that Company or its Customers are likely to engage in; and (c) any information which, if disclosed, would be detrimental to Company or its Customers, whether or not such information is identified as Confidential Information.

By way of example, and without limitation, Confidential Information shall include information about Company's, its Customers', or Potential Customers' products, processes, business, plans, research, programs, teaching techniques, formulas, trade secrets, inventions, discoveries, improvements, research and development and test results, specifications, data, know-how, formats, strategies, forecasts, unpublished financial data, information, budgets, projections, and customer and supplier identities, characteristics, agreements, and like information.

Employee agrees that Employee's employment relationship with Company results in a Confidential Relationship with Company. Employee agrees that during and after his/her employment relationship with company, that Employee will keep confidential, and not disclose to any third party, make use of, or allow a third party to make use of any Confidential Information except for the benefit of Company and at Company's written direction prior to such disclosure or use. Employee further agrees not to cause the transmission, removal, or transport of Confidential Information or Inventions from Company's place of business without the prior written approval of Company's Officers.

In the event that Employee desires to publish the results of his or her work for Company through literature or speeches, Employee agrees to submit such literature or speeches to any Officer at least [#] days before dissemination of such information for a determination of whether such disclosure may destroy trade secret status or be highly prejudicial to the interests of Company or its Customers, or whether disclosure may constitute an invasion of their privacy. Employee agrees not to publish, disclose, or otherwise disseminate such information without prior written approval of an Officer of Company. Employee acknowledges that he/she is aware that the unauthorized disclosure of Confidential Information of Company, its Customers, or Potential Customers, may be highly prejudicial to their interests, an invasion of privacy, and an improper disclosure of trade secrets.

3. Non-Competition - No Soliciting During Employment. As a condition to Employee's compensation, Employee agrees that during his/her employment relationship with Company, that he/she will not engage in any business that competes with Company, disrupt, damage, impair, or interfere with the business of Company by way of interfering with or raiding Company's employees, or disrupting Company's relationships with its Customers, Potential Customers, agents, vendors, representatives, or otherwise. Employee further agrees that Employee will not, directly or indirectly, for himself or herself or on behalf of, or in conjunction with any other person, firm, partnership, or corporation, divert or take away or attempt to divert or take away, call on, solicit or attempt to solicit the business or patronage of any of Company's customers, patrons, suppliers, including but not limited to those with whom he/she became acquainted while engaged as an Employee in Company's business.

4. Prior Knowledge and Inventions. Employee has disclosed on Exhibit A anything that Employee knows about Company's Confidential Information. Other than such disclosures, Employee does not know anything about Company's Confidential Information. Employee has also disclosed on Exhibit A a list of inventions that Employee has made to date, and that Employee wants to exclude from the application of this Agreement.

5. Prior Relationships and Return of Prior Employer's Property. Employee warrants that he/she is not aware of any prior obligations which would prevent Employee from executing this Agreement or interfering with its terms and spirit. Additionally, Employee warrants that he/she will not disclose to Company any proprietary information, trade secrets, or Confidential Information of others. Employee further warrants that he/she has returned all property and Confidential Information belonging to all prior employers.

6. Disclosure of Inventions. Employee will promptly disclose in writing to Company, all discoveries, developments, designs, ideas, improvements, inventions, formulas, processes, techniques, know-how, and data (whether patentable or registerable under copyright or similar statutes) made, conceived, reduced to practice, or learned by Employee (either alone or jointly with others) during the period of his/her employment, that are related to or useful in the business of Company, or which results from tasks assigned to Employee by Company, or from the use of the premises owned, leased, or otherwise acquired by Company (all of the foregoing are referred to in this Agreement as "Inventions").

7. Assignment of Inventions. Employee acknowledges and agrees that all Inventions belong to and shall be the sole property of Company and shall be Inventions of Company subject to the provisions of this Agreement. Employee assigns to Company all right, title, and interest Employee may have, or may acquire, in and to all Inventions. Employee agrees to sign and deliver to Company (either during or subsequent to his/her employment) such other documents as Company considers desirable to evidence the assignment of all rights of Employee, if any, in any Inventions to Company and Company's ownership of such Inventions.

Any provision in this Agreement requiring Employee to assign rights to an Invention does not apply to any invention for which no equipment, supplies, facility, or trade secret information of Company was used and which was developed entirely on Employee's own time, and (a) which does not relate either to the business of Company or to Company's actual or demonstrably anticipated research or development, or (b) which does not result from any work performed by Employee for Company.

8. Power of Attorney. In the event Company cannot obtain Employee's signature on any document necessary to apply for, prosecute, obtain, or enforce any patent, copyright, or other right or protection relating to any Invention, whether due to mental or physical incapacity or any other cause, Employee hereby irrevocably designates and appoints Company and each of its duly authorized officers and agents as his/her agent and attorney-in-fact, to act for and on his/her behalf and stead to execute and file any such document and to do all other lawfully permitted acts to further the prosecution, issuance, and enforcement of patents, copyrights, or other rights or protections with the same force and effect as if executed and delivered by Employee.

9. Delivery of Documents and Data on Termination of Employment. In the event of termination (voluntary or otherwise) of Employee's employment with Company, Employee agrees, promptly and without request, to deliver to and inform Company of all documents and data pertaining to his/her employment and the Confidential Information and Inventions of Company or its Clients, whether prepared by Employee or otherwise coming into his or her possession or control, and, if applicable, to sign Company's Exit Letter. Employee will not retain any written or other tangible material containing any information concerning or disclosing any of the Confidential Information or Inventions or Company or its Clients. Employee understands that the unauthorized taking of any of Employee's trade secrets may be a crime under certain penal codes. Employee further understands that such unauthorized taking of Company's trade secrets could result in civil liability and that willful misappropriation may result in an award against Employee.

10. Obligations after Termination of Employment. In the event of termination (voluntary or otherwise) of Employee's employment with Company,

Employee agrees that he/she will protect the value of the Confidential Information and Inventions of Company and Clients and will prevent their misappropriation of disclosure. Employee will not disclose or use to his/her benefit (or benefit of a third party) or to the detriment of Company or its Clients any Confidential Information or Invention. Employee further agrees that for a period of two years immediately following termination (voluntary or otherwise) of Employee's employment with Company, Employee shall not interfere with the business of Company by inducing an employee to leave the Company's employ or by inducing a consultant to sever the consultant's relationship with the Company.

11. Injunctive Relief. Because Employee's breach of this Agreement may cause Company irreparable harm for which money damages are inadequate, Employee agrees that Company will be entitled to injunctive relief to enforce this Agreement, in addition to damages and other available remedies.

12. Understanding. Employee acknowledges and agrees that the protections set forth in this Agreement are a material condition to his/her employment with and compensation by Company.

13. [*If Employment At-Will*] Employment and compensation can be terminated, with or without cause, and with or without notice, at any time, at the option of Company or Employee. Nothing contained in this Agreement shall limit or otherwise alter the foregoing.

[*Add boilerplate clauses as needed*]

CONFIDENTIALITY AGREEMENT
NON-DISCLOSURE—NON-COMPETITION—NON-CIRCUMVENTION

This agreement is entered into this [*date*] by and between [*name*], [*an individual, partnership, corporation*] having its principal offices at [*location*] (hereinafter referred to as "Disclosing Party"), and [*name*], [*an individual, partnership, corporation*] having its principal offices at [*location*] (hereinafter referred to as "Receiving Party") for the purpose of preventing the unauthorized disclosure or use of Confidential Information (as defined below) which may be disclosed to Receiving Party for the purpose of pursuing the establishment of a business relationship or negotiating any contract or agreement between Disclosing Party and Receiving Party, and for the unauthorized competition and circumvention of Disclosing Party in any contract or agreement for which Receiving Party learns as a result of this Agreement with Disclosing Party.

For purposes of this Agreement, Confidential Information shall mean: [*describe what is to be kept confidential, e.g., proprietary techniques, products, formulas, inventions, discoveries, formats, patents, processes, Disclosing Party's business plans, agreements, research, programs, teaching techniques, trade secrets, research and development, specifications, data, know-how, formats, strategies, forecasts, unpublished financial data, information, budgets, projections and customer and supplier identities and characteristics, customer lists, customer leads or potential customers, marketing strategies, copyrightable works of authorship, trademarks and service marks, and like information.*] Confidential Information shall also be defined broadly and shall include the following: (a) any information that has commercial value or other utility in the business of Disclosing Party or that Disclosing Party is likely to engage in; and (b) any information which, if disclosed, would be detrimental to Disclosing Party or its Customers, whether or not such information is identified as Confidential Information.

NOW THEREFORE IN CONSIDERATION of the mutual covenants, agreements, representations, and warranties, and in exchange for good and valuable consideration, the receipt and sufficiency of which is hereby acknowledged, the Parties hereby agree as follows:

1. Effective Date. This Agreement shall become effective on the earlier of the first date of execution of this Agreement or the date that any Confidential Information (as defined herein) was or is first disclosed to Receiving Party, whichever comes first.

2. Non-Disclosure. Receiving Party acknowledges that the Confidential Information is essential to the goodwill of the business of Disclosing Party. Receiving Party shall hold and maintain the Confidential Information in strictest confidence and in trust for the sole and exclusive benefit of Disclosing Party. Receiving Party shall not use for its own benefit, publish, or otherwise disclose to others, or permit the use by others for their benefit or to the detriment of Disclosing Party, any of the Confidential Information. Receiving Party shall carefully restrict access to the Confidential Information to those of its officers, directors, and employees who clearly need such access in order to participate on behalf of Receiving Party in the analysis and negotiation of a business relationship or any contract or agreement, or the advisability thereof, with Disclosing Party.

Receiving Party warrants and represents that Receiving Party will advise each of the persons to whom Receiving Party provides access to any of the Confidential Information under the foregoing sentence that such persons are strictly prohibited from making any use, publishing, or otherwise disclosing to others, or permitting others to use for their benefit or to the detriment of Disclosing Party, and of the Confidential Information. Receiving Party shall take all necessary action to protect the confidentiality of the Confidential Information, except for its disclosure as stated in this paragraph, and agrees to indemnify Disclosing Party against any and all losses, damages, claims, or expenses incurred or suffered by Disclosing Party as a result of Receiving Party's breach of this Agreement. In the event of termination (voluntary or otherwise) of this Agreement, Receiving Party agrees that he/she/it will protect the value of the Confidential Information of Disclosing Party and will prevent their misappropriation of disclosure. Receiving Party will not disclose or use to his/her/its benefit (or benefit of a third party) or to the detriment of Disclosing Party or its Customers any Confidential Information.

3. Non-Circumvention. As a condition to entering into this Agreement, Receiving Party agrees that he/she/it will not engage in any business that competes with Disclosing Party, disrupt, damage, impair, or interfere with the business of Disclosing Party by way of interfering with or raiding Disclosing Party's employees, or disrupt Disclosing Party's relationships with its customers, potential customers, agents, vendors, representatives, or otherwise.

Receiving Party further agrees that he/she/it will not, directly or indirectly, for himself/herself/itself or on behalf of, or in conjunction with any other person, firm, partnership, or corporation, divert or take away or attempt to divert or take away, call on or solicit or attempt to solicit the business or patronage of any of Disclosing Party's customers, patrons, suppliers, including but not limited to those with whom he/she/it became acquainted as a result of Receiving Party's relationship with Disclosing Party.

4. Non-Competition. Receiving Party agrees that during the term of this Agreement and for a period of [*one or two*] years immediately following termination (voluntary or otherwise) of this Agreement, Receiving Party will not by himself/herself/itself or on behalf of any other person, firm, partnership, or corporation, engage in the business that is the same as Disclosing Party's within a radius of [*not more than 50 miles from the city of (city) and its outlying areas in the state of (state)*]; nor call on or solicit or attempt to solicit the business or patronage of any person, firm, corporation, or partnership for the purpose of selling similar services or goods sold by Disclosing Party within a radius of not more than 50 miles from the city of [*city*] and its outlying areas in the state of [*state*]; nor interfere with the business of Disclosing Party by inducing an employee to leave Disclosing Party's employ or by inducing a consultant, customer, supplier, vendor, and the like to sever a relationship it has with the Disclosing Party.

[***Add boilerplate clauses as needed***]

CONFIDENTIALITY LEGEND

This document contains information that is the confidential and proprietary property of [*owner*]. It constitutes trade secrets and may not be copied, published, or disclosed to others, or used for any purpose other than review, without the express prior written consent of an authorized officer of [*owner*].

EMPLOYMENT APPLICATION

AN EQUAL OPPORTUNITY EMPLOYER

Date: ____________________

Please Print

Name: ______________________________ Telephone No. (______)____________________

Present Address:

____

Employment Desired:

What hours are you available for work? ____________ Salary at last job: ____________

If hired, on what date can you start work? ____________ Salary desired: ____________

Personal Information:

Are you at least 18 years old? [ ] yes [ ] no

If hired, can you show evidence of your U.S. citizenship or proof of legal right to work in the U.S.?

[ ] yes [ ] no

Do you have any limitation on your ability to perform duties of the job that you are applying?

[ ] yes [ ] no

School	Name & Address	No. of Years Completed	Did you graduate?	Degree or Diploma
High School				
College/ University				
Vocational/ Business				

Employment History: List below all present and past employment starting with your most recent employer (up to 5 years).

Name of Employer: ______________________________

Address: ______________________________

Type of Business: ______________ Supervisor's name: ______________

Your position and duties: ______________________________

____

Date of employment: From ______________ To ______________

Weekly pay: Starting ______________ Ending ______________

Reason for Leaving: ______________________________

Name of Employer: ______________________________

Address: ______________________________

Type of Business: ______________ Supervisor's name: ______________

Your position and duties: ______________________________

____

Date of employment: From ______________ To ______________

Weekly pay: Starting ______________ Ending ______________

Reason for Leaving: ______________________________

References: List below two persons who have knowledge of your work performance within the last three years.

Name: ______________ Occupation: ______________

Telephone No. (____)______________ Number of Years Acquainted: ______________

Name: ______________ Occupation: ______________

Telephone No. (____)______________ Number of Years Acquainted: ______________

Please read and sign below:

I hereby certify that I have not knowingly withheld any information that might adversely affect my chances for employment and that the answers given by me are true and correct to the best of my knowledge. I further certify that I, the undersigned applicant, have personally completed this application. I understand that any omission or misstatement of material fact on this application or on any document used to secure employment shall be grounds for rejection of this application or for immediate discharge if I am employed, regardless of the time elapsed before discovery. I hereby authorize [*company*] to thoroughly investigate my references, work record, education, and other matters related to my suitability for employment. I understand that nothing contained in the application or conveyed during any interview which may be granted is intended to create an employment contract between me and [*company*].

____

INTERVIEW QUESTIONS

AN EQUAL OPPORTUNITY EMPLOYER

If hired, on what date can you start work? If clerical: type? how fast?

____

Computer experience? IBM or MAC? What programs?

____

Salary desired: Current salary (or salary at last position):

____

If we asked your last employer what your three best attributes were, what would he/she say?

____

What would he/she say is the number one thing that you need to improve on?

____

At your last job, how many days were you absent because of sickness? times for tardiness?

____

What did you like best about your last job? Dislike most? Why did you leave?

____

Do you have any commitments that will take you out of the area within the next year?

____

In what area of town do you live in? How long have you lived in [*city*]?

____

If hired, would you have reliable means of transportation to and from work?

____

Do you smoke?

____

[*date*]

Dear [*First Name*]:

Welcome to [*company*]. The purpose of this letter is to offer you a position with our company and to convey some information to you regarding our company and the offered position.

Your job title: ______________________________
Hire date: ______________________________
Starting time: ______________________________
Report to: ______________________________
Rate of pay: ______________________________

We assume that you have carefully reviewed and will abide by any agreement which you might have signed with your current or previous employers regarding company information and materials before commencing work with us.

We hire all personnel on an at-will status. Thus, this letter is not to be construed as a contract of employment, but rather is simply informational. I have enclosed a copy of our At-Will Employment Agreement for your review. If it meets with your approval, please sign and bring it with you on your first day of employment. If you have any questions, please do not hesitate to call me.

We look forward to working with you.

Sincerely,

[*New Employer*]

AT-WILL EMPLOYMENT AGREEMENT

This agreement is made this [*date*], between [*employer*] (hereinafter referred to as "Employer"), and [*employee*] (hereinafter referred to as "Employee").

Recitals

Employer is engaged in the [*type of business*] business and maintains an office in [*location*]; and Employee is willing to be employed by Employer, and Employer is willing to employ Employee on the terms, covenants, and conditions set forth. NOW THEREFORE IN CONSIDERATION of the mutual covenants, agreements, representations, and warranties, and in exchange for good and valuable consideration, the receipt and sufficiency of which is hereby acknowledged, Employer and Employee hereby agree as follows:

Agreement

1. Nature and Place of Employment. Employer employs, engages, and hires Employee as [*position*] at the offices of [*employer*], and Employee accepts and agrees to such hiring, engagement, and employment. Subject to the supervision and pursuant to the orders, advice, and directions of Employer, Employee's duties shall include the following tasks: [*describe tasks*] and perform such other duties as are customarily performed by one holding a similar position in like circumstances in business, in the industry, and shall also additionally render such other and unrelated services and duties as may be assigned to Employee from time to time by Employer.

2. Manner of Performance of Employee's Duties. Employee agrees that Employee will at all times faithfully, industriously, and to the best of Employee's ability, experience, and talent, perform all of the duties that may be required of and from Employee pursuant to the express and implicit terms of this agreement, to the reasonable satisfaction of Employer. Such duties shall be rendered at [*location*], and at such other place or places as Employer shall in good faith require, or as the interests, needs, business, and opportunities of Employer shall require or make advisable.

3. Employees Lack of Authority to Bind Employer Without Consent. Employee shall not have the right to make any contracts or commitments for or on behalf of Employer without first obtaining the express written consent of Employer.

4. Duration of Employment. This agreement shall be in effect from [*date*], until it is terminated, which may be done by either party at will, with or without cause.

5. Compensation. Employer shall pay Employee, and Employee agrees to accept from Employer, in full payment for Employee's services under this agreement, compensation at the rate of $[*amount*] dollars per hour, payable [*every week, two weeks, semi-monthly, monthly*], on [*each Friday, the second and fourth Fridays, etc.*] of each month.

6. Devotion by Employee to Business. Employee shall work during the regular hours of [*9:00 a.m. until 5:00 p.m.*] Monday through Friday, and shall have [*1/2 or 1*] hour off without pay for lunch during each of these days. During working hours, Employee shall devote the whole of Employee's time attention and energies to the performance of Employee's duties and shall not, either directly or indirectly, alone or in partnership, be connected with or concerned in any other business or pursuit during the term of employment.

7. Vacation Days, Holidays, Personal Days. Employer shall give Employee a vacation allowance and personal leave as provided in the Employee Handbook of Employer. The time for such vacation is to be approved by Employer. In addition, Employee shall be entitled to such paid or unpaid leave and holidays as stated in the Employee Handbook. *OR* Employee shall be entitled to [#] days of vacation with pay after one year of consecutive employment, the time for such vacation to be taken at a time or times approved by Employer. Employee shall not accumulate more than [#] days vacation. In addition to vacation, Employee shall have the following designated holidays:

New Year's Day	Martin Luther King Day
President's Day	Memorial Day
Independence Day	Labor Day
Thanksgiving Day	Friday after Thanksgiving
Christmas Day	

In addition to vacation and holidays, Employee shall be entitled to [#] days of personal leave at a rate of [*one-quarter, one-half*] day for each month of service, up to a total of [#] days per year. Personal leave may not be carried forward from one year to the next. To reward Employee with perfect attendance, Employer will pay [#] days salary to Employee if such Employee does not use any personal leave for one year of continuous employment.

8. Non-Disclosure of Information Concerning Business. Employee further specifically agrees that Employee will not at any time, in any fashion, form, or manner, either directly or indirectly, divulge, disclose, or communicate to any person, firm, or corporation in any manner whatsoever any information of any kind, nature, or description concerning any manners affecting or relating to the business of Employer, including without limiting the generality of the foregoing, the [*list information of concern*] or any other information of, about, or concerning the business of Employer, its manner of operation, its plans, or other data of any kind, nature, or description without regard to whether any of all of the foregoing matters would be deemed confidential, material, or important, the parties stipulating that, as shown between them, the matters are important, material, and confidential and gravely affect the effective and successful conduct of the business of employer, and its goodwill, and that any breach of the terms of this paragraph is a material breach of this agreement.

[Add boilerplate clauses as needed]

EMPLOYMENT AGREEMENT
WITH STOCK OPTIONS

This Agreement is effective this [*date*] between [*name*] (hereinafter referred to as "Employer"), and [*name*] (hereinafter referred to as "Employee").

Recitals

Employer is engaged in the [*type of business*] and maintains an office at [*location*]; and Employee is willing to be employed by Employer, and Employer is willing to employ Employee on the terms, covenants, and conditions set forth herein.
NOW THEREFORE IN CONSIDERATION of the mutual covenants, agreements, representations, and warranties, and in exchange for good and valuable consideration, the receipt and sufficiency of which is hereby acknowledged, the Employer and Employee hereby agree as follows:

Agreement

1. Nature and Place of Employment. Employer employs, engages, and hires Employee as [*manager/supervisor*] at the office of Employer, and Employee accepts and agrees to such hiring, engagement, and employment, subject to the supervision and pursuant to the orders, advice, directions, and control by Employer. Furthermore, Employee agrees to devote Employee's entire time and attention during employment hours throughout the period of employment exclusively to the business of Employer, which shall have the right at any time to change or modify the work and duties to be performed by Employer.

2. Employee's Duties. Employee's duties shall include the following tasks: [*describe tasks*]. Employee agrees that Employee will at all times faithfully, industriously, and to the best of Employee's ability, experience, and talent, perform all of the duties that may be required of and from Employee pursuant to the express and implicit terms of this Agreement, to the reasonable satisfaction of Employer. Such duties shall be rendered at Employer's principal place of business located in [*state*] and at such other place or places, as Employer shall in good faith require, or as the interests, needs, business, and opportunities of Employer shall require or make advisable.

3. Employees Lack of Authority to Bind Employer Without Consent. Employee shall not have the right to make any contract whatsoever, oral or in writing; or institute, bring, or cause to be brought, any suit, action, or proceeding in any court, civil or criminal, in Employee's own name or in the name of Employer or make any other commitments for or on behalf of Employer without first obtaining the express written consent of Employer; and any such unauthorized contracts or commitments shall be null and void.

4. Duration of Employment.
[If At-Will] This contract shall be in effect from [*date employment begins*] until it is terminated, which may be done by either party at will, with or without cause. Termination of Employee's employment shall not be in limitation of any other right or remedy Employer may have under this Agreement or in law, in equity, or under any other provision of any Agreement between the parties.

[If Term Employment] This contract shall be in effect from [*date*], and shall continue for a period of [*# of months/years*] until [*date*]. Except that the employment of Employee may be terminated at any time prior to the expiration date as listed below: (a) for incompetence, insubordination, or violation of any rule or regulation that may be established from time to time for the conduct of Employer's business, or for breach or neglect of any duty or obligation of Employee under this Agreement; (b) for any disability or incapacity of Employee to perform duties properly for a consecutive period of [#] days; or if in Employer's reasonable opinion, Employee is not efficient, conscientious, and productive; (c) on the destruction of Employer's premises by fire or otherwise, or on discontinuance of Employer's business due to any other cause; (d) at any time that the business conducted by Employer shall be unprofitable as determined by Employer in its absolute discretion; and (e) upon thirty (30) days written notice from Employee to Employer, that Employee shall terminate this Agreement. If Employee terminates this Agreement, Employer shall be under no obligation to

Employee for any expenses or otherwise, except to pay to Employee his or her salary or wages to the date of termination less the amount of any advances made by Employer to Employee.

Termination of Employee's employment shall not be in limitation of any other right or remedy Employer may have under this Agreement or in law, in equity, or under any other provision of any Agreement between the parties. At the expiration of the period of time, if neither party notifies the other in writing that this Agreement will be terminated, then this Agreement shall be extended on a [*monthly/yearly*] basis.

5. Compensation. Employer shall pay Employee, and Employee agrees to accept from Employer, in full payment for Employee's services under this Agreement, compensation at the rate of $[*amount*] dollars per [*month, year*], payable in [*weekly, biweekly, semi-monthly, monthly*] installments on [*dates*] and on each month thereafter during the term of this Agreement.

[If stock is part of compensation package, add the following] In addition to salary, Employer shall pay Employee [*number*] shares of the common stock of Employer upon execution of this agreement. Such shares shall be fully vested at the time of issuance. Pursuant to such stock issuance and as a condition precedent to its taking effect, Employee agrees to execute a Shareholders' Buy/Sell Agreement with Employer and existing Shareholders. Employee further agrees that all stock purchased by Employee is restricted and may not be transferred, sold, or otherwise disposed of except in accordance with the terms of such Shareholder's Agreement.

In the event that Employee's employment with Employer is terminated for whatever reason (which shall include, but not be limited to: death, voluntary resignation, or total disability) so that Employee is no longer an employee of Employer, then Employer shall have the option to purchase any shares owed by Employee and the other Shareholders shall have the option to purchase any shares for which Employer does not exercise its option as per the terms of the above mentioned Shareholders' Buy/Sell Agreement.

6. Option to Purchase Common Stock. [*If Employee continues in the service of Employer for (x) months from the date of this Agreement,*] Employee shall have the option [*while employed*] to purchase [*number*] shares of the common stock of Employer for the purchase price of $[*amount*] dollars per share. The terms of such purchase shall be that Employee cannot purchase over [*number of shares per each of the years of employment*]. Pursuant to Employee's first purchase and as a condition precedent to its taking effect, Employee agrees to execute a Shareholders' Buy/Sell Agreement with Employer and existing Shareholders. Employee further agrees that all stock purchased by Employee is restricted and may not be transferred, sold, or otherwise disposed of except in accordance with the terms of such Shareholders' Agreement.

In the event that Employee's employment with Employer is terminated for whatever reason (which shall include, but not be limited to: death, voluntary resignation, or total disability) so that Employee is no longer an employee of Employer, then Employer shall have the option to purchase any shares owed by Employee and the other Shareholders shall have the option to purchase any shares for which Employer does not exercise its option as per the terms of the above mentioned Shareholders' Buy/Sell Agreement.

7. Automobile Expenses. Employer agrees to reimburse Employee for all normal operating expenses incurred in the use of a vehicle in conjunction with normal work responsibilities, including gas, oil, tires, batteries, other normal maintenance, and any repairs that may be normally required. Employer will not pay for extraordinary or other automobile expenses.

8. Reimbursement for Entertainment Expenses. Employer shall reimburse Employee for such reasonable, ordinary, and necessary business expenses for entertainment, provided such entertainment was pursuant to Employer's written directions and provided that the value of such expense shall not exceed a total of $[*amount*] in any taxable year, upon the condition that Employee shall incur such expense in connection with Employee's services for Employer, and after presentation by Employee of appropriate invoices and documentation to Employer showing: (a) the amount of expenditure; (b) the time, place, and nature of expense; (c) the business reason for the expense and the business benefit derived or expected to be derived therefrom; and (d) the names, occupations, addresses, and other data concerning individuals entertained sufficient to establish their business relationship to Employer.

9. Devotion by Employee to Business. Employee shall work as many hours as reasonably necessary to complete any tasks or duties required of one in a similar position in the same industry in like circumstances. During working hours, Employee shall devote all of Employee's time, attention, knowledge, and skill solely and exclusively to the business and interest of Employer, and Employer shall be entitled to all of the benefits, profits, or other issues arising from or incident to any and all work, services, and advice of Employee, and Employee expressly agrees that during the term of this Agreement, Employee will not be interested, directly or indirectly, in any form, fashion, or manner, as partner, officer, director, stockholder, advisor, employee, or in any other form or capacity, in any other business similar to Employer's business or any allied trade, provided, however, that nothing in this agreement contained shall be deemed to prevent or limit the right of Employee to invest any of Employee's surplus funds in the capital stock or other securities of any corporation whose stock or securities are publicly owned or are regularly traded on any public exchange, nor shall anything in this agreement contained be deemed to prevent Employee from investing or limit Employee's right to invest Employee's surplus funds in real estate.

Employee shall communicate and channel to Employer all knowledge, business, and customer contacts, and any other matter of information that could concern or be in any way beneficial to the business of Employer; provided however, that nothing shall be construed as requiring such communications where the information is lawfully protected from disclosure as a trade secret of a third party.

10. Vacation, Holidays, Personal Days. Employer shall give Employee a vacation allowance and personal leave as provided in the Employee Handbook of Employer. The time for such vacation is to be approved by Employer. In addition, Employee shall be entitled to such paid or unpaid leave and holidays as stated in the Employee Handbook. *OR* Employee shall be entitled to [#] days of vacation with pay after one year of consecutive employment, the time for such vacation to be taken at a time or times approved by Employer. Employee shall not accumulate more than [#] days vacation. In addition to vacation, Employee shall have the following designated holidays:

New Year's Day	Martin Luther King Day
President's Day	Memorial Day
Independence Day	Labor Day
Thanksgiving Day	Friday after Thanksgiving
Christmas Day	

In addition to vacation and holidays, Employee shall be entitled to [#] days of personal leave at a rate of [*one-quarter, one-half*] day for each month of service, up to a total of [#] days per year. Personal leave may not be carried forward from one year to the next. To reward employee with perfect attendance, Employer will pay [#] days salary to Employee if such Employee does not use any personal leave for one year of continuous employment.

11. Non-Disclosure of Trade Secrets. Employee specifically agrees that Employee will not at any time during the term of Employee's employment agreement or thereafter, in any fashion, form, or manner, either directly or indirectly, divulge, disclose, or communicate to any person, firm, or corporation in any manner whatsoever any trade secret or other information of any kind, nature, or description concerning any manners affecting or relating to the business of the Employer, including without limiting the generality of the foregoing: [*the names, buying habits, or practices of any of its customers, its marketing methods and related data, the names of any of its vendors or suppliers, costs of materials, the prices it obtains or has obtained or at which it sells or has sold its products or services, sales costs, lists or other written records used in Employer's business, compensation paid to Employees and other terms of employment, policies and procedures, merchandising or sales techniques, details of training methods, contracts or licenses, computer programs, business systems, or any other information of, about, or concerning the business of Employer, its manner of operation, its plans, or other data of any kind, nature, or description*] without regard to whether any of all of the foregoing matters would be deemed confidential, material, or important, the parties stipulating that, as shown between them, the matters are important, material, and confidential and gravely affect the effective and successful conduct of the business of Employer, and its goodwill, and that any breach of the terms of this section is a material breach of this agreement; except that Employee shall be allowed to impart any information to the business or affairs of Employer to those Employees of Employer who are entitled to receive such information.

From time to time during the term of this Agreement, additional confidential information or knowledge of whatever kind, nature, or description concerning matters affecting or relating to Employer's business may be developed or obtained. Employee specifically agrees that all such additional confidential information or knowledge shall be deemed by the parties to this Agreement to be included within the terms of this section and to constitute important, material, and confidential trade secrets that affect the successful conduct of Employer's business and its goodwill, so that any breach of any terms of this paragraph relating to such additional confidential information or knowledge is a material breach of this Agreement.

If any confidential information or other matter described in this section is sought by legal process, Employee will promptly notify Employer and will cooperate with Employer in preserving its confidentiality in connection with any legal proceeding.

12. Inventions—Materials. All ideas, inventions, processes, patents, trademarks, and other developments or improvements in plant, machinery, processes, or otherwise, conceived by Employee, alone or with others, during the term of the employment that are within the scope of Employer's business operations, or that relate to Employer's work or projects, or that Employee developed on his own time by using Employer's equipment, supplies, facilities, or trade secret information are the exclusive property of Employer; and upon termination of this Agreement, Employee shall do all acts necessary to give effect to this paragraph, and at Employer's expense, Employee shall do all acts necessary to assist Employer to obtain a patent, trademark, or the like, in the name of Employer.

All computers, equipment, notebooks, documents, memorandums, reports, files, samples, books, correspondence, lists, other written and graphic records, and the like, affecting or relating to the business of Employer, which Employee shall prepare, use, construct, observe, possess, or control shall be and remain the exclusive property of Employer; and upon termination of this Agreement, Employee agrees to deliver promptly to Employer the same to Employer's business, and all copies of such materials, which are or have been in Employee's possession or under Employee's control.

13. Covenant Not to Solicit Business. Employee agrees that during the term of this Agreement, Employee will not by himself or herself or on behalf of any other person, firm, partnership, or corporation, engage in the business that is the same as Employer's within a radius of [*50 miles from city*] and its outlying areas in the state of [*state*]; nor call on or solicit or attempt to solicit the business or patronage of any person, firm, corporation, or partnership for the purpose of selling similar [*services/items*] sold by Employer within a radius of [*50 miles from city*] and its outlying areas in the state of [*state*].

Employee further agrees that Employee will not, directly or indirectly, for himself or herself or on behalf of, or in conjunction with any other person, firm, partnership, or corporation, divert or take away or attempt to divert or take away, call on or solicit or attempt to solicit the business or patronage of any of Employer's customers, patrons, suppliers, including but not limited to those on whom he or she called, or whom he or she solicited, or with whom he or she became acquainted while engaged as an Employee in Employer's business.

Employee agrees that, in the event of violation by Employee of this covenant not to compete, Employee will pay as liquidated damages to Employer the sum of $[*state reasonable amount*] dollars per day, for each day or part thereof that Employee continues to so break the covenant. It is recognized and agreed that damages in such event are irreparable and difficult to determine, and that this Agreement with respect to liquidated damages shall in no event limit Employer's right to injunctive or other relief.

[*Add boilerplate clauses as needed*]

EMPLOYEE HANDBOOK

Note: This form is a general outline covering topics which are commonly found in an employee handbook. It is less "fill-in-the-blank" than the other forms presented in this section and more instructional as to the type of information that should be presented in each part of the handbook. However, you will find that most of the sections and language in this form will become essential parts of your company's employee handbook.

President's Message. The President should welcome the employees to the company with a message that is friendly and conveys that the intent of the employee handbook is to assist new employees in getting to know the company and its policies.

YOUR EMPLOYMENT WITH [*COMPANY*]

Your Employment Here. This section should include the reasons for the employee handbook. It should include statements about the following:

- the handbook is provided to answer common questions posed by employees.
- employees should read it thoroughly and carefully and learn its contents.
- if an employee has a question about company policies which is not answered by the handbook, he or she should feel free to ask any key personnel of the company.
- the policies and practices set out in the manual are not a contract and are not intended to imply a contractual relationship (if the employer wishes to employ at-will employees).
- this version of the handbook replaces all earlier handbooks and takes precedence over all memoranda and oral descriptions of the terms and conditions of employment.
- a request to discard any old handbooks to avoid confusion.

Equal Employment Opportunity Is Our Policy. Every employer is required to comply with federal and state laws regarding discrimination, handicaps, etc., and each employer should take the steps necessary to make sure that his or her company is in compliance with such laws. Without such assurance, the employer risks litigation and problems. At the very least, this section should include a statement regarding the following:

- the company is an equal employment opportunity employer where employment decisions are based on merit and business needs and not on race, color, citizenship status, national origin, ancestry, sex, sexual orientation, age, religion, creed, physical or mental disability, physical handicap, medical condition, marital status, or veteran status.
- it is company policy to comply with the law regarding reasonable accommodation for handicapped and disabled employees.

At-Will Employment. This section should include a statement regarding the at-will nature of the employment relationship, if the employer desires such a relationship. The following suggestions may be helpful:

- the employee is free to terminate his or her employment with the company at any time, with or without a reason.
- the company has the right to terminate the employee's employment at any time, with or without a reason.
- the relationship created by this situation is called "at-will" employment.
- apart from the policy of at-will employment and those policies required by law, the company may change its policies or practices at any time without further notice.

Employment Status. This section should describe the types of employees that will be hired by the company. For example, the company may hire full-time, part-time, and temporary employees. The following suggestions may be helpful:

- introductory employees—employees who have not yet completed the introductory period.
- regular full-time employees—employees who have completed their introductory period and work 40 hours or more per week.
- regular part-time employees—employees who have completed their introductory period and work less than 40 hours per week.
- temporary employees—employees who are hired for a specific period or specific project, and who do not fit into one of the above classifications.

New Hires. This section should explain the nature of the employment relationship when first hired. It should explain the new hire's rights and duties and should at least include a statement regarding the following:

- the employee has the right to work in the United States and that, upon commencement of work, the new employee will be asked to provide original documents verifying his or her right to work in the United States. It should further state that if the employee cannot at any time verify his or her right to work in the United States, the Immigration Reform and Control Act of 1986 may obligate the company to terminate the employment.
- the new hire is considered an introductory employee for the first [#] months of employment. A statement should further spell out whether the employee will or will not earn any benefits, such as vacation, sick pay, or personal holidays during the introductory period.
- the introductory period shall not be construed as a probationary period which implies subsequent permanent employment; nor does a successful completion of the introductory period guarantee continued employment.
- the introductory period may be extended because of permitted time off taken by the employee.
- the relationship is at-will during the introductory period or afterwards during the entire course of employment.

Work Schedules. This section should set forth the desired work schedules or include a statement that the schedules will be determined according to each employee's employment contract (if one is used) or as informed by the employee's supervisor.

Rest and Meal Breaks. This section should include a statement regarding company policies on rest and meal breaks. Check with federal and state laws to make sure the company is in compliance with both. You might include something like the following:

- if you work three hours or more, you may take a ten-minute break. If you work five hours or more, you may take a ten-minute break and a thirty-minute meal break, which should be scheduled with your supervisor. If you work seven hours or more, you may take two ten-minute breaks and a thirty-minute meal break. All ten-minute breaks must be taken on company premises. Your supervisor will inform you of where you can take your breaks.

Personnel Records. This section should explain company policies on keeping personnel records. Make sure that this section complies with federal and state regulations. You might include statements like the following:

- the company keeps a personnel file on each employee. With exceptions, the contents of each employee's file is open for inspection by that employee at reasonable times and at reasonable intervals at the employee's request. The employee may make copies of certain papers in his or her file.
- all employees have the duty to inform the company of any personal changes such as change in address, phone number, marital status, or changes in the number of dependents.
- the company will keep all personnel records private, unless required by law to release certain information.

Separation Procedures. This section should state what procedures are necessary when an employee leaves the company. It should include language requesting that the employee return all supplies, keys, and other company property.

Business Ethics. This section should set forth company policies regarding gifts and avoiding the appearance of improprieties. It should include a statement that the company expects its employees to act in accordance with the highest standards of business ethics both on and off company premises and while conducting business on the company's behalf.

Confidential Information. This section should inform the employee that he or she may come into possession of trade secrets or confidential information which belongs to the company, and that such information, whether about the company, its customers, suppliers, or employees is strictly confidential. You might include statements like the following:

- all confidential information must not be disclosed to anyone, including family members outside the company, or to any company employee who is not entitled to the information, either during or after your employment.
- any doubts about the confidentiality of information should be resolved in favor of confidentiality.

Conflict of Interest. This section should discuss conflicts of interests and state activities which could raise questions of a conflict. You should at least include a statement regarding the following:

- employees are expected to avoid situations which create an actual or potential conflict with the company's interests or that could interfere with the employee's duty and ability to best serve the company.
- employees who are unsure about whether a conflict exists should consult his or her supervisor.

• engaging in any other employment or personal activity during company work hours, or using the company's name, stationery, supplies, equipment, or other property for personal purposes can be deemed a conflict.
• when a conflict of interest is found to exist, the conflict may result in discipline or, when appropriate, termination of employment.

Inspections of Work Stations and Personal Belongings. This section should include a discussion of the right to privacy issues which have surfaced recently and which have been construed against employers. You might include statements similar to the following:

• [*Company*] reserves the right to search work stations, desks, company vehicles, lunchboxes, lunch bags, briefcases, purses, coats, and other personal property of employees, and their contents, for illegal drugs, alcohol, weapons, and stolen property (which is collectively referred to as "contraband").
• [*Company*] will conduct searches only when there is reasonable cause to believe the employee has contraband in his or her possession. However, any contraband in plain view may be confiscated at any time. (Reasonable cause means facts that would lead a person of reasonable prudence and knowledge to believe that contraband is located on the person or in the area to be searched.)
• When contraband is not in plain view, but management has reasonable cause to believe that contraband is on company property, management will ask for the employee's permission to conduct the search.
• Employees have no reasonable expectation of privacy in, and may not withhold permission for, company searches of company-supplied containers, including desks, toolboxes, and company vehicles.

Use of Computer Files and E-Mail. This section should discuss the company's right to inspect and access computer information and work-related electronic information. You might include statements like the following:

- **Company's Right to Access Information.** Although employees may have personal access codes to voicemail, e-mail, and computer network systems, [*company*] has the right to access and inspect such systems at all times, whether unannounced or not, for business purposes. Employees have the duty to report all access codes and changes to such codes immediately and on a constant basis. Employees may not use pass codes that are unknown to the company. Employees must backup copies of e-mail and voicemail and maintain them for future reference for business and legal reasons.

- **Systems Use Restricted to Company Business.** Employees are expected to use the e-mail, voicemail, and computer network systems for company business only and not for personal purposes.

- **Forbidden Content.** Employees are prohibited from using the company's information systems in any way that may be disruptive or offensive to others, including, but not limited to, the transmission of sexually explicit messages, ethnic or racial slurs, or anything that may be construed as harassment, discriminatory, or disparagement of others.

- **Password Security and Integrity.** Employees are prohibited from disclosing their access code to others and from using the access codes of other employees to gain access to their e-mail and voicemail messages.

Employees are warned that such personal or other inappropriate use of company's information systems will result in disciplinary action up to and including termination.

Use of Telephone and 800 Numbers. This section should discuss your company policies regarding making personal telephone calls. You might include language like the following if long distance is a concern:

All phones are to be use for business use only. No long distance calls for personal use will be tolerated and any violation of this section may result in discharge and the employee may be required to pay for such charges.

YOUR PAY AT [COMPANY]

Pay Periods. This section should discuss employees pay periods. You might include a statement like the following:

Paydays are on a [*weekly, bi-weekly, semi-monthly, monthly basis*] and paychecks are distributed [*every Friday, every 2nd and 4th Fridays, on the first (1st) and fifteenth (15th) day of each month, monthly*]. Your paycheck will include your pay for all time worked, including overtime.

Overtime. This section should discuss non-exempt and exempt status of employment. Perhaps you might include statements like the following:

Some employees are exempt from overtime pay. Exempt employees are paid on a salary basis and are commonly in executive, administrative, or professional positions.

Non-exempt employees are paid either a salary or on an hourly basis, and receive overtime pay for time worked in excess of eight hours per day or 40 hours per work week.

If you are non-exempt, and are required to work overtime, your pay is paid at one and a half times the regular hourly rate if you work more than eight hours per day or 40 hours per week, or for the first eight hours if you work the seventh day of a work week.

Non-exempt employees who have to work more than 12 hours in one day (a day begins at midnight) or more than eight hours on the seventh working day in a work week (each work week begins on Monday), are paid at two times their regular hourly rate for the excess hours.

Days or hours when you are paid but do not work, such as vacations, holidays, or sick leave, do not count as time worked for computing overtime.

You must obtain permission from your supervisor to work overtime. If you work overtime without permission, you may be disciplined up to and possibly including discharge.

Payroll Deductions. This section should discuss federal and state required payroll deductions. You might include a statement like the following:

We are required by federal and state laws to make the following deductions from your pay: (a) federal income tax; (b) state income tax; (c) Federal Insurance Contributions Act (FICA) (social security and Medicare); and (d) State Disability Insurance (SDI). If you marry, divorce, or change the number of exemptions in your family, you are required to immediately report the change to personnel or your supervisor.

Garnishment. This section should discuss the company's obligation to comply with wage garnishments. You might include a statement like the following:

If we receive an order to garnish an employee's wages, federal or state laws require that we comply with that order. A garnishment will reduce the garnished employee's take-home pay. If we are forced to comply with multiple wage garnishment, we may elect to discipline or discharge the employee because such multiple garnishment takes valuable company time and money.

YOUR POTENTIAL BENEFITS AT [COMPANY]

Paid Leave. This section should discuss benefits that the company will offer its employees. It should state which employees are entitled to which benefits. The following categories and statements might be helpful:

Vacations. If you are a regular, full-time employee, you are entitled to paid vacation days after one year of continuous service. Part-time employees are entitled to paid vacation at half the number of days as full-time employees after one year of continuous service. Temporary and introductory employees are not entitled to paid vacation days. Time off is paid on the basis of your base hourly rate, excluding premiums and overtime compensation, if any.

After one year of continuous service and continuing each subsequent year, regular, full-time employees accrue [# *of days*] vacation days per year of employment and part-time employees accrue half the number of days as full-time employees. All employees are asked to submit vacation requests as soon as possible. The company will schedule vacations based on seniority and the operational needs of the company.

All vacation requests must be approved in advance by your supervisor. You cannot accrue vacation time beyond the year in which it is earned. You may not take vacation before you earn it, unless you obtain written permission from your supervisor. If permission is granted, the vacation will be considered a salary advance. If you take more vacation than you have earned, and then leave the company, the amount of unearned vacation you took will be deducted from your final paycheck. If you are on a leave of absence or are suspended, you will not earn vacation benefits.

Company Holidays. The company provides the following paid holidays each year: [*specify, e.g., New Year's Day; President's Day; Memorial Day; Independence Day; Labor Day; Thanksgiving Day; Friday after Thanksgiving; and Christmas Day*]. When a holiday falls on a Saturday, it is observed the preceding Friday. When it falls on a Sunday, it is observed the following Monday. Holidays that fall during a scheduled vacation do not count as a vacation day used.

Sick/Personal Leave. Regular, full-time employees accrue sick/personal leave from the date of employment at a rate of [*one-half day, one day*] for each month of service, up to a total of [*six, twelve*] days per year. Part-time employees are entitled to paid sick/personal leave on the same terms and at half the number of days as full-time employees. Temporary and introductory employees are not entitled to paid sick/personal days. Suspended employees do not accrue sick/personal leave and are not paid for sick/personal days.

Employees cannot rollover sick/personal leave from one year to the next. However, to reward employees with perfect attendance, [*company*] shall pay [*six, twelve*] days salary to any eligible employee who does not use any sick/personal leave for one year. For purpose of calculating this bonus, a year will begin on the employee's anniversary date and end on the day before his or her next anniversary date.

If you are sick or are requesting personal leave, you must tell your supervisor within one half hour of the beginning of your shift unless it is extremely unusual for you to do so, or you will not receive sick/personal pay for that day. If you cannot inform your supervisor within the time required, you are required to have a member of your family or a friend call your supervisor within the required time frame.

If you are hospitalized or out sick for more than seven calendar days for an injury or illness that is not work-related, you should apply for State Disability Insurance (SDI) benefits. These benefits will be deducted from your sick pay. We can supply the form you will need to apply for SDI, but it is your responsibility to make the application.

YOUR JOB PERFORMANCE AT [COMPANY].

This section should discuss reviews, attendance, performance, and tardiness. You might use statements like the following:

Evaluations. Your supervisor may review your job performance with you on a regular basis. The purposes of these evaluations are: (a) to evaluate the strengths and weaknesses of your work; (b) to communicate these to you; (c) to get feedback from you regarding your position and your thoughts of the company; and (d) to set mutually satisfactory future performance goals.

Your supervisor may prepare a written assessment of your job performance and, if so, you will meet with your supervisor to discuss the evaluation. When you meet with your supervisor, you are encouraged to ask specific questions and to comment about your evaluation. You will be allowed to write your own comments on the evaluation form and to sign it to show that you have read it and discussed it. Signing it does not mean that you agreed to its contents, but rather only that you have read it. You may request a copy of the assessment for your records. A good performance evaluation does not guarantee a pay raise, because pay increases may not occur every year, nor is it a promise of continued employment.

Attendance and Absences. If you cannot report to work, you are expected to call your supervisor and tell him or her that you will not be coming in and when you expect to return. If you do not know your return date, you must call your supervisor each day within one hour of the beginning of your regularly scheduled day. If you are absent three days without contacting your supervisor, we will assume you have voluntarily quit your job at the end of the third day.

If you know in advance that you are going to be absent, you must schedule the absence with your supervisor at least one week in advance. Excessive absences and failure to report absences on time will lead to discipline, up to and including discharge. Absences are excessive if they occur frequently or if they show a pattern. Absences immediately before or after holidays and weekends are suspect. Frequent absences for minor complaints such as a headache or stomachache are also suspect.

Tardiness. You must arrive at your job location and be ready to start work at the beginning of your work day. Be ready to resume work on time after authorized rest and meal periods. Tardiness may lead to discipline up to and including discharge. We know that traffic or weather conditions may cause you to be late once in a while. However, if this happens on a continuous basis, or if you demonstrate a pattern of tardiness, you may be disciplined up to and including discharge.

POLICIES GOVERNING UNPAID TIME OFF. This section should discuss federal and state required leaves of absences. You need to discuss the contents of this section with legal counsel in your state. The following categories should be discussed:

Medical Leave: Non-Occupational Disability
Medical Leave: Occupational Disability
Pregnancy Leave
Military Service
Jury Duty
Death in Immediate Family

COMPANY RULES STRICTLY ENFORCED. This section is essential. The following lists are intended to show some violations you may want to consider. The lists are not all-inclusive and you should consider other violations as well:

Violations for Which You Will Be Discharged

- Malicious or willful destruction or damage to company property or supplies.
- Malicious or willful destruction or damage to property of an employee or others.
- Stealing or removing without permission company property.
- Stealing or removing without permission property of an employee, customer, or visitor.
- Obtaining your job by lying or giving false or misleading information.

- Falsifying any employment documents or records and other acts of dishonesty.
- Possessing firearms, weapons, and hazardous devices/substances on company property.
- Possession, use, or sale of alcoholic beverages or illegal drugs on company property.
- Reporting for duty under the influence of alcohol or illegal drugs.
- Insubordination, including improper conduct toward supervisor and refusal to perform tasks.
- Fighting on company property.
- Harassing, threatening, intimidating, or coercing a supervisor or another employee.
- Giving company products away or at a discount in violation of company policies.
- Pleading guilty to or being convicted of any crime other than a minor traffic violation.
- Failure to follow company procedures for maintaining the confidentiality of the company's confidential and proprietary information and trade secrets.

Violations for Which You Will Be Disciplined

- Unsatisfactory job performance.
- Not following an established safety rule.
- Tardiness or excessive absence from work or your work area.
- Leaving the premises or your job during working hours without supervisor's permission.
- Horseplay or other action that is dangerous or that disrupts work.
- Smoking in non-smoking areas or where No Smoking signs are posted.
- Working unauthorized overtime.
- Use of abusive or vulgar language.
- Carelessness or negligence in doing your job.
- Using company equipment, materials, or supplies without permission.

• Possessing or removing company or employee food or other items without permission.
• Sleeping while on duty.
• Inappropriate appearance or grooming.

The type of discipline will depend on how bad the violation is and the specific facts and circumstances of the conduct. Discipline includes oral or written warnings, suspension, or discharge. We have the right to determine what discipline is appropriate. There is no standard series of disciplinary steps the company must follow. In certain circumstances, your conduct may lead to immediate discharge. Further, as previously stated, either you or the company may terminate your employment at any time without cause on notice to each other; our discipline procedures are not meant to imply any contrary policy.

Personal Safety and Company Security. We believe that your work environment should be safe, secure, and free from harassment. To accomplish this, all employees are required to act in a professional manner toward fellow employees, customers, and third parties involved in the work environment. To maintain confidentiality of company's trade secrets and confidential information, all employees are required to follow company rules regarding premises security.

Your Responsibilities. If you see an unsafe condition, you must immediately report it your supervisor. You must also report all accidents, no matter how minor you think they may be. All employees are required to learn the location of the first aid kit, fire extinguishers, stairs, and exits.

Tell your supervisor of any equipment breakdown as soon as it happens. If the breakdown requires emergency repairs, your supervisor will try to deal with the emergency situation. All employees are required to attend safety training seminars put on by the company.

General Security. All employees will be required to sign an employment agreement with confidentiality clauses. Breach of the agreement may give us a cause of action against any employee and third parties including but not limited to an action for breach of contract, breach of confidence, breach of implied or express covenants, or an action in tort.

Crime. Your safety is our biggest concern. For your safety, you must follow these procedures if a crime occurs while you are on the premises:

- Cooperate fully with the person committing the crime.
- Try to keep your fellow employees as safe as possible.
- As quickly as possible after the crime is committed, call for needed medical help.
- As quickly as possible after the crime is committed, contact the local police department.
- As quickly as possible after the crime is committed, write down all the details of the crime.
- List the names of the employees at the scene and get written statements from them.
- If customers are present, ask them to stay until the police come or get their names and where they can be reached.
- Do not try to be a "hero."

On-the-Job Injuries. If any employee is seriously injured on the job, he or she must get medical treatment immediately. If necessary, call an ambulance and contact your supervisor immediately. If the injury is less serious, make arrangements to have the employee taken to the hospital or a doctor.

Workers' Compensation. If you are injured while performing your job, you may be covered by the company's workers' compensation insurance. You must report your injury to your supervisor as quickly as possible, no matter how minor it is and even if you feel you do not need medical treatment. The supervisor must make a report of the injury to appropriate personnel as soon as possible after the injury happens. Claims for workers' compensation benefits should be made to appropriate key personnel.

Substance Abuse. The illegal use, sale, or possession of narcotics, drugs, or controlled substances while on the job or on company property will result in immediate discharge. Conviction for the illegal use, sale, or possession of narcotics, drugs, or controlled substances off duty or off company property may also result in discharge. If you are arrested for a drug-related offense and are awaiting trial, you will be suspended without pay: (a) until all charges against you are dismissed; (b) until you plead guilty; or (c) until your trial results in a verdict. If you plead guilty or are convicted of a drug-related crime, your employment with us with be terminated.

The legal use of controlled substances, such as prescription drugs prescribed by a licensed physician or over-the-counter medications that you buy at the store is allowed. However, if you cannot do your job satisfactorily because you are taking prescription or over-the-counter medicine, you may be discharged or obliged to take a leave of absence if the doctor concludes that you cannot do your job safely and efficiently.

Your Appearance. A professional appearance is essential to your job. You must practice good grooming and personal hygiene and dress appropriately in professional, appropriate clothing or in a neat and clean uniform, if required to do so. T-shirts, sweatshirts, and jeans are not professional nor appropriate unless the Company exercises casual days and authorizes such apparel.

Harassment. Verbal, physical, visual, and sexual harassment of co-workers, third parties, and members of the public is absolutely forbidden. Harassment can take many forms. A few examples of prohibited harassment (for illustrative purposes only) include: (a) racial, sexual, or ethnic jokes and insults; (b) sexually suggestive or unwelcome touching, or obscene gestures; (c) insulting cartoons, sexually suggestive or lewd pictures or photographs; and (d) harassment because of terminal illness.

Sexual harassment may consist of unwelcome sexual advances, deprecating sexual remarks, references to women as "honey," "doll," "dear," or an environment demeaning to women.

If you think that you or one of your co-workers has been the victim of harassment, you must report the incident and the names of the persons to your supervisor immediately. If you do not report harassment, it cannot be investigated. Your cooperation is crucial. There will be no retaliation against you by management for making a complaint of sexual harassment. If you are afraid to report harassment to your supervisor, you should report it to appropriate key personnel.

TERMINATION OF YOUR EMPLOYMENT. This section is needed to discuss the situations which will trigger the termination of the employment relationship. The following statements may be helpful:

We will consider that you have voluntarily terminated your employment if you do any of the following: (a) resign from the company; (b) fail to return from an approved leave of absence on the date specified by company; or (c) fail to report to work and fail to call in for three work days in a row.

You may be terminated for poor performance, misconduct, excessive absences, tardiness, or other violations of the company rules. However, your employment is at-will, and you and the company have the right to terminate your employment for any legal reason or no reason, on notice to each other.

We may need to terminate your employment because of reorganization, job elimination, economic downturns, or lack of work. Should we decide that such a termination is necessary, we will try to give as much advance notice as is practical.

RECEIPT OF THIS EMPLOYEE HANDBOOK. It is essential that your employees sign a copy of the handbook (not their own) or a separate form for company files to acknowledge that they have received the handbook. The following acknowledgment may be helpful:

I acknowledge that I have been given a copy of the [*company*] Employee Handbook. I agree that I have read and will follow the information and rules in this handbook.

Dated: ____________________ ____________________________

Signature of Employee

PERFORMANCE EVALUATION

Employee: ______________________ **Date of Hire:** ______________________

Evaluator: ______________________ **Date of Evaluation:** ______________________

The following scale is a guideline for rating each category:

5 = **Outstanding.** Performance well beyond expectation.
4 = **Above Expectation.** Performance above average.
3 = **Meets Expectations.** Performance at average level.
2 = **Below Expectations.** Performance is below average.
1 = **Unsatisfactory.** Performance is unacceptable.

CRITERIA	1	2	3	4	5
Performance					
Completes tasks quickly					
Quality of completed work					
Productivity					
Works independently					
Communication					
Reports to supervisor					
Communicates to clients/customers skillfully and effectively					
Communicates to staff personnel skillfully and effectively					
Uses time efficiently (e.g., does employee waste time talking, etc.)					
Interpersonal Skills					
Working relationship with other staff personnel					
Working relationship with clients/customers					
Attendance					
Punctuality					
Absenteeism					
Overall attendance record					
Knowledge/Skills					
Meets job requirements					
Applies knowledge/skills to do job					
Increases knowledge and skills					

Evaluator's comments: ____

____

Employee's comments: ____

____

Signatures: ____

EMPLOYEE WARNING

[ ] RECORD OF VERBAL WARNING
[ ] WRITTEN WARNING
[ ] NOTICE OF SUSPENSION

Name of Employee: ______________________ Date of Warning: ________________

Reason for Warning/Notice:

____

____

To Avoid Further Discipline, Employee Should:

____

____

Next Disciplinary Step Proposed:

____

____

Employee Response:

____

____

Warning Given By: ______________________ Signature: ______________________

Suspension Dates: ______________________ Effective from _________ to _________

For Written Warning Only

By signing this warning, I acknowledge that I have been counseled as noted above. I understand that my signing is simply an acknowledgement of receiving this counsel and not an admission of wrongdoing.

Employee Signature: __________________________ Date:____________

COMPLAINT FORM FOR SEXUAL HARASSMENT

It is our policy that all of our employees be free from sexual harassment. Please use this form to report sexual harassment, so that we may investigate and take appropriate disciplinary or other action when the facts show that there has been sexual harassment. Please provide as much factual detail as you can so we can properly investigate it.

You can file this form with your supervisor. If the complaint concerns conduct by your supervisor or you do not wish to file the complaint with your supervisor for some other reason, you should file the complaint with Human Resources or any member of executive management.

Description of events or conduct that are the basis of the complaint (attach additional pages if needed):

____

____

____

We will undertake every effort to handle the investigation of your complaint in a confidential manner. In that regard, we will disclose the contents of your complaint only to those persons having a need to know.

In signing this form below, you authorize us to disclose the information you have provided, and may in the future provide, with respect to your complaint, to the extent that we believe we must release that information to adequately investigate your claim.

Charges of sexual harassment are very serious because of the harm caused to the alleged person harassed and the potential sanctions that may be taken against the alleged harasser. It is therefore very important that you report the facts as accurately and completely as possible and that you cooperate fully with us as we will fully cooperate with you.

I acknowledge that I have read and understand the above statements. I hereby authorize [*company*] to disclose the information I provide as it finds necessary in pursuing its investigation of sexual harassment.

______________________	______________________
Date	Signature of Employee

[*date*]

Company
Company Address
City, State, Zip

Dear [*Company*]:

I, the undersigned, acknowledge and warranty that I do not have in my possession, nor have I failed to return, any confidential information or copies of such information or trade secrets, or other documents or materials, equipment, or other property belonging to [*company*] or its customers.

I further acknowledge and warranty that I have complied with and will continue to comply with all the terms of the [*Confidentiality Agreement, Invention Assignment Agreement, etc.*] which I signed.

I further agree that I will keep all confidential information and trade secrets confidential and I will neither use them nor participate in the unauthorized disclosure of them or any information that could be detrimental to the interests of [*company*] or its customers, whether or not such information is identified as confidential information by the company or its customers.

I will further comply in all respects to the terms I agreed to in all Confidentiality and Invention Assignment Agreements to which I was a party.

____
Employee

AGENCY AGREEMENT

This agreement is made this [*date*] by and between [*company*] (hereinafter called "Company"), located at [*address*], and [*individual*], an individual doing business as [*name*], located at [*address*].

Recitals

1. [*Company*] holds the manufacturing and marketing rights to the [*products*].

2. [*Individual*] desires to market and commercialize the products (as defined herein) in the sales territory (as defined herein), and [*company*] has agreed to designate [*individual*] as its sole and exclusive agent for such purposes within the territory and as its exclusive agent within the territory for such purposes.

Definitions

The following terms as used in this Agreement shall have the meaning as defined with respect to each such term.

1. Effective Date. "Effective Date" shall be the date of execution of this Agreement by the last party to so execute.

2. Net Sales. "Net Sales" shall mean the gross invoice price of any product sold by [*individual*] or any dealer, distributor, or any other person or entity directly or indirectly related to any person or entity introduced to company by individual in accordance with the terms of this agreement within the sales territory, less the following deductions as applicable: cash, trade, or quantity discounts allowed and taken, if any; sales, use, value-added, tariff, import, or export duty or other taxes imposed and actually withheld or paid upon particular sales; foreign government withholding; transportation charges; and allowances or credits to customers because of rejections or returns as reflected in company's sales returns and allowances accounts for the sales territory, provided that such terms are (a) attributable to sales made directly by individual, and (b) certified by company's independent auditor as being correct. The products shall be considered "sold" when payment is received from the purchaser.

3. Products. "Products" shall mean [*describe products*].

4. Territory. "Territory" shall mean [*worldwide, specific territory*].

In consideration of the above, and for other good and valuable consideration, the sufficiency and receipt of which is hereby acknowledged, the parties hereby agree as follows:

Agreement

1. Recitals and Definitions Part of Agreement. The above recitals and definitions are a material part of this Agreement.

2. Appointment as Exclusive Agent. Company hereby appoints [*individual*] as its exclusive sales representative to sell and market the products in and throughout the sales territory.

3. Acceptance of Appointment. [*Individual*] hereby accepts such appointment and agrees to sell and promote the Products subject to the provisions and conditions of this Agreement.

4. Term. This Agreement shall run from its effective date for a period of one year, and shall renew automatically each additional year, provided that [*Individual*] is in compliance with the terms of this Agreement.

5. Company's Duties.

a) Company shall not quote, offer to sell, or sell the Products to any purchasing agent, public or private, or any existing or potential customer located in the Territory, and shall refer all such inquiries to [*individual*].

b) Company shall forward to [*individual*] all inquiries applicable to the Territory received for the Products.

c) Company shall furnish to [*individual*], upon request, pricing, delivery, and technical information covering the products as it may relate to [*individual's*] sales efforts, and shall exercise its best efforts to promptly furnish [*individual*] with replacements and parts at no cost for products which expire or prove defective within any applicable period of warranty. Company shall bear sole responsibility for pricing the products.

d) Company shall pay to [*individual*] all commissions when due.

e) Company shall maintain adequate product liability insurance to cover reasonably foreseeable claims that may be made against the products.

f) Company shall provide [*individual*] with the best quotes/rates offered by company to any of its other dealers/distributors/agents for the products during the term of this agreement.

6. Commissions. [*Individual's*] compensation hereunder shall consist of commissions of [*amount*] percent (%), which will be paid on the net sales price of all products sold within the sales territory by individual or any person or entity introduced to company by individual in accordance with the terms of this agreement. The parties agree that no other commissions will be paid by company, unless the parties subsequently agree otherwise in a writing signed by all parties.

7. When Commissions Are Earned. Commissions shall be earned on all orders at such time as the order is accepted by company and company receives payment from the purchaser. All commissions shall be payable in U.S. currency and shall be paid proportionately to the payments effected by the purchaser to company. Commissions shall be paid [*state payment terms*].

8. Individual's Duties. Individual warrants that individual shall:

a) Use his/her best efforts to sell, promote, and locate and identify potential dealers and distributors for the products.

b) Devote such time as is reasonably necessary for the above-described purposes.

c) Conduct his/her business in his/her own name, pay his/her expenses, and the cost of all of his/her employees.

9. Warranties. Any warranties given to a customer will be made by company or the applicable product manufacturer and [*individual*] shall have no responsibility thereunder. Notwithstanding anything to the contrary herein, [*individual*] shall maintain full responsibility for any representations made by his/her sales force, employees, agents, sublicensees, officers, or directs which induce a customer to purchase any of the products in reliance on such representations, and where such representations prove to be false and were not in accordance with the specifications and capabilities of the products specified in information provided by company to individual.

[*Add boilerplate clauses as needed*]

CONSULTING AGREEMENT

This Agreement is made this [*date*] between [*name*] (hereinafter referred to as "Company"), located at [*address*], and [*name*] (hereinafter referred to as "Consultant").

Recitals

WHEREAS, Company is engaged in the [*type*] business; and Consultant is willing to consult with Company on business and [*type of business matters*], and the Parties are willing to contract with each other on the terms, covenants, and conditions set forth herein.

NOW THEREFORE IN CONSIDERATION of the mutual covenants and promises of the parties, and exchange for good and valuable consideration, the receipt and sufficiency of which is hereby acknowledged, Company and Consultant covenant and agree as follows:

Agreement

For a period of [*state length of time*] following the date of execution of this Agreement, Company shall employ Consultant under the following terms and conditions:

1. Compensation. Company shall pay Consultant an aggregate remuneration of $[*amount*], payable as follows: [*state payment terms*].

2. Duties. Consultant shall make himself or herself available to advise and assist Company in the business affairs, management, or training and orientation of Company's business. During this consultation period, Company shall have the right to consult with Consultant for a reasonable time, not to exceed [*number*] hours during each calendar month. Whether or not Company consults with Consultant during any calendar month, Consultant shall be paid $[*amount*] at the beginning of each calendar month during the consultation period.

[*Add boilerplate clauses as needed*]

SPECIALLY COMMISSIONED
WORK AGREEMENT

This agreement is made this [*date*] by [*company*] (hereinafter referred to as "Company"), with its principal place of business located at [*address*], and [*commissioned business or individual*] (hereinafter referred to as "Programmer"), with his/her principal place of business located at [*address*], with respect to certain rights in [*specify what individual is commissioned to do, e.g., create a software program (hereinafter called the "Software Program" or "Program")*].

1. Work Commissioned. Company engages Programmer, and Programmer agrees to be engaged, on the terms and conditions of this Agreement, to complete and deliver one final version of a Software Program for Company's use.

2. Programmer's Duties. Programmer shall deliver to Company a complete and first version of the Software Program in content and form satisfactory to Company on or before [*date*]. Programmer shall make any additions to, deletions from, alterations of, or revisions in the Software Program which Company, in its sole judgment, determines are necessary to render the Software Program satisfactory to Company. Nothing in the foregoing shall be deemed to obligate Company to afford Programmer the opportunity to revise the Software Program.

3. Compensation. In full consideration for all services rendered by Programmer and for all rights granted or relinquished by Programmer under this Agreement, Company shall pay Programmer the sum of $[*amount*] dollars, payable on delivery and acceptance by Company of the complete and satisfactory Software Program [*or payable as follows*].

4. Ownership of Program. Company shall own all right, title, and interest in and to the Software Program, the work associated with the Software Program, and all additions to, deletions from, alterations of, or revisions in the Software Program and the work, and all drafts, notes, concepts, ideas, suggestions, and approaches related thereto or contained therein, or other materials developed or furnished by Programmer for the production of the Software Program, and each element and part thereof.

Without limiting the foregoing, Programmer hereby acknowledges that Programmer's work and services hereunder and all results and proceeds thereof are works done under Company's direction and control and have been specially ordered or commissioned by Company to be published by Company, and that all such services, results, and proceeds shall be considered a Work Made for Hire. As between Programmer and Company, Company shall be considered the author of the Program for purposes of copyright and shall own all the rights in and to the copyright in Company's name. To the extent such rights do not vest in Company as a "Work Made For Hire," Programmer further grants, assigns, and transfers to Company all of Programmer's right, title, and interest in and to the Program and all materials contained therein and proceeds thereof, Company shall have the sole and exclusive right throughout the universe in all languages and in perpetuity to use and exploit all or any part of the Program and all or any part of any material contained therein or prepared therefor, whether or not used therein, in any format or version, by any means and in any media, whether now known or hereafter developed.

Without limiting the foregoing, Programmer hereby waives any and all claims that Programmer may now or hereafter have in any jurisdiction to so-called "moral rights" or rights of "droit moral" with respect to the results and proceeds of Programmer's work and services hereunder. Programmer shall execute such further instruments as Company may request to establish, maintain, or protect its rights in and ownership of the Properties.

5. Relationship as Independent Contractor. Programmer is an independent contractor and shall be solely responsible for any unemployment or disability insurance payments, or any social security, income tax, or other withholdings, deductions, or payments which may be required by federal, state, or local law with respect to any sums paid Programmer hereunder. Programmer shall not be entitled to any employee benefits of whatever nature from Company.

6. No Authority to Bind. Programmer is not Company's agent or representative and has no authority to bind or commit Company to any agreements or other obligations.

7. Termination. Company may terminate this Agreement if Programmer fails to deliver the final Software Program to Company by the time specified in Paragraph 2 (except where such delay is caused by circumstances beyond Programmer's control and Programmer has promptly notified Company of such delaying circumstances) or if Company determines, in its reasonable judgment, that the Software Program is not satisfactory. If this Agreement is terminated for any other reason, Company shall have the right, without further obligation to Programmer, to the first and final versions of the Software Program, and to use the Program in any manner it deems appropriate, including, without limitation, editing, altering, and revising the Program, and shall pay Programmer a reasonable amount to be agreed upon by the parties.

8. Representations and Warranties. Programmer represents and warrants to Company that Programmer has full power and authority to make this Agreement; that in performing under this Agreement, Programmer will not violate the terms of any agreement with any third party; that the Software Program, and all elements and parts thereof, as finally determined by Company to be satisfactory, will not infringe any statutory or common-law copyright, will not be libelous or obscene, will not violate any right of privacy or publicity, or otherwise violate any law or any person's personal or property rights.

9. Indemnification. Programmer shall indemnify Company and hold Company harmless against any liabilities, losses, damages, costs, or expenses, including attorney's fees, arising from any claim, action, or proceeding based upon or in any way related to any breach or alleged breach of the foregoing warranties and representations. These warranties and representations shall survive termination of this Agreement for any reason.

10. Programmer's Remedy. Programmer's remedy, if any, for any breach of this Agreement by Company shall be solely in money damages and Programmer shall look solely to Company for recovery of such damages. Programmer waives and relinquishes any right Programmer might otherwise have (a) to obtain injunctive or equitable relief for any reason, and (b) to proceed against any third party with respect to any dispute arising under this Agreement.

[*Add boilerplate clauses as needed*]

INDEPENDENT CONTACTOR AGREEMENT

This Agreement is entered into on this [*date*], by and between [*company*] ("Company"), whose business address is [*location*], and [*independent contractor*] ("Independent Contractor"), whose business address is [*location*].

Recitals

WHEREAS, Company is engaged in [*type of business*], and maintains an office at [*location*]; and

WHEREAS, Independent Contractor is in the business of [*describe business*] and maintains an office at a location other than at Company's place of business; and

WHEREAS, Company requires [*sales of its products*] on a continuing basis for efficient operation of its business, and Independent Contractor is willing to provide such services on the terms and conditions set forth in this Agreement.

NOW THEREFORE IN CONSIDERATION of the mutual covenants, agreements, representations, and warranties, and in exchange for good and valuable consideration, the receipt and sufficiency of which is hereby acknowledged, the parties hereby agree as follows:

Agreement

1. Recitals Part of Agreement. Recitals are a material part of this Agreement.

2. Services to Be Provided. Independent Contractor agrees to perform the following [*sales and sales related*] services pursuant to the terms and conditions of this Agreement: [*provide general description of services*].

3. Term. The initial term of this Agreement shall begin on the date of this Agreement, and shall continue for a period of [*years*], unless terminated sooner pursuant to the provisions of this Agreement. *[If renewal is desired]* Upon expiration of the initial term of this Agreement, this Agreement shall automatically renew on the same terms and conditions for successive [*number of years*] periods, unless either party notifies the other that the arrangement is not to continue beyond the ensuing year.

4. Declaration of Relationship Between Parties. The parties to this Agreement intend and agree that Independent Contractor, in handling sales and services, shall act as an independent contractor and shall have control of his or her work and the manner in which it is performed. Independent Contractor shall adhere to all laws and ethical standards applicable to [*salespersons*] and shall perform in a manner consistent with generally accepted procedures for his or her profession. Independent Contractor is not to be considered an agent or employee of Company and is not entitled to the benefits provided by Company to any employee or future employee, including, but not limited to, compensation insurance, unemployment insurance, and pension plans. Independent Contractor shall be free to contract for similar services to be performed for other owners while he or she is under this Agreement with Company. Company may, during the term of this Agreement, engage other Independent Contractors to perform the same work that Independent Contractor performs hereunder.

5. Control of Work by Independent Contractor. Independent Contractor shall have sole control of the manner and means of performing under this Agreement, and he or she shall complete it according to his or her own means and methods of work. Independent Contractor is not required to follow a routine or a schedule established by Company. The operation of Company's business does not require Independent Contractor's work to be supervised or controlled in the performance of such service.

6. Furnishing Supplies and Equipment. Company shall furnish [*list supplies and equipment that company will supply*] to Independent Contractor for work to be performed by Independent Contractor. Other than the above mentioned items, Independent Contractor shall furnish his or her own supplies at his or her own expense.

7. Expenses Incurred by Independent Contractor. Independent Contractor is solely responsible for expenses incurred by Independent Contractor in the performance of services for Company. Company shall not reimburse Independent Contractor for such expenses.

8. Right of Company to Supervise and Inspect. Independent Contractor shall have the authority to control and direct the performance of the work done under this Agreement. However, the work shall be subject to Company's general right of inspection and supervision.

9. Limitation on Delegation of Personal Services by Independent Contractor. The work and services provided for herein shall be performed personally by Independent Contractor, and no person other than Independent Contractor shall be engaged in such work or services except on written approval of Company, provided that this provision shall not apply to secretarial, clerical, or similar incidental services needed by Independent Contractor to assist in the performance of this Agreement.

10. Compensation. As compensation for performance hereunder, Company shall pay Independent Contractor the sum of $[*amount*] dollars per [*product*] sold to be paid as follows: [*list terms of payment*].

11. Liability of Independent Contractor - Negligence. Independent Contractor shall be responsible for performing the work under this Agreement in a skillful manner and shall be liable for his or her negligence. Company shall have no right of control over the manner in which the work is to be done and shall therefore not be charged with the responsibility of preventing risk to Independent Contractor or third parties. All work shall be done at Independent Contractor's risk.

12. Indemnification of Company. Independent Contractor shall indemnify Company against all liability or loss, and against all claims or actions based upon or arising out of injury to or death of persons, or damage to or loss of property, caused by acts or negligence of Independent Contractor in connection with the performance of this Agreement.

13. Restriction on Use or Disclosure of Information or Secrets. During the term of this Agreement, Independent Contractor will be dealing with information of a confidential nature that is Company's property and used in the course of Company's business. Independent Contractor will not disclose to anyone, directly or indirectly, either during the term of this agreement or at any time thereafter, any such information, or use it other than in the course of this Agreement with Company.

14. Termination. Either party has the right to terminate this Agreement, with or without cause, with thirty (30) days written notice to the other party.

[*Add boilerplate clauses as needed*]

DISTRIBUTION AGREEMENT

This agreement is made and entered into on [*date*], by and between [*name*] (hereinafter referred to as "Manufacturer"), whose business address is located at [*address*], and [*name*] (hereinafter referred to as "Distributor"), whose business address is located at [*address*].

Recitals

WHEREAS, Manufacturer is the manufacturer and owner of [*list products or state "the products listed in Exhibit A"*] (referred to as the "Products"); and

WHEREAS, Manufacturer reserves to itself the unqualified right to manage its business in all respects, including but not limited to, the right to maintain or alter the Products, formulas, or ingredients for the Products, and labeling or packaging of all the Products; and

WHEREAS, Distributor wishes to act as a [*wholesale*] distributor of the Products in the territory described herein (referred to as the "Territory"), in accordance with the terms and conditions set forth herein;

NOW THEREFORE IN CONSIDERATION of the mutual covenants, agreements, representations, and warranties, and in exchange for good and valuable consideration, the receipt and sufficiency of which is hereby acknowledged, the parties hereby agree as follows:

Agreement

1. Recitals Part of Agreement. Recitals are a material part of this Agreement.

2. Term. The initial term of this Agreement shall be for a period of [*number of months, years*], commencing [*date*] and ending [*date*]. This Agreement shall be renewed at the expiration of the current term for successive periods of one year each, unless either party gives written notice of termination to the other no later than thirty (30) days before the close of the current term.

3. Territory. The territory shall be [*intrastate, interstate, the United States, worldwide*].

4. Purchase of Products. Distributor agrees to purchase from Manufacturer such quantities of the Products as are required to maintain a reasonable supply sufficient to meet the demand of Distributor's customers. The prices, credit terms, and any other terms and conditions of sale for the Products, which Manufacturer shall determine, shall be stipulated on each invoice provided to Distributor. All orders received by

Manufacturer are subject to its acceptance in its sole discretion, and Manufacturer shall have no liability if it is unable to supply the Products for any reason.

5. Obligations of Distributor. Distributor agrees to use its best efforts during the term of this Agreement to sell and to actively promote, in all lawful ways and to the maximum extent possible, the sale of the Products in the Territory. Distributor understands that the Manufacturer may, from time to time, add items to the list of Products, withdraw items from the list of Products, and add other distributors of the Products in [*the Territory, other territories*] without obligation to Distributor. Any products which Manufacturer for any reason ceases to manufacture shall be automatically deleted from the list of Products without obligation to Distributor. This Agreement shall be deemed a single agreement governing all of the Products, notwithstanding that various Products may be listed on different versions of Exhibit A.

6. Performance Standards. During each month of the initial term of this agreement, Distributor shall achieve the performance standards set forth below: [*state performance terms*].

7. Distributor's Representations and Warranties. Distributor represents and warrants that: a) it holds all necessary federal, state, and local licenses and permits for Distributor to distribute the Products in the Territory in accordance with applicable laws; b) within the knowledge of Distributor, there are no actions or proceedings pending or contemplated that would in any way jeopardize any such licenses or permits; and c) Distributor has all appropriate authority to perform this agreement and that such performance will not violate any agreement to which Distributor is a party.

8. Termination. Either party may terminate this Agreement with or without cause upon [*30,90*] days written notice to the other party during the initial term or during any renewal term.

[Add boilerplate clauses as needed]

IN WITNESS WHEREOF, the parties hereto have executed this Agreement, the day and year first written above.

Manufacturer:	Distributor:
By:________________________ President	By:________________________ President

PURCHASE ORDER TERMS AND CONDITIONS

1. All artwork, drawings, sketches, writings, photographs, ideas, concepts, comp art, and other property created hereunder, including all materials incorporated therein and all preliminary or other copies thereof (the "Materials"), remain the property of [*name*] (the "Seller"), and shall not be considered specially ordered for a Customer as a "Work Made for Hire" and Seller does not assign his/her/its rights, title, and interest in the Materials to Customer. Seller shall own all right, title, and interest in the Materials, including without limitation all versions of all negatives, plates, dyes, molds, prints, paintings, artwork, sketches, etchings, drawings, mechanical, or any other work, comp art, or material or property produced, developed, or fabricated for use in performance of this Agreement, and Customer agrees that should it desire to obtain any right, title, or interest in such Materials from Seller, that Customer shall enter into a separate agreement for such purpose and only upon making such an agreement shall Seller agree to execute documents necessary to perfect the transfer of such rights and title.

2. Seller's rights in the Materials shall include, but not be limited to: a) unrestricted and exclusive reproduction rights throughout the world, with name credit if Seller desires, for advertising, trade, art purposes, or any other lawful purpose; b) the exclusive right throughout the world to protect the Materials by copyrights, patents, or trademarks in Seller's name and for its benefit, including the right to secure extensions and renewals of such copyrights, patents, and trademarks in Seller's name and for its benefit; c) the right to alter, retouch, or crop the Materials in any way; d) the right to license, distribute, assign, or transfer any right, title, interest, or copyright in the Materials or otherwise dispose of the Materials or any portion thereof for any purpose and in any manner; and e) all subsidiary and renewal rights.

3. Completed Materials shall be to Customer's reasonable satisfaction and Customer shall be entitled to return any Materials which are not reasonably satisfactory. Customer bears all risk of loss or damage to the Materials upon execution of this Agreement. The parties agree time of completion and delivery of Materials is not considered of the essence.

4. Customer acknowledges that upon execution of this Agreement, Seller shall expend time and money in accordance with Seller's performance herein, and should Customer cancel this order at any time prior to acceptance of Materials, that Customer shall pay all costs, whether direct or indirect, incidental or consequential, incurred by Seller in the performance of Seller's obligations prior to such cancellation, including any amount which shall exceed the price specified on the reverse side of this order; and in addition, Seller has all rights to keep all payments made by Customer to Seller. Seller shall have the right to terminate this Agreement in the event Customer fails to make any payments due pursuant to this Agreement, provided however, nothing herein shall prevent Seller from bringing suit based on Customer's breach of contract.

5. Customer gives Seller permission to use Customer's name in connection with the purchase of Materials, in all forms and media and in all manners, including but not limited to exhibition, display, advertising, and trade uses, without violating Customer's rights of privacy that Customer may possess in connection with this Agreement. Customer agrees that Customer will not intentionally destroy, damage, alter, modify, or change the Materials in any way whatsoever. If any alteration of any kind occurs after receipt by Customer, whether intentional or accidental and whether done by Customer or others, the Materials shall no longer be represented to be the work of Seller with Seller's written consent. Customer agrees to see that the Materials are properly maintained.

6. Customer represents and warrants that Customer is free and has full right to enter into this Agreement and perform all obligations hereunder.

7. Customer's signature on the front of this order shall indicate Customer's agreement to all of the above terms and conditions.

[*Add boilerplate clauses as needed*]

PROMISSORY NOTE

$________________________

For value received, the undersigned Borrower, promises to pay in lawful money of the United States, to the order of [*note holder*] (hereinafter referred to as "Note Holder"), on demand the principal sum of $[*amount*] dollars, with interest on the amount so advanced, at an interest rate of [*ten percent (10%) per annum*] or the highest legal rate, whichever is lower.

Debtor waives presentment, demand, protest, and the right to assert any statute of limitations. Debtor agrees to pay the actual expenditures made in any attempt to collect the amount due pursuant under this Promissory Note. Debtor further agrees that this Note is not assumable without the written consent of Note Holder and that any such nonconsentual assignment shall be null and void.

Signed at [*location*] on this [*date*].

____________________________ ____________________________

Borrower Witness

PROMISSORY NOTE — INSTALLMENT TERMS

$______________________

For value received, the undersigned Borrower, promises to pay in lawful money of the United States, to the order of [*note holder*] (hereinafter referred to as "Note Holder"), the principal sum of $[*amount*] dollars, with interest on the amount so advanced, at an interest rate of [*ten percent (10%) per annum*] or the highest legal rate, whichever is lower. Payments are to be made to Note Holder in monthly installments of $[*amount*] dollars including interest, commencing on [*date*] and continuing on the [*first, last, etc.*] day of each consecutive month until paid in full. All payments shall be applied first to accrued interest and then to principal. This Promissory Note may be prepaid in whole or in part at any time without penalty. If not paid off sooner, this Promissory Note is due and payable in full on [*date*]. All payments due under this Promissory Note shall be paid to [*note holder*] at [*location*] or at such reasonable place as the holder may designate in writing from time to time. Should default be made in the payment of any amount when due, then Note Holder, without notice to Debtor, may then accelerate the payment or performance of any or all Debtor's obligations under this Agreement; and in the event of such acceleration by Note Holder, the entire amount of principal, accrued interest, and late charges due hereunder shall, at the election of Note Holder, become immediately due and payable to Note Holder by Debtor. Debtor waives presentment, demand, protest, and the right to assert any statute of limitations. Debtor agrees to pay the actual expenditures made in any attempt to collect the amount due pursuant under this Promissory Note. Debtor further agrees that this Note is not assumable without the written consent of Note Holder and that any such nonconsentual assignment shall be null and void.

Signed at [*location*] on this [*date*].

______________________________ ______________________________

Borrower Witness

PROMISSORY NOTE WITH SECURITY AGREEMENT

This Promissory Note and Security Agreement ("Agreement") is made this [*date*], by and between [*name*] ("Secured Party"), an individual located at [*address*], and [*debtor.1*], [*a (state) corporation*], located at [*address*], and [*debtor.2*], an individual located at [*address*]. [*Debtor.1 and debtor.2*] are hereafter collectively referred to as "Debtor."

Recitals

WHEREAS, on or about [*date*], Secured Party and Debtor entered into a Sale of Assets Agreement for the sale of substantially all of the assets of the business known as [*name of business*] located at [*address*] (the "Sales Agreement"); and

WHEREAS, pursuant to the Sales Agreement, Debtor agreed to execute this Promissory Note and Security Agreement;

NOW THEREFORE IN CONSIDERATION of the foregoing and following promises, covenants, conditions, and premises, and for other good and valuable consideration, the adequacy, sufficiency, and receipt of which is hereby acknowledged, the parties hereby agree as follows:

Agreement

1. Recitals Part of Agreement. The recitals are a material part of this Agreement.

2. Principal Repayment. Debtor hereby promises to pay, in lawful money of the United States, to the order of Secured Party, the principal sum of $[*amount*] together with interest at the rate stated in this agreement, in [*number*] equal monthly installments beginning on [*date*] and continuing on the [*first day*] of each consecutive month until [*ending date*].

3. Interest. Debtor agrees to pay to Secured Party, interest on the amount so advanced, at an interest rate of [*ten percent (10%) per annum*] or the highest legal rate, whichever is lower, all due and payable each month on the first day of each month beginning [*same date*] and continuing until all principal and interest amounts are repaid in full.

4. Total Monthly Payments. Provided that the highest rate of interest allowed by law is greater than or equal to [*ten percent (10%) per annum*], then the total monthly payment required to be made to Secured Party by Debtor hereunder will be $[*amount*] for each of the [*number*] of installments due hereunder.

5. Application of Payments. Payments shall be first credited to accrued but unpaid interest, then late charges, with the remainder thereof being credited to principal. Failure of Debtor to make any payment within five (5) days of the date that it is due shall subject Debtor to an administrative late charge equal to [*ten percent (10%)*] of the payment then due. Interest shall continue to accrue on any and all past due principal, interest, and late charges at the rate provided this Agreement.

6. Acceleration. Should the security interests be impaired or threatened, or should default be made in the payment of any amount when due, then Secured Party, without notice to Debtor, may then accelerate the payment or performance of any or all Debtor's obligations under this Agreement; and in the event of such acceleration by Secured Party, the entire amount of principal, accrued interest, and late charges due hereunder shall, at the election of the Secured Party, become immediately due and payable to Secured Party by Debtor.

7. Collection Costs. Debtor agrees to pay the actual expenditures made in any attempt to collect the amount due pursuant to the Promissory Note hereunder.

8. Secured Transaction. On the terms and conditions stated in this Promissory Note, Debtor hereby grants to Secured Party a security interest in and to all of the property listed on Exhibit A, attached hereto and incorporated by reference herein (the "Collateral") and the proceeds or products of such Collateral. Debtor further consents to the acceptance of substituted security for this Promissory Note.

9. Waiver or Presentment, Notice of Dishonor and Protest. Debtor waives presentment, demand, and protest, and the right to assert any statute of limitations.

10. Debtor's Obligations Secured by this Agreement. The obligations of Debtor secured by this Agreement are as follows: a) to pay the obligations to Secured Party when they are due; b) to pay all expenses, including attorney's fees and court costs, incurred by Secured Party in the perfection, preservation, realization, enforcement, and exercise of its rights under this agreement; c) to indemnify Secured Party against loss of any kind, including reasonable attorney's fees and costs, caused to Secured Party by reason of its interest in the collateral; d) to conduct Debtor's business efficiently and without voluntary interruption; e) to preserve all rights and privileges held by debtor's business; f) to keep Debtor's business property in good repair; g) to pay all taxes when due; h) to give Secured Party notice of any litigation that may have a material adverse effect on the business; i) not to change the name or place of business, or to use a fictitious business name, without first notifying Secured Party in writing; j) not to sell, lease, transfer, or otherwise dispose of the Collateral except as authorized by Secured Party in writing; k) not to permit liens on the Collateral, except existing liens and current tax liens; l) to maintain fire and extended coverage insurance on the Collateral in the amounts and under policies acceptable to Secured Party, naming Secured Party under a lender's loss payable clause, and to provide Secured Party with the policies and certificates at Secured Party's request; m) not to use the Collateral for any unlawful purpose or in any way that would void any effective insurance; n) to permit Secured Party, its representatives, and its agents to inspect the Collateral at any time, and to make copies of records pertaining to it, at reasonable times at Secured Party's request; o) to perform all acts necessary to maintain, preserve, and protect the Collateral; p) not to move the Collateral from the following location without first obtaining Secured Party's agreement in writing: location of Collateral: [*state location*]; q) to notify Secured Party promptly in writing of any default, potential default, or any development that might have a material adverse effect on the Collateral; r) to execute and deliver to Secured Party all financing statements and other documents that Secured Party requests, in order to maintain a first perfected security interest in the Collateral; s) to furnish Secured Party the reports relating to the Collateral at Secured Party's request; t) *[if collateral includes receivables]* not to make or agree to make any reduction in the original amount owing on a receivable, or to accept less than the original amount in satisfaction of a receivable, except before default or potential default, when Debtor may do so in the ordinary course of business and in accordance with its present policies; u) to deliver to Secured Party: (i) duplicate invoices for each account, bearing the language of assignment as Secured Party specifies; (ii) the originals of all instruments and documents constituting Collateral, endorsed and assigned as Secured Party requests; and (iii) proceeds (except cash proceeds collected in the ordinary course of business, unless Debtor is in default); and v) Debtor promises to pay all expenses incurred by Secured Party in connection with the collection of the proceeds, including expenses of and incidental to accounting, correspondence, collection effort, reporting to account or contract debtors, filing, recording, and recordkeeping.

11. Appointment of Attorney in Fact. Debtor hereby appoints Secured Party, or any other person whom Secured Party may designate, as Debtor's attorney in fact.

12. Debtor Covenants, Warrants, and Represents as Follows: a) Debtor is a [*corporation/partnership*] duly organized, validly existing, and in good standing under the laws of the jurisdiction of its organization, and has all necessary authority to conduct its business wherever it is conducted; b) Debtor has been authorized to execute and deliver this Promissory Note and Security Agreement. The Promissory Note and Security Agreement is a valid and binding obligation of Debtor. The agreement creates a perfected, first priority security interest enforceable against the collateral in which Debtor now has rights; and will create a perfected, first priority security interest enforceable against the Collateral in which Debtor later acquires rights, when Debtor acquires those rights; c) neither the execution and delivery of this Promissory Note and Security Agreement, nor the taking of any action in compliance with it, will (i) violate or breach any law, regulation, rule, order, or judicial action binding on Debtor, any agreement to which Debtor is a party, Debtor's articles of incorporation or bylaws; or (ii) result in the creation of a lien against the collateral except that created by this Promissory Note and Security Agreement; d) no default or potential default exists; e) Debtor owns and has possession of the collateral, subject only to those liens and adverse claims identified in the Exhibit A; and f) if any of the collateral consists of fixtures, the Collateral subject to this Promissory Note and Security Agreement includes those fixtures. Debtor has provided Secured Party all information needed to make the fixture filings required to give Secured Party's security interest in that fixture Collateral priority over all third parties with an interest in the real property to which the fixtures are attached.

13. Debtor Will Be in Default under This Agreement If: a) Debtor fails to pay any installment when due, or its entire indebtedness to Secured Party when due, at stated maturity, on accelerated maturity, or otherwise; b) Debtor fails to make any remittances required by this agreement; c) Debtor commits any breach of this agreement, or any present or future rider or supplement to this agreement, or any other agreement between Debtor and Secured Party evidencing the obligation or securing it; d) any warranty, representation, or statement, made by or on behalf of Debtor in or with respect to the agreement, is false; e) the Collateral is lost, stolen, or damaged; f) there is a seizure or attachment of, or a levy on, the Collateral; and g) Debtor ceases operations, is dissolved, terminates its existence, does or fails to do anything that allows obligations to become due before their stated maturity, or becomes insolvent or unable to meet its debts as they mature.

14. When an Event of Default Occurs: a) Secured Party may: (i) declare the obligations immediately due and payable without demand, presentment, protest, or notice to Debtor, all of which Debtor expressly waives; (ii) terminate any obligation to make future advances; (iii) exercise all rights and remedies available to a Secured Party after default; (iv) perform any of Debtor's obligations under this agreement for Debtor's account. Any money expended or obligations incurred in doing so, including reasonable attorney's fees and interest at the highest rate permitted by law, will be charged to Debtor and added to the obligation secured by this agreement; b) Secured Party's notice of the time and place of public sale of the Collateral, or the time on or after which a private sale or other disposition of the Collateral will be made, is reasonable if sent to Debtor in the manner for giving notice at least five days before the public or private sale; c) Debtor must: (i) assemble the Collateral and make it and all records relating to it available to Secured Party as Secured Party directs; (ii) allow Secured Party, its representatives, and its agents to enter the premises where all or any part of the Collateral, the records, or both may be, and remove any or all of it.

15. Termination. This Promissory Note and Security Agreement will continue in effect even though from time to time there may be no outstanding obligations or commitments under this agreement. The agreement will terminate when: a) Debtor completes performance of all obligations to Secured Party, including, without limitation, the repayment of all indebtedness by Debtor to Secured Party; b) Secured Party has no commitment that could give rise to an obligation to Secured Party involving the Collateral described herein; and c) Debtor has notified Secured Party in writing of the termination.

16. Miscellaneous. Debtor will pay all costs and expenses of collection, including reasonable attorney's fees and court costs. No waiver by Secured Party of any breach or default will be a waiver of any breach or default occurring later. A waiver will be valid only if it is in writing and signed by Secured Party. Debtor's representations and warranties made in this Promissory Note and Security Agreement will survive its execution, delivery, and termination. This Promissory Note and Security Agreement will bind and benefit the successors and assignees of the parties, but Debtor may not assign its rights under the agreement without Secured Party's prior written consent. This contract will be governed by the laws of [*state*], as amended from time to time. This Promissory Note and Security Agreement is the entire agreement, and supersedes any prior agreement or understandings, between Secured Party and Debtor relating to the Collateral.

17. Notices. Notices under this security agreement are considered to be served five (5) days after they are deposited in the United States mail, with prepaid first-class postage, addressed as follows:

DEBTOR:

____

____

____

Attention:______________________

SECURED PARTY:

____

____

____

Attention:______________________

Either party may change its address for service of notice, by notice to the other.

Dated: _________________________

____

Debtor

____

Secured Party

EXHIBIT A

1. Collateral:

____

____

2. Location of Debtor's chief executive office:

____

____

3. Location of inventory Collateral:

____

____

4. Location of records relating to receivables:

____

____

5. All the names under which Debtor has conducted his/her/its business:

____

____

6. All liens and adverse claims to which the Collateral is subject:

____

____

7. All financing statements except those naming Secured Party in which Debtor is the Debtor:

____

____

8. If any Collateral consists of fixtures, the location, legal description, and name of the owner of the real property to which it is affixed:

____

____

Debtor will notify Secured Party in writing before any change occurs in any of the above.

COPYRIGHT ASSIGNMENT

WHEREAS, [*company*] (hereinafter referred to as "Assignor"), [*an individual, partnership, corporation*] organized under the laws of the state of [*state*], with its principal place of business at [*location*], has authored and licensed certain literary and other works, the copyrights of which are more specifically described in Exhibit A; and

WHEREAS, [*company*] (hereinafter referred to as "Assignee"), [*an individual, partnership, corporation*] organized under the laws of the state of [*state*], is desirous of acquiring the entire rights, title, and interest in all such copyrighted works.

Agreement

NOW THEREFORE IN CONSIDERATION of the mutual covenants and promises of the Parties, and in exchange for good and valuable consideration, the receipt and sufficiency of which is hereby acknowledged, Assignor does hereby assign unto Assignee all rights, title, and interest in the copyrighted works.

1. Copyright. In addition to the precise copyrights being assigned as more specifically described in Exhibit A, derivatives of such copyrights are hereby assigned and Assignor conveys the right to Assignee to perfect all such rights in the copyrighted works.

2. Geographical Scope. This assignment is effective within the borders of the United States and it extends globally to all foreign countries, whether or not such copyright has been used, sold, or is registered in such foreign countries.

3. Consideration. Consideration for the assignment is provided by the parties in Exhibit A.

4. Goodwill. Goodwill in each copyright, whether registered or not, is transferred by this assignment from Assignor to Assignee.

5. Title Henceforth in the Assignee. Upon execution of this assignment, Assignor expressly recognizes and agrees that, from this date forward, Assignee is the exclusive owner of each of the copyrights and the goodwill each represents.

6. Representation of Understanding. All parties to this assignment acknowledge and agree that the terms of this assignment are contractual and not mere recital, and all parties represent and warrant that they have carefully read this assignment, have fully reviewed its provisions with their attorneys, know and understand its contents, and sign the same as their own free acts and deeds. It is understood and agreed by all parties to this assignment that execution of this assignment may affect rights and liabilities of substantial extent and degree and with the full understanding of that fact, they represent that the covenants and releases provided for in this assignment are in their respective best interests.

[*Add boilerplate clauses as needed*]

State of [*state*]

County of [*county*]

On [*date*] before me, [*notary*], notary, personally appeared [*name*], personally known to me (or proved to me on the basis of satisfactory evidence) to be the person(s) whose name(s) is/are subscribed to the within instrument and acknowledged to me that he/she/they executed the same in his/her/their authorized capacity(ies), and that by his/her/their signature(s) on the instrument the person(s), or the entity upon behalf of which the person(s) acted, executed the instrument.

Witness my hand and official seal.

(Seal) Signature ________________

Notary

EXHIBIT A

[*State name of author, title of work, copyright registration number, date of filing, and consideration paid for copyright assignment*]

TRADEMARK ASSIGNMENT

WHEREAS, [*name*], an individual whose business is located at [*address*] (hereinafter referred to as the "Assignor"), has adopted, used, and is using the mark [*mark*] which was registered with the U.S. Patent and Trademark Office on [*date*] with [*registration number*]; and

WHEREAS, [*company*], a corporation organized under the laws of the State of [*state*], with its principal place of business at [*address*] (hereinafter referred to as the "Assignee"), is desirous of acquiring said mark and registration thereof;

NOW THEREFORE IN CONSIDERATION of the mutual covenants and promises of the Parties, and in exchange for good and valuable consideration, the receipt and sufficiency of which is hereby acknowledged, Assignor does hereby assign unto said Assignee, all right, title, interest in and to said mark, together with the goodwill of the business in which the mark is used (or that part of the goodwill of the business connected with the use of and symbolized by the mark) and the registration thereof.

Agreement

1. Trademark. The precise trademarks being assigned are more specifically described in Exhibit A and Assignor conveys the rights to Assignee to perfect all such rights in the trademarks.

2. Geographical Scope. This assignment is effective worldwide.

3. Consideration. Consideration for the assignment is provided by the parties in Exhibit A.

4. Goodwill. Goodwill in each trademark, whether registered or not, is transferred by this assignment from Assignor to Assignee.

5. Ownership Henceforth in the Assignee. Upon execution of this assignment, Assignor expressly recognizes and agrees that from this date forward that

Assignee is the exclusive owner of each of the trademarks and the goodwill each represents.

6. Representation of Understanding. All parties to this assignment acknowledge and agree that the terms of this assignment are contractual and not mere recital, and all parties represent and warrant that they have carefully read this assignment, have fully reviewed its provisions with their attorneys, know and understand its contents, and sign the same as their own free acts and deeds. It is understood and agreed by all parties and signatories to this assignment that execution of this assignment may affect rights and liabilities of substantial extent and degree and with the full understanding of that fact, they represent that the covenants and releases provided for in this assignment are in their respective best interests.

[*Add boilerplate clauses as needed*]

State of [*state*]

County of [*county*]

On [*date*] before me, [*notary*], notary, personally appeared [*name*], personally known to me (or proved to me on the basis of satisfactory evidence) to be the person(s) whose name(s) is/are subscribed to the within instrument and acknowledged to me that he/she/they executed the same in his/her/their authorized capacity(ies), and that by his/her/their signature(s) on the instrument the person(s), or the entity upon behalf of which the person(s) acted, executed the instrument.

Witness my hand and official seal.

(Seal) Signature ____________________

Notary

EXHIBIT A

[*Show specimens of registered trademark, trademark title, registration number, date of registration, and consideration paid for trademark assignment*]

PATENT ASSIGNMENT

WHEREAS, [*name*] (hereinafter referred to as the "Inventor") has invented a certain new and useful invention described in and identified by United States Patent Number [#], dated [*date*] (hereinafter referred to as "Patent"); and

WHEREAS, [*company*], a [*corporation, partnership*] organized under the laws of the State of [*state*] with its principal place of business at [*address*], (hereinafter referred to as the "Assignee") is desirous of acquiring the entire right, title, and interest in the Patent;

NOW THEREFORE IN CONSIDERATION of the mutual covenants and promises of the Parties, and in exchange for good and valuable consideration, the receipt and sufficiency of which is hereby acknowledged, Assignor does hereby assign unto said Assignee all right, title, interest in and to said patent.

Agreement

1. Patent. The precise patent and patent claims being assigned are more specifically described in Exhibit A and Assignor conveys the rights to Assignee to perfect all rights in the patents.

2. Geographical Scope. This assignment is effective worldwide.

3. Consideration. Consideration for the assignment is provided by the parties in Exhibit A.

4. Ownership Henceforth in the Assignee. Upon execution of this assignment, Assignor expressly recognizes and agrees that from this date forward that Assignee is the exclusive owner of the Patent and the patent claims and the goodwill each represents.

5. Representation of Understanding. All parties to this assignment acknowledge and agree that the terms of this assignment are contractual and not mere recital, and all parties represent and warrant that they have carefully read this assignment, have fully reviewed its provisions with their attorneys, know and understand its contents, and sign the same as their own free acts and deeds. It is understood and agreed by all parties to this assignment that execution of this assignment may affect rights and liabilities of substantial extent and degree and with the full understanding of that fact, they represent that the covenants and releases provided for in this assignment are in their respective best interests.

6. Inventor's Representation and Warranty. Inventor warrants and represents that Inventor has not entered into any Assignment, contract, or understanding in conflict with this Agreement.

[*Add boilerplate clauses as needed*]

State of [*state*]

County of [*county*]

On [*date*] before me, [*notary*], notary, personally appeared [*name*], personally known to me (or proved to me on the basis of satisfactory evidence) to be the person(s) whose name(s) is/are subscribed to the within instrument and acknowledged to me that he/she/they executed the same in his/her/their authorized capacity(ies), and that by his/her/their signature(s) on the instrument the person(s), or the entity upon behalf of which the person(s) acted, executed the instrument.

Witness my hand and official seal.

(Seal) Signature ______________________

Notary

EXHIBIT A

[*Attach patent registration,patent claims and description, patent number, date of issuance, sand consideration paid for patent assignment*]

Section II

Business Letters

Copyrights and Trademarks

Letter 1. Permission to Use Copyrighted Materials. Use this letter to request permission from the copyright owner to use his or her copyrighted works.

Letter 2. Cease and Desist Letter for Infringement of Copyrighted Materials. Use this letter to demand that an infringer cease using your copyrighted works.

Letter 3. Cease and Desist Letter for Infringement of Trademark or Confusing Mark. Use this letter to demand that an infringer cease using a mark that is the exact same or so similar to yours that it is likely to confuse the public as being yours.

Credit and Collection

Letter 4. Nice Collection Letter. Use this letter as a friendly reminder to the debtor that his or her account is overdue. It is possible that the debtor has innocently overlooked the account, so be polite in requesting the amount due.

Letter 5. In-Between Collection Letter. Use this letter to make a second request to the debtor that his or her account is overdue. If you do not receive a response from the debtor after allowing 10 days to pass from the date of mailing this letter, contact the debtor by telephone and attempt to negotiate a payment plan. Be polite but firm. Get commitments of amounts that the debtor will pay and the dates of when payments will be made. Follow up to make sure the debtor abides by the new promises.

Letter 6. Tough Collection Letter. Use this letter as a final demand before taking stronger collection action. Tell the debtor that you will be forced to hand over the matter to a collection agency or attorney if payment is not received by a certain date. Also, inform the debtor that he or she could be liable for collection and court costs if such collection procedures become necessary. If you do not hear from the debtor after a reasonable time, not to exceed 30 days from the date of mailing the letter, pursue your collection and/or court options.

Letter 7. Request Change in Payment Terms. Use this letter to inform a creditor that you are experiencing financial challenges when you cannot make payments as you have agreed to do. The creditor will appreciate the notice and will probably be amenable to working out a reasonable payment plan with you.

Letter 8. Accept Payment Adjustments. Use this letter if you have received notice from a debtor asking to change the repayment terms on a debt owed to you. If you agree with the proposed terms, state your confirmation with the understanding that the debtor must adhere to the newly proposed terms, regardless of whether he or she faces another change in financial picture in the future. If you cannot accept the proposed terms, let the debtor know and, if possible, suggest alternative terms that are acceptable.

Letter 9. To Check Writer Regarding Returned Check. Use this letter to inform a check writer that his or her check was returned for insufficient funds. If you have a policy of replacing the check with a certified check, ask the check writer to comply with your policy and do not forget to request an amount owed to cover payment of your bank's insufficient funds charge.

Letter 10. Inquiry to Credit Bureau for Bad Credit Report. Use this letter when denied credit or a loan because you were the subject of a bad credit report from a credit bureau.

Letter 11. Prevent Reporting of Bad Credit/Dispute Collection Matter. Use this letter when you disagree that you owe a debt and need to place the alleged creditor on notice that you dispute the claim. Include a demand that the creditor not contact any credit reporting agency to affect your credit until you get the opportunity to resolve the matter. Provide your best assessment of the facts and request additional information, if needed.

Letter 12. Settlement of Disputed Account. Use this letter when you dispute the validity or amount of a claim, but want to offer a settlement to put the matter behind you. Make sure not to use language that admits any liability.

Contracts and Sales

Letter 13. Cease and Desist Unlawful Business Practices. Use this letter if a competitor is using unlawful practices against your business by interfering with your customers, your contracts, or your potential customers and contracts and/or is disparaging your business's goodwill and reputation.

Letter 14. Confirm Oral Agreement. Use this letter to follow up on and confirm a prior oral agreement. Transcribing your oral agreements into writing will enhance your chances that the deal will go the way that you intend. Without such a writing, the chances of litigation later on is much more likely.

Letter 15. Modify Contract Terms. Use this letter to modify terms of a contract.

Letter 16. Assignment of Contract. Use this letter to assign your rights, title, and interests in a contract (if your rights are assignable). Make sure to include language that it is the assignee's responsibility to notify the other party to the contract.

Letter 17. Notice of Breach of Contract. Use this letter to notify a party to a contract that the party is in breach of its terms.

Letter 18. Conditional Acceptance of Non-Conforming Goods. Use this letter if you have received non-conforming goods and you want to keep the goods under a condition that the seller reduce the purchase price.

Letter 19. Rejection of Defective or Inferior Products. Use this letter if you have received non-conforming goods and want the seller to make arrangements to pick up the goods.

Letter 20. Rescind Contract Because of Misrepresentation. Use this letter if you believe you were induced into entering into a contract because of the other party's misrepresentations.

When writing business letters using the forms in Section II, you may have questions about how to fill them in or how to relate them to your business situation. How specific do you need to be? How "legal" should it sound? Use the tips on the following pages to finalize your letters.

TIPS FOR LETTER WRITING

TIP #1
Don't be too formal

Many good writers make the mistake of being too formal and impersonal all the time in their writings. They use stiff language and forget all the pleasantries that they normally would use in person. They demand too much and use even more "legalese" than I tried to avoid when I was in law school. Do not make the mistake of drafting formal, demanding letters in all situations. Leave the legalese to collect dust on old legal book shelves. Try being friendly when the situation is warranted. As the saying goes, you catch more flies with honey than vinegar.

TIP #2
Be positive and don't say too much

Put the reader in the right frame of mind with your letter. Write from a positive angle and see if you can help the reader achieve his or her goals while, at the same time, achieving yours. Remember, many have often regretted their speech, never their silence. Say what you need to say, but don't say too much. You are creating a written document that can be used in your favor or against you. Oftentimes, the written letter says too much and puts the writer in a worse position than had he or she not written it. Do not let this happen to you.

TIP #3
Remember your intended goals

Keep your intended goals in mind when writing any letter. You want to get your desired result, not send the reader scampering in the opposite direction creating ill will and a negative attitude about you and your business. Also, do not write a letter when you do not have a goal in mind. Remember, you must know the harbor you are headed for in order to catch the wind to take you there.

TIP #4
Do unto others

Think about the intended reader's position. What is causing her actions? What situation does he face? If you have the upper hand in a situation, seek a solution that benefits both. Remember, a great man shows his greatness by the way he treats little men, and a little man may become a big man someday and be in the position to help the great man.

TIP #5
Write to communicate, not to impress

Too many people want to impress themselves with their own writing. They use gigantic words when big ones will do. They write to show the world that they learned a new five syllable word. They use technical language when addressing a laymen audience. Do not make this mistake. Write to communicate, not impress.

TIP #6
Don't write emotional letters in business situations

People with good causes lose support for their position because they present issues in an emotional way. No one likes to read a letter wrought with emotion. Do not bully the other side and attack them. Do not whine and cry "life is unfair." Stick to the facts at hand and try to solve the problem the best that you can. If you do, you will have a better chance of finding a workable solution. If your letter is too emotional, you may not have a second chance.

TIP #7
Choose your paper carefully

The language that you choose in your business letter is not the only factor that will have an impact on the reader. The quality of the paper and your spelling impacts the reader as well. If you use low-quality paper, you may have a more difficult time convincing a bank to give you credit. If you have typographical errors or write the request in unreadable handwriting, you may really damage your chances of success. This is not to say that you should spend an enormous amount of money on the most expensive embossed paper on the market. Choose paper that will make corrections that are invisible to the average eye and review your letters carefully so that they are not filled with spelling or other errors.

TIP #8
Signing on the dotted line

Your signature is a very important and legal part of any letter that you write. You should use your title in all situations. This will help prevent personal liability in certain situations. As shown in the following example, if you are operating as a corporation, you should always place the corporate name above the signature line and sign as a corporate officer:

Anthony Animal Rescue Foundation (AARF)

By: ______________________________

Lynne Frasier, President

TIP #9
Be sure your letter is received

In each of the preceding letter writing situations, it is a good idea to send one letter by certified mail and a second one by regular first class mail. If the letter writing and telephone negotiations do not get the results you desire, be prepared to take further action—because ignoring the problem only means delaying a bigger and more serious challenge later on.

Certified Mail/Return Receipt Requested

[*date*]

Dear [*Name of Copyright Owner*]:

We have devoted years of service in public education. Today, we are developing a program to educate the public on [*describe topic*]. The program consists of a ten-minute video presentation and is being introduced to present the timely issue of [*subject*]. We are contacting you because you are the author of [*copyrighted work*] and we would like to use a [*clip, quote, paragraph, story, anecdote*] of the work in our program.

We plan to limit our use of the [*clip to (state planned usage)*]. Such use is of tremendous value to educate the public on the benefits of [*subject*]. We will not use it in any advertising or for our commercial advantage. Additionally, we will limit our presentation to [*describe areas of presentation*].

We respectfully request your support as the copyright holder to allow us the right to use the [*clip, quote, etc.*] free of charge. Please let us know if we can count on your support. Thank you for your consideration and your time.

Sincerely,

[*Proposed User of Copyrighted Works*]

Certified Mail/Return Receipt Requested

[*date*]

Dear [*Name*]:

It has come to our attention that you have placed our original, creative and copyright protected [*photograph, quote, clip*] in an advertisement in volume [*x*], number [*y*], of [*magazine or newspaper*]. This advertisement unlawfully misappropriates and misuses our original and creative photographic work and deprives us of the benefits, privileges, and profits from the exclusive use of our copyrighted work.

We have not authorized your use of this photo for your own commercial purposes and, therefore, as the copyright owners, we demand that you immediately cease and desist from using and from permitting any third party to use this photograph.

We further demand that you pay us a licensing fee of $[*amount*] for your unauthorized exploitation of our [*photograph, quote, clip*] to date. Please contact us immediately so we can resolve this matter. If we do not hear from you within ten days from the date of this letter, we will be forced to pursue further action against you.

Sincerely,

[*Copyright Owner*]

Letter 3. Cease and Desist Letter for Infringement of a Trademark

Certified Mail/Return Receipt Requested

[*date*]

Dear [*Name*]:

Recently, we learned that you began to use the mark [*describe mark*] for your [*services*]. Since [*date*], we have been using and have established the right to use our registered trademark [*mark*] for our [*services*].

Because of the similarity of both marks and because you are in the same industry as our company, the use of your mark is likely to confuse the public into believing that your services are associated with our services. Since this is misleading and confusing to the public, and has consequently deprived us of the benefit of goodwill attached to our registered trademark, we demand that you immediately cease and desist from using and from permitting any third party to use [*your mark as it exists at the present time*].

Please call this office at once to clear up this matter. If we see further evidence of your infringing use, we we will have no other choice other than to proceed in an action against you—which is an action that I am sure none of us wants.

Sincerely,

[*Trademark Owner*]

Certified Mail/Return Receipt Requested

[*date*]

Dear [*Name*]:

As you know, we [*state the services that you rendered or the products that you sold*] on [*date of services/sale of product*].

Your payment of $[*amount*] has not arrived within the [*amount of time passed*]. We are sure that this is an oversight and ask that you please send it today. If we are forced to spend time collecting overdue accounts receivable, we will not be able to offer our valued clients, such as yourselves, our current [*prices/rates*].

If you have already sent your payment to us, please accept our thanks.

Sincerely,

[*Company*]

Certified Mail/Return Receipt Requested

[*date*]

Dear [*Name*]:

As you know, we promised to provide [*services or products*] in exchange for your payment of $[*amount*]. We undertook our duties and performed our side of the bargain on [*date*]. However, today, your balance due continues to be $[*amount*] and we must ask that you please send payment immediately.

We are trying to avoid bringing legal action against you for your failure to pay. After all, your goodwill is important to us and we do not want to take any action which might jeopardize your reputation and cause you embarrassment or added expense. Yet, we think that you will agree that our position is a fair one: (1) we were happy to provide you with credit based on your promise to pay according to the terms of our agreement; (2) we have contacted you numerous times but you have not held up to your end of the bargain; and (3) now, we must soon consider the possibility of taking legal action against you to secure payment of the monies due.

We are hopeful that you will act promptly and forward $[*amount*] in full payment on your account or that you will call to set up a reasonable payment plan. As you can imagine, we do not want to be forced into a costly decision where neither of us wins. Please call us within ten days to discuss this urgent matter.

Sincerely,

[*Company*]

Letter 6. Tough Collection Letter

Certified Mail/Return Receipt Requested

[*date*]

Dear [*Name*]:

As you know, we have provided [*describe services or products sold*] over [*x*] months ago with the understanding that you would pay $[*amount*]. As the attached statement reflects, you have not abided by the terms of our agreement, and despite our numerous attempts to request payment on this account, $[*amount*] remains unpaid.

THIS IS YOUR FINAL NOTICE

If you would like to avoid legal action, please contact us immediately and pay the required payment in full. This is our last attempt to contact you before we must turn your account over to collection without further notice. If this matter goes that far, you will also be liable for all legal and court-related expenses incurred as a result of this account. Such an action may also have and adverse effect on your credit rating.

We regret that if we do not hear from you within ten days from the date of this letter, we shall be forced to pursue our legal options to enforce your legally binding agreement with us.

Sincerely,

[*Company*]

Certified Mail/Return Receipt Requested

[*date*]

Dear [*Creditor*]:

We have been experiencing financial difficulties the past few months and ask that you work with us so we can pay our outstanding payment due of $[*amount*]. As you know, our agreement with you is to pay as follows: [*state originally agreed-upon payment terms*].

While we are financially unable to pay that amount at the present time, we ask that you consider the following substituted payment schedule: [*state proposed payment terms*]. I have enclosed the first proposed payment of $[*amount*]. If you accept this payment with our additional promise to pay all future payments as per the proposed substituted term, we will be able to improve our financial situation and remain your good customer.

We have enjoyed working with you and are sorry for any inconvenience that our financial difficulties may have caused you. We hope that you will allow us to work it out. Please call to discuss this matter further.

Sincerely,

[*Debtor/Customer*]

Certified Mail/Return Receipt Requested

[*date*]

Dear [*Customer/Debtor*]:

We have received your letter, dated [*enter date*], regarding your proposed changes for repaying your current balance due of $[*amount*].

[*If substituted terms are okay*]
We will agree with your proposed terms, which are as follows: [*state terms*]. However, please understand that we will only agree to such new terms under the condition that you agree to adhere to these new terms regardless of another change in your financial picture. Please call to discuss this matter.

[*If substituted terms are not okay*]
It is unfortunate, but we cannot agree to your proposed payment terms as stated in your letter. However, we understand that you are experiencing financial difficulties and would like to assist you by offering the following terms for repayment of your balance due [*state terms*]. If you agree to our proposed repayment plan, you must also agree to adhere to these new terms regardless of another change in your financial picture. Please call to discuss this matter.

[*If applicable*]
We are happy to assist you through this unfortunate time.

Sincerely,

[*Creditor*]

Certified Mail/Return Receipt Requested

[*date*]

Dear [*Customer/Debtor*]:

I am sorry to report that your check number [#] in the amount of $[*amount*] has been returned to us for insufficient funds.

We are sure that this is a result of a simple error. However, we must insist that you replace the insufficient funds check immediately. Therefore, please bring or send to our office [*a certified check, money order, replacement check*] in the amount of $[*amount*] plus $20.00 to cover the insufficient funds charge assessed to our account by our bank due to this matter.

If you are experiencing financial difficulties, please contact us at once. It is important that we speak to you immediately to maintain your good credit. If payment is not made within 24 hours, we will be forced to pursue this matter further.

Thank you for your cooperation.

Sincerely,

[*Creditor*]

Certified Mail/Return Receipt Requested

[*date*]

Dear [*Credit Bureau*]:

We have recently been turned down for credit because of a report issued by your bureau. As we understand it, the reason for your denial is as follows: [*state reason for the bureau's denial of your credit application*].

We dispute [*the bureau's reasons*] and offer our explanation as follows: [*state why the credit report was incorrect, e.g., you have not missed any payments as per the report suggests or you have resolved a dispute over charges that were paid*].

Please contact us immediately so we can to resolve this matter. Our credit rating is important to us and vital to our existence. Thank you.

Sincerely,

[*Receiver of Bad Credit Report*]

Certified Mail/Return Receipt Requested

[*date*]

Dear [*Name*]:

This letter responds to your collection letter, dated [*date*], regarding the above account. It serves as notice that we are disputing this account as to its validity and amount with respect to our liability.

Under the authority of the Fair Credit Reporting Act and applicable consumer protection statutes, we demand that you do not you cause any negative credit reporting information to be released with respect to our company or any of our principals until this dispute is resolved.

So that we may attempt to resolve this matter efficiently and effectively, please provide us with any information or documentation supporting your claim which reflects any liability on our part for any debts due [*company*].

We look forward to resolving this matter as quickly as possible and await your timely response.

Thank you for your cooperation.

Sincerely,

[*Company*]

Certified Mail/Return Receipt Requested

[*date*]

Dear [*Name*]:

As we have discussed, this letter will reduce to writing our prior oral agreement to settle our account with you. To reiterate our discussion, we disagree over the amount due your company; however, to promote goodwill between us and without admitting any liability, we are prepared to pay $[*amount*] as per the following agreed upon terms in full settlement and release of all claims regarding our current account with you: [*state amount and terms that you are willing to pay.*]

Please sign below to show your acceptance of the above described payment terms to settle and release all claims regarding our current account due. We are happy to put this matter behind us so we can move forward with a mutually beneficial relationship with you and your company.

Sincerely,

[*Company*]

AGREED AND ACCEPTED

I, [*name*], authorized representative of [*company*], agree to the accept $[*amount*] as per the terms stated in this letter in full settlement and release of all claims regarding your current account with [*company*].

____

Authorized Signatory

Certified Mail/Return Receipt Requested

[*date*]

Dear [*Business Owner*]:

It has come to our attention that in order to persuade prospective purchasers into purchasing [*goods*] from you, and to attempt to persuade them not to purchase, or to disparage or interfere with the purchases already made by third parties from our company, you have knowingly and maliciously made false statements to your prospective purchasers, to our actual and prospective purchasers and to the public in general about the [*goods*] that our company is authorized to sell.

You have specifically referred to our [*goods*] as "seconds" and "without warranty" from the manufacturer. Such conduct is unlawful and a serious and continuing threat to our company's business reputation and goodwill. Furthermore, your unlawful actions interfere with our contractual relations with our customers. They are without any justification and excuse, malicious, willful, wanton, reckless, and done for the purpose of promoting your business over ours and unlawfully taking away business from our company. Because of such wrongful, malicious, and tortious conduct, our company is damaged from interference with actual sales, loss in prospective business, loss in reputation and goodwill, and unfair trade practices involving trade disparagement and unfair competition.

This notice is to demand that you immediately cease and desist from all of your unlawful activities involving our company. Should we hear from any of our customers or potential customers that you have not ceased all unlawful activity as described above, we will be forced to take this matter further, in an action that we are sure no one wants to pursue. It may include a court action, and should we prevail in such an action, you could also be liable for our attorney's fees and costs.

Sincerely,

[*Company*]

Certified Mail/Return Receipt Requested

[*date*]

Dear [*Party to Oral Agreement*]:

This letter serves as confirmation of our oral agreement to enter into a contract for the purchase of [*goods, services*] at a price of $[*amount*] on the following terms: [*state terms*]. If you agree with the terms as I have stated herein, please sign one copy of this letter and return it to me in the self-addressed stamped envelope. The other copy is for your files.

If you have questions, please contact me at your earliest convenience. We look forward to working with you on this matter.

Sincerely,

[*Other Party to Oral Contract*]

AGREED AND ACCEPTED

I, [*name*], authorized representative of [*company*], agree that this letter correctly states our prior oral agreement and by this writing I confirm to be bound by such oral agreement.

____

Authorized Signatory

Certified Mail/Return Receipt Requested

[*date*]

Dear [*Party to Contract*]:

As we discussed, this letter will serve as our agreement to amend our existing contract, dated [*date*] which is attached hereto and incorporated by reference herein. As discussed, we shall amend the original terms of the contract as follows: [*state changes to contract terms*] and all other terms of our original contract shall remain the same and in full force.

If you agree with the terms as stated herein, please sign one copy of this letter amendment and return it to me in the self-addressed stamped envelope. The other copy is for your files.

If you have questions, please contact me at your earliest convenience.

Sincerely,

[*Other Party to Contract*]

AGREED AND ACCEPTED

I, [*name*], authorized representative of [*company*], agree to the above specified written amendments of the contract, dated [*date*]. I further agree that all other terms of our original contract shall remain the same and in full force.

____

Authorized Signatory

Letter 16. Assignment of Contract

Certified Mail/Return Receipt Requested

[*date*]

Dear [*Assignee*]:

With this letter, we hereby assign all of our rights, title, and interests in the contract entered into between [*ourselves, our company*] and [*name of third party*], which is attached hereto and incorporated by reference herein.

Please note that we are making this assignment without any warranties, representations, or collateral assurances with regard to the assigned [*goods, subject matter*]. As we have discussed, you have the duty to notify [*third party*] of this assignment so that [*third party*] can perform its duties under the contract directly to you.

Please sign below to acknowledge your acceptance of this assignment.

Sincerely,

[*Assignor*]

AGREED AND ACCEPTED

I, [*name*], authorized representative of [*company*], agree to the assignment as presented in the above terms. I further agree that the assignment is made without any representations, warranties, or collateral assurances regarding the subject matter of the assignment.

____

Assignee

Certified Mail/Return Receipt Requested

[*date*]

Dear [*Party to Contract*]:

As you know, we entered into a contract, dated [*date*] which is attached hereto and incorporated by reference herein. Under the terms of our agreement, we agreed to [*perform services, deliver products, etc.*] and you agreed to [*pay amount, perform services*]. We undertook our duties and performed our side of the bargain on [*date*] and this gave rise to your duty to perform. However, although we have repeatedly asked for your performance, nothing has been done to provide it.

Thus, this letter serves as our notice to you of your failure to perform your duties under our agreement. We urge you to perform as required. Contact this office immediately by return mail to assure us that you are taking the necessary steps to perform your obligations under our agreement. Otherwise, we will be forced to take legal action against you.

Sincerely,

[*Non-Breaching Party*]

Letter 18. Conditional Acceptance of Non-Conforming Goods

Certified Mail/Return Receipt Requested

[*date*]

Dear [*Party to Contract*]:

We received delivery from you regarding our purchase order number [*number*] dated [*date*]. While inspecting the goods, we noticed that our order called for [*x*], but instead you delivered [*y*], and for this reason, the delivered goods are non-conforming. As non-conforming goods, we are not obligated to accept them; however, we will do so under the following conditions: [*state conditions, e.g., you reduce the purchase price by $ __________ and credit our balance due so that our amended purchase price will be $ _________*].

If our terms are agreeable to you, we will accept your non-conforming goods. If you do not accept our terms, we hereby reject your non-conforming goods as defective as the term is used in our industry and you will need to contact us to make arrangements to return them to you.

Please contact us within ten days from the date of this letter. If we do not hear from you within that time, we will assume that you do not accept our offer and, thus, we will reject the goods and return them to you. Thank you for your needed attention to this matter.

Sincerely,

[*Receiver of Non-Conforming Goods*]

Certified Mail/Return Receipt Requested

[*date*]

Dear [*Party to Contract*]:

We have received delivery from you regarding our purchase order number [*number*] dated [*date*]. While inspecting the goods, we noticed that our order called for [*x*], but instead you delivered [*y*], and for this reason, the delivered goods are non-conforming.

As non-conforming goods, we are not obligated to accept them. We hereby reject the goods as defective as the term is used in our industry and ask that you make arrangements to have them returned to you. Since we have paid for delivery of conforming goods as per the above purchase order, we request an immediate full refund [*or, we refuse to make payment for this product/service*].

Thank you for your prompt attention to this matter. We will hold the goods for a reasonable time; however, we cannot accept responsibility for their safe storage.

Sincerely,

[*Receiver of Non-Acceptable, Non-Conforming Goods*]

Certified Mail/Return Receipt Requested

[*date*]

Dear [*Name*]:

The purpose of this letter is to inform you of why our agreement entered into with you on [*date*] is [*unenforceable, not valid, etc.*].

The reasons are as follows: [*state reasons, e.g., misrepresentation to induce the contract, fraud, mutual mistake by the parties*]. Since the contract is [*unenforceable, not valid, etc.*], we hereby rescind the agreement [*and request an immediate return of the amount paid by us as a deposit*].

We strongly suggest your prompt attention to this matter. If we do not hear from you within ten days of the date of this letter, we shall be forced to pursue further action to protect our position.

Sincerely,

[*Company*]

Section III

Government Forms

Intellectual Property Forms

Intellectual property is a body of law generally comprising copyrights, trademarks, and patents. Copyrights protect the originality of authorship, such as writings from an author; trademarks indicate the source of goods and services, like the golden arches indicates McDonald's Hamburgers®; trade names identify a business or occupation, like General Motors® identifies the automaker of Chevrolets and other automobiles; and patents protect novel inventions or discoveries, like the Macintosh® Powerbook or Apple® computer. Each of these "intellectual property" areas is separate and distinct.

The forms, procedures, and instructions necessary to obtain registration of copyrights, trademarks, and patents are included in this section. Generally, the instructions are easy to understand and the forms easy to fill out. The below listed information should provide further insight into these areas and the procedures for obtaining, preparing, and filing the registration forms included in this section.

Forms 1-4. U.S. Copyright Registration. To be capable of copyright registration, a work must be original and fixed in tangible form. Works that are capable of registration include literary works, musical works including any accompanying lyrics, sound recordings, dramatic works including any accompanying music, pantomimes and choreographic works, pictorial and graphic works, motion pictures, audiovisual works, and visual works including toys, sculptors, photography, and the like.

Some works of authorship cannot be protected by copyright. They include: a) ideas, systems, processes, procedures, concepts, methods; b) lists of ingredients, contents, or as a general rule, forms; c) titles of works, and names of products or services, even if they are novel or distinctive; d) names of businesses, organizations, or groups; e) catch words, slogans, short phrases, and familiar symbols for familiar designs; and f) information that is in the public domain (common property and property that contains no original authorship) such as

Form 1 Copyright Form TX	To register literary works such as books, catalogs, directories, computer programs, manuals, databases, architectural drawings, advertising copy, compilations of information, etc.
Form 2 Copyright Form PA	To register works of performing arts such as music with or without words, lyrics with or without music, dramatic works with or without music, pantomimes and choreographic works, motion pictures and other audiovisual works.
Form 3 Copyright Form SR	To register published or unpublished sound recordings.
Form 4 Copyright Form VA	To register works of visual arts such as 3-dimensional sculptures like dolls, toys, and sculptures, 2-dimensional artwork including paintings, drawings, logos, computer graphics, artwork on posters, commercial prints, as well as 2-dimensional artwork on useful items, reproductions, maps, photographs, jewelry designs, technical drawings, and architectural works.

standard charts, measuring devices, tables, or lists taken from government public sources.

Not everyone can register a work for copyright protection at the federal registry. Those eligible include only: 1) the author who creates the work; 2) if the work has been transferred, the owner of the exclusive rights in the work; or 3) the authorized agent of the copyright owner. If you fit one of the mentioned categories and want to register your copyrightable work, all you need to do is select the proper registration form from this section, prepare it according to the instructions included with the form, and forward the completed form, along with a "deposit" of the work (as described in the instructions) and the filing fee to the Register of Copyrights, at the Copyright Office, located in the Library of Congress, Washington, DC 20540.

The type of work that you want to register determines the form to use. For literary works such as books, manuals, architectural drawings, computer programs, databases, etc., use FORM TX and prepare it according to the instructions on the form. For dramatic or musical works with or without lyrics, use FORM PA, unless you desire protection for the sound recording, in which case you should use FORM SR. For works of visual art, like photographs, sculptors, toys, artwork, and work on two- and three-dimensional objects, use FORM VA.

It is not necessary to register your work for copyright protection but if you do not register: a) you will not be able to file a lawsuit for copyright infringement; b) certain remedies will not be available to you in a court of law (attorneys' fees and statutory damages); and c) registration provides prima facie evidence that the facts in the registration documents are true, which shifts the burden of proof concerning those facts from the copyright owner to the other party in the event of a lawsuit.

The length of time for registration varies, depending on the amount of material the copyright office receives and the personnel available. However, a general rule of thumb is that registration takes approximately 4 - 6 months from the date of filing the application. Since the Register of Copyrights receives over 600,000 applications annually, you will not be able to check on the status of your application for at least 4 months.

Once you obtain your certificate of registration for works created on or after January 1, 1978, your registration is valid for your life plus 50 years, if you are the sole author. When two or more authors create a joint works, the copyright registration is valid for the life of the last surviving author plus 50 years. If the copyright was prepared within the scope of employment, the registration is valid for 75 years from the date of first publication or 100 years from the date of creation, whichever comes first. For works created prior to January 1, 1978, the copyright registration is valid for basically 75 years from first publication (if renewed at 28 years after first published).

Whether or not you avail yourself of the registration process, you should use the copyright notice. For visually perceptible copies, this notice is the following three elements: 1) the symbol "©" or "copyright"; 2) the year of first publication of the work; and 3) the name of the owner of copyright in the work. The copyright notice for phonorecords of sound recordings should contain the following: 1) the symbol "the letter P in a circle"; 2) the year of first publication of the sound recording; and 3) the name of the owner of copyright.

Before March 1, 1989, notice was mandatory on all published works, and any work first published before that date had to bear the notice or the copyright owner jeopardized losing his/her/its copyright protection. Today, notice is optional. However, its use is recommended because it informs the public that the work is protected by copyright, it identifies the copyright owner, it shows the year of first publication, and in the event of infringement of the work a court will not allow a defendant to claim "innocent infringement," which reduces the amount of damages the infringer would pay to the copyright owner. You should affix the notice to copies or phonorecords of the work in such a manner and location as to give reasonable notice of your copyright claim.

If you want to use a work that is protected by copyright, you should contact the copyright owner and obtain permission to use it or inquire about obtaining a license to do so. Depending on the purpose and character of your use, (like whether you intend to use it for your commercial gain or for educational purposes) and other factors, you may even be able to use it or a portion of it without obtaining permission of the copyright owner if it fits under certain exemptions under copyright law. However, generally if you use the copyrighted work without permission or without a license to do so, all the copyright owner will need to do is to establish ownership and copies of protectible portions of the copyrighted work to establish a copyright infringement claim against you.

If you are found liable for copyright infringement, the owner's remedies can include an injunction against you, impoundment and destruction of the alleged infringing materials, and either their actual damages and any additional profits from you, or statutory damages, which are currently between $500 and $20,000 for any one work infringed, with a willfulness factor permitting increases up to $100,000 for each infringement.

Copyright protection originates from the U.S. Constitution, Patent and Copyright Clause. In effect, it states that to promote progress of the useful arts and to encourage the steady stream of creative material into the marketplace, authors should have an exclusive right to use their own original expressions for a certain length of time to the exclusion of everyone else. This right subsists from creation and cannot be abandoned due to non-use. However, registration is a prerequisite to a suit for infringement and to certain remedies. Therefore, use the forms listed in this section to avail yourself of your entire rights of protection under the copyright laws.

Form 5. U.S. Trademark Application. A trademark is anything that identifies and distinguishes the goods of a business. It can be a number of things. For example, it can be a name, like Guess®, a symbol like your company logo, a slogan, like "don't leave home without it®", or a device, like the Coca-Cola® bottle, among others. If the mark is used to identify a service, it is called a service mark. Generally, trademarks appear on products or packaging and service marks appear in advertising and on business cards, stationery, letterheads, and signs.

Not every mark is capable of being a trademark. Included in this category are marks that are merely ornamental or falsely suggest a connection with persons, institutions, or national symbols, and marks that are immoral, deceptive, scandalous or merely descriptive, geographic, or primarily a surname.

A trademark or service mark can exhibit a wide range of strength depending upon how it is classified. The strongest marks are those which are arbitrary or fanciful because they are coined words having no intrinsic meaning or words which have no rational connection to the product. Examples of such marks include Exxon® or Kodak®. The next strongest category are those which are suggestive, which while not really descriptive of the product's qualities, nevertheless suggest some benefit or property of the product. The next category of marks are descriptive of the product or service which they identify. Finally, those marks which are not protected by trademark law are generic marks. Marks which have lost trademark status because they became generic include kleenex, aspirin, and cellophane.

To be eligible for trademark registration at the Federal Trademark Office, the owner of the mark must sell his/her goods or services across state lines. Trademark registration is not required for trademark protection, but the owner should consider registration because: a) without it, the owner risks losing the exclusive right to use the mark; b) another person or entity may acquire superior rights over the owner; c) the owner does not have access to the federal courts to bring an infringement action against an alleged infringer; d) there is a presumption of ownership with registration; e) statutory damages are allowed with registration; and f) the trademark owner can protect against importation of goods bearing infringing marks.

The federal registration process is involved and lengthy. It begins with filing the application, complete with drawings and specimens if the application is for a mark that is already in use in the stream of commerce. The application included in this section is an In-Use Application. If the mark is not yet in use, the application is an Intent-to-Use Application and the rules relating to such applications are complicated and more restrictive than for In-Use Applications. If you are interested in filing an Intent-to-Use Application, contact the U.S. Department of Commerce, Patent and Trademark Office in Washington, DC 20231 to get the application and instructions.

Assuming you want to use the application included in this section, all you need to do is to follow the directions that accompany the form and forward the form to the Trademark Office with the required specimens (as described in the instructions) and filing fee. Once that office receives the application, it will be assigned to a trademark examining attorney and he or she will conduct a search and either approve or reject the mark for registration.

If the mark is rejected, the trademark attorney must give reasons for the rejection. You will have six months to respond to the rejection. The examining attorney will either approve or reject that response. Such a process may be repeated until the examiner either approves the application for publication or issues a final refusal. This process can become complicated and may take over a year to resolve. If a final refusal is ordered, the registration process is terminated, unless you appeal the final refusal.

If the mark is approved for registration, it is published in the primary register, known as the *Official Gazette*. With certain exceptions, anyone who believes that he or she would be damaged by registration of the mark has thirty days after publication to file his/her opposition to the registration. If someone opposes the mark, an opposition proceeding is held to determine whether the mark is eligible for registration. If no opposition is filed within the publication period or if an opposition is filed and dismissed, a certificate of registration is prepared.

Once you receive the certificate of registration, you may use the statutory notice ® or its equivalents ™ or SM. You may not use the ® designation while your application is pending and owners of common law trademarks (marks not registered) are never entitled to use the ® symbol.

Trademark rights stem from the Commerce Clause which grants Congress the power to regulate commerce. Use and protection can extend indefinitely if the mark is used on a continuous basis and registration is renewed within the proper renewal term, which is currently 10 years from the date of registration, subject to cancellation if you do not file an affidavit during the sixth year of registration specifying certain information.

If you want to use another's registered mark, explain that it is a registered mark of the respective owner/holder. Make it clear that you are not claiming ownership of the mark, but are rather using or referring to their mark. If you follow this procedure for every mark that you refer to, you should not get into trouble with the trademark owner. For example, If you want to refer to the "Whopper® sandwich," make a statement to the effect that "the Whopper® is a trademark of Burger King®."

If you use a mark without the owner's consent, or if you use a mark that is so similar to another's mark that your use is likely to confuse the public into believing an association exists between your mark and the owner of the other trademark or service mark, you could be liable for trademark infringement. Do not risk such an infringement action.

Form 6. State Trademark Application. For the few of you who will restrict your sales and services to intrastate activity, you should obtain state registration of your trademark or service mark. Call the Trademark Office or Secretary of State in your state for details (see the Appendix). The registration process is basically the same as for federal marks and as shown here for the state of Illinois; however, most states do not provide registration unless the mark is in use. In other words, intent-to-use applications are generally available only at the federal registry.

Form 7. U.S. Patent Application. Design patents are granted to anyone who invents a new, original, and ornamental design for an article of manufacture. The purpose of the design patent is to promote progress in the decorative arts by encouraging the creation of ornamental designs.

In contrast, utility patents are granted to those who invent technology. The purpose of the utility patent is to promote the progress of science. A utility patent can be granted on any novel and non-obvious useful product, process, method, machine, manufacture, composition, or any useful improvement thereof. Items that are not eligible for a utility patent include laws of nature, scientific principles, mathematical formulas, methods of doing business, and improvements in a device which take only mechanical skills to develop.

Only the inventor can apply for a patent. If you are the inventor, you can use the application form listed in this section to apply for a patent or you can obtain a patent application from the U.S. Patent Office located in Washington, DC 20231. If you are an individual or small business, you should include the verified statement claiming small entity status to get a discount in fees.

Prepare your application according to the instructions that accompany the form and forward the application along with the correct filing fee to the U.S. Patent Office. Do not wait too long after completing your invention or discovery to obtain a patent, as you may not be able to obtain one if the invention is in public use or for sale in the United States for more than one year prior to filing your patent application. If you are not the inventor, you cannot obtain a patent. The inventor can subsequently sell his/her interest in the patent to you, but the application must still be filed in the inventor's name.

Once you obtain a patent, you will receive, for a limited period (which is changing due to GATT), the federal right to exclude others from making, using, or selling your design or invention. Upon expiration of the patent, this federal right will no longer exist. When the monopoly ends, it ends, as does your exclusive right to make the design or invention to the exclusion of others. The length of time when a patent will expire will vary depending upon the type of patent you obtain. You should seek legal counsel experienced in patent matters if you have questions or want to ensure that you have correctly prepared your patent application.

Business Related Forms

The forms included in this section are common to businesses. Read about each form and determine if your company needs to prepare such a form.

Form 8. Fictitious Business Name Statement. A business must file a Fictitious Business Name Statement under the following conditions: a) where the business name of a proprietorship (or partnership) does not reflect the owner's (or partners') surname or if the business name implies additional owners; or b) where a corporation conducts business under a name different than the corporate name.

Filing a Fictitious Business Name Statement is done in four easy steps: a) obtain a blank Statement from the County Clerk/Recorder or Newspaper of General Circulation in your area and prepare it according to the instructions on the back of the form; b) file the Statement with the County Clerk/Recorder in the county where the principal place of business exists; c) publish your company's intent to use the name in a Newspaper of General Circulation in the same county where you filed the Statement; and d) within 30 days after publishing the notice, file an Affidavit of Publication with the County Clerk/Recorder.

Once filed, the name is generally protected in that county for five years. Before five years is up, renew your right to use the name by performing the same procedures as discussed above for the original filing. Filing this statement enables your company exclusive use of the name in counties where the statement is filed.

The Fictitious Business Name Statement in this section is an example of such a form used in San Diego, California. The form in your county will look similar. To get such a form in your area, call your county recorder or perhaps try a legal stationery store.

Form 9. IRS SS-4—Federal Employer Identification Number. Unless you are able to use your social security number for business tax purposes, you must obtain a Federal Employer Identification Number (FEIN) from the Internal Revenue Service (IRS). This number is used to identify your business for income tax, payroll, and other federal purposes, and the IRS requires that you apply for the number if you or your business fits one of the following categories: a) you do not have an FEIN and you will be or currently are: (i) paying wages; (ii) required to use an FEIN on any return, statement, or other document, even if you are not an employer; (iii) required to withhold taxes on income; b) you will become the new owner of an existing business, even if the business does not have employees; except that if you will become the new owner by acquiring its stock, then use the FEIN of the corporation; c) you are forming a partnership or corporation; or d) you are incorporating your sole proprietorship or partnership.

The form in this section is an example of an FEIN application. You can copy this form or obtain an original from any IRS office. Follow the instructions that accompany the form and file the FEIN application with the IRS location listed in the instructions for your area. Once the IRS processes the application, it will send you the nine-digit number, which incidentally, is the number needed to establish a bank account, elect Subchapter S corporate status, make a tax deposit, or file a tax return—so obtain your FEIN as soon as possible. The amazing news regarding this form is that there is no filing fee.

Form 10. IRS SS-8—Independent Contractor Factors. If you hire independent contractors, you will not have to pay social security tax, federal or state unemployment tax, or workers' compensation. Since this is very favorable for employers, the IRS scrutinizes independent contractor relationships very carefully to determine if the relationship should be reclassified as an employer-employee relationship. In its assessment, the IRS uses 20 factors to determine whether a worker is an employee or an independent contractor.

These factors can be found on IRS Form SS-8, shown in this section. You can use this form or you can obtain IRS Form SS-8 from any IRS office. If you are planning to hire independent contractors, peruse this form before doing so. Also, contact the state taxing authority and workers' compensation board in your state, because they use independent contractor factors of their own which should also be considered before you structure your business relationship with persons whom you want to be categorized as independent contractors.

Form 11. IRS Form 2553—Subchapter S Election. A corporation that elects Subchapter "S" status is a regular corporation which, in effect, is taxed like a partnership, yet has the limited liability of a corporation. The corporation must qualify as a small business before it can elect such status. The small business qualifies under the federal regulations if it meets all of the following requirements: a) it has 35 or fewer shareholders; b) it does not have any corporation, partnership, or non-resident alien as a shareholder; c) it issues only one class of stock (sometimes the IRS will treat shareholder loans as a second class of stock, so you must be very cautious when preparing loan documents); and d) it is an eligible domestic corporation.

Once it is determined that the corporation can qualify for S status, the business owners must elect this status by filing the proper documents with IRS. Form 2553 in this section is the proper form to federally elect this status. Follow the instructions provided with the form, and file it with the IRS at the address listed on the form for your particular state. There is no fee for electing this status. You may also want to contact your state taxing authority to see if the corporation is required to make a state election. If so, that department will be able to send you the proper forms and instructions for filing.

Forms 12 & 13. UCC-1 and UCC-3 Statements. If you are going to purchase a business, you must understand what "perfecting a security interest" means. You must also know how the following terms relate to each other: "debtor," "security interest," "secured party," and "collateral." A "debtor" is a person who has incurred a debt. If the debtor grants to the person to whom the debt is owed, interest in certain property to secure the debt, the interest is called a "security interest." The person to whom the secured debt is owed is known as a "secured party." The property in which the security interest is held is called "collateral."

Perfecting a security interest means that the secured party can keep the collateral if the debtor fails to make payments. Generally, one perfects a security interest either by filing a financing statement, which is the most popular method of perfection, or by taking possession of the collateral. To perfect a security interest by filing a financing statement, the secured party obtains a "UCC-1—Standard Financing Statement" from any legal stationery store. The secured party fills out the UCC-1 as per the instructions on the form, listing the equipment or assets which will be the subject of protection. The debtor signs the UCC-1 and the secured party files it with the appropriate government agency. Once the UCC-1 is filed, the secured party's interest is perfected.

If you are about to purchase a business with equipment and assets, or if you are going to purchase all or substantially all of the assets of a business, you need to search the records of the Secretary of State and/or County Recorder to determine if the equipment or assets are free and clear. To make such a search, you will need to obtain a UCC-3 Form—Request for Information or Copies from any legal stationery store in your area. After preparing the form according to its instructions, file it along with the nominal fee with the proper government agency that handles the collateral subject to your particular transaction. The UCC-3 search will determine if the assets or equipment are tied up by someone else.

Form UCC-1—Standard Financing Statement and Form UCC-3—Request for Information or Copies are included in this section. Because these forms are for California, do not use these exact forms—each state requires it own format. Instead, obtain similar forms from any legal stationery store in your area and prepare and record them as instructed on the form.

TIPS FOR OBTAINING AND PREPARING GOVERNMENT FORMS

TIP #1
Ask a lot of questions

When you contact a government agency to obtain government forms, first ask to speak to a person who could answer some questions about the form before you order it. Talk with that person and explain in detail what you are trying to accomplish. Make sure that the person understands your goals so he or she can suggest the proper form. Do not be afraid to ask questions and do not let the agency personnel bully you. If you do not ask enough questions, chances are that you will end up with the wrong form, filing instructions, or other information needed to properly prepare or file the correct form.

TIP #2
Do not forget the filing fee

If you want to file a government form, chances are that there will be a filing fee. If such a fee is required, make sure to include it with the documents that you want filed. If you do not include it, it will only delay the process and cause you to have to deal with the situation twice.

TIP #3
Read the instructions

Government forms generally come with instructions on how to fill them out. Read the instructions carefully to ensure that they are properly followed. If you do, chances are that you will get your desired results handling the matter only once. If you do not, chances are you will spend additional time and money straightening out a problem or correcting the document later on.

TIP #4
Be patient

Some government agencies receive hundreds of thousands of the same documents. Thus, it may take awhile to process your document. At the time of filing your document, find out the typical return time and wait patiently, contacting the agency only when it's reasonable to do so.

TIP #5
File with the proper agency at the proper location

Make sure to send your completed documents to the proper agency at the proper location. This information should be included in the instructions that accompany the form. Make sure that you follow the filing instructions so your documents are not returned for improper filing. Where you file may depend on where you live.

TIP #6
Be nice

If you have a problem obtaining or trying to file a document, call the agency and ask to speak to a supervisor. When you get that person's ear, be nice. Chances are that the person with whom you are speaking is probably not the cause of your problem. On the other hand, he or she can probably help you. For every minute that you direct your anger to that person, you give up sixty seconds of getting him or her on your side.

Filling Out Application Form TX

Detach and read these instructions before completing this form.
Make sure all applicable spaces have been filled in before you return this form.

BASIC INFORMATION

When to Use This Form: Use Form TX for registration of published or unpublished nondramatic literary works, excluding periodicals or serial issues. This class includes a wide variety of works: fiction, nonfiction, poetry, textbooks, reference works, directories, catalogs, advertising copy, compilations of information, and computer programs. For periodicals and serials, use Form SE.

Deposit to Accompany Application: An application for copyright registration must be accompanied by a deposit consisting of copies or phonorecords representing the entire work for which registration is to be made. The following are the general deposit requirements as set forth in the statute:

Unpublished Work: Deposit one complete copy (or phonorecord).

Published Work: Deposit two complete copies (or one phonorecord) of the best edition.

Work First Published Outside the United States: Deposit one complete copy (or phonorecord) of the first foreign edition.

Contribution to a Collective Work: Deposit one complete copy (or phonorecord) of the best edition of the collective work.

The Copyright Notice: For works first published on or after March 1, 1989, the law provides that a copyright notice in a specified form "may be placed on all publicly distributed copies from which the work can be visually perceived." Use of the copyright notice is the responsibility of the copyright owner and does not require advance permission from the Copyright Office. The required form of the notice for copies generally consists of three elements: (1) the symbol "©," or the word "Copyright," or the abbreviation "Copr."; (2) the year of first publication; and (3) the name of the owner of copyright. For example: "© 1995 Jane Cole." The notice is to be affixed to the copies "in such manner and location as to give reasonable notice of the claim of copyright." Works first published prior to March 1, 1989, **must** carry the notice or risk loss of copyright protection.

For information about notice requirements for works published before March 1, 1989, or other copyright information, write: Information Section, LM-401, Copyright Office, Library of Congress, Washington, D.C. 20559-6000.

PRIVACY ACT ADVISORY STATEMENT
Required by the Privacy Act of 1974 (Public Law 93-579)

AUTHORITY FOR REQUESTING THIS INFORMATION:
- Title 17, U.S.C., Secs. 409 and 410

FURNISHING THE REQUESTED INFORMATION IS:
- Voluntary

BUT IF THE INFORMATION IS NOT FURNISHED:
- It may be necessary to delay or refuse registration
- You may not be entitled to certain relief, remedies, and benefits provided in chapters 4 and 5 of title 17, U.S.C.

PRINCIPAL USES OF REQUESTED INFORMATION:
- Establishment and maintenance of a public record
- Examination of the application for compliance with legal requirements

OTHER ROUTINE USES:
- Public inspection and copying
- Preparation of public indexes
- Preparation of public catalogs of copyright registrations
- Preparation of search reports upon request

NOTE:
- No other advisory statement will be given you in connection with this application
- Please keep this statement and refer to it if we communicate with you regarding this application

LINE-BY-LINE INSTRUCTIONS

Please type or print using black ink.

1 SPACE 1: Title

Title of This Work: Every work submitted for copyright registration must be given a title to identify that particular work. If the copies or phonorecords of the work bear a title or an identifying phrase that could serve as a title, transcribe that wording *completely* and *exactly* on the application. Indexing of the registration and future identification of the work will depend on the information you give here.

Previous or Alternative Titles: Complete this space if there are any additional titles for the work under which someone searching for the registration might be likely to look or under which a document pertaining to the work might be recorded.

Publication as a Contribution: If the work being registered is a contribution to a periodical, serial, or collection, give the title of the contribution in the "Title of this Work" space. Then, in the line headed "Publication as a Contribution," give information about the collective work in which the contribution appeared.

2 SPACE 2: Author(s)

General Instructions: After reading these instructions, decide who are the "authors" of this work for copyright purposes. Then, unless the work is a "collective work," give the requested information about every "author" who contributed any appreciable amount of copyrightable matter to this version of the work. If you need further space, request Continuation sheets. In the case of a collective work such as an anthology, collection of essays, or encyclopedia, give information about the author of the collective work as a whole.

Name of Author: The fullest form of the author's name should be given. Unless the work was "made for hire," the individual who actually created the work is its "author." In the case of a work made for hire, the statute provides that "the employer or other person for whom the work was prepared is considered the author."

What is a "Work Made for Hire"? A "work made for hire" is defined as (1) "a work prepared by an employee within the scope of his or her employment"; or (2) "a work specially ordered or commissioned for use as a contribution to a collective work, as a part of a motion picture or other audiovisual work, as a translation, as a supplementary work, as a compilation, as an instructional text, as a test, as answer material for a test, or as an atlas, if the parties expressly agree in a written instrument signed by them that the works shall be considered a work made for hire." If you have checked "Yes" to indicate that the work was "made for hire," you must give the full legal name of the employer (or other person for whom the work was prepared). You may also include the name of the employee along with the name of the employer (for example: "Elster Publishing Co., employer for hire of John Ferguson").

"Anonymous" or "Pseudonymous" Work: An author's contribution to a work is "anonymous" if that author is not identified on the copies or phonorecords of the work. An author's contribution to a work is "pseudonymous" if that author is identified on the copies or phonorecords under a fictitious name. If the work is "anonymous" you may: (1) leave the line blank; or (2) state "anonymous" on the line; or (3) reveal the author's identity. If the work is "pseudonymous" you may: (1) leave the line blank; or (2) give the pseudonym and identify it as such (for example: "Huntley Haverstock, pseudonym"); or (3) reveal the author's name, making clear which is the real name and which is the pseudonym (for example, "Judith Barton, whose pseudonym is Madeline Elster"). However, the citizenship or domicile of the author **must** be given in all cases.

Dates of Birth and Death: If the author is dead, the statute requires that the year of death be included in the application unless the work is anonymous or pseudonymous. The author's birth date is optional but is useful as a form of identification. Leave this space blank if the author's contribution was a "work made for hire."

Author's Nationality or Domicile: Give the country of which the author is a citizen or the country in which the author is domiciled. Nationality or domicile must be given in all cases.

Nature of Authorship: After the words "Nature of Authorship," give a brief general statement of the nature of this particular author's contribution to the work. Examples: "Entire text"; "Coauthor of entire text"; "Computer program"; "Editorial revisions"; "Compilation and English translation"; "New text."

3 SPACE 3: Creation and Publication

General Instructions: Do not confuse "creation" with "publication." Every application for copyright registration must state "the year in which creation of the work was completed." Give the date and nation of first publication only if the work has been published.

Creation: Under the statute, a work is "created" when it is fixed in a copy or phonorecord for the first time. Where a work has been prepared over a period of time, the part of the work existing in fixed form on a particular date constitutes the created work on that date. The date you give here should be the year in which the author completed the particular version for which registration is now being sought, even if other versions exist or if further changes or additions are planned.

Publication: The statute defines "publication" as "the distribution of copies or phonorecords of a work to the public by sale or other transfer of ownership, or by rental, lease, or lending"; a work is also "published" if there has been an "offering to distribute copies or phonorecords to a group of persons for purposes of further distribution, public performance, or public display." Give the full date (month, day, year) when, and the country where, publication first occurred. If first publication took place simultaneously in the United States and other countries, it is sufficient to state "U.S.A."

4 SPACE 4: Claimant(s)

Name(s) and Address(es) of Copyright Claimant(s): Give the name(s) and address(es) of the copyright claimant(s) in this work even if the claimant is the same as the author. Copyright in a work belongs initially to the author of the work (including, in the case of a work made for hire, the employer or other person for whom the work was prepared). The copyright claimant is either the author of the work or a person or organization to whom the copyright initially belonging to the author has been transferred.

Transfer: The statute provides that, if the copyright claimant is not the author, the application for registration must contain "a brief statement of how the claimant obtained ownership of the copyright." If any copyright claimant named in space 4 is not an author named in space 2, give a brief statement explaining how the claimant(s) obtained ownership of the copyright. Examples: "By written contract"; "Transfer of all rights by author"; "Assignment"; "By will." Do not attach transfer documents or other attachments or riders.

5 SPACE 5: Previous Registration

General Instructions: The questions in space 5 are intended to show whether an earlier registration has been made for this work and, if so, whether there is any basis for a new registration. As a general rule, only one basic copyright registration can be made for the same version of a particular work.

Same Version: If this version is substantially the same as the work covered by a previous registration, a second registration is not generally possible unless: (1) the work has been registered in unpublished form and a second registration is now being sought to cover this first published edition; or (2) someone other than the author is identified as copyright claimant in the earlier registration, and the author is now seeking registration in his or her own name. If either of these two exceptions apply, check the appropriate box and give the earlier registration number and date. Otherwise, do not submit Form TX; instead, write the Copyright Office for information about supplementary registration or recordation of transfers of copyright ownership.

Changed Version: If the work has been changed and you are now seeking registration to cover the additions or revisions, check the last box in space 5, give the earlier registration number and date, and complete both parts of space 6 in accordance with the instructions below.

Previous Registration Number and Date: If more than one previous registration has been made for the work, give the number and date of the latest registration.

6 SPACE 6: Derivative Work or Compilation

General Instructions: Complete space 6 if this work is a "changed version," "compilation," or "derivative work" and if it incorporates one or more earlier works that have already been published or registered for copyright or that have fallen into the public domain. A "compilation" is defined as "a work formed by the collection and assembling of preexisting materials or of data that are selected, coordinated, or arranged in such a way that the resulting work as a whole constitutes an original work of authorship." A "derivative work" is "a work based on one or more preexisting works." Examples of derivative works include translations, fictionalizations, abridgments, condensations, or "any other form in which a work may be recast, transformed, or adapted." Derivative works also include works "consisting of editorial revisions, annotations, or other modifications" if these changes, as a whole, represent an original work of authorship.

Preexisting Material (space 6a): For derivative works, complete this space and space 6b. In space 6a identify the preexisting work that has been recast, transformed, or adapted. An example of preexisting material might be: "Russian version of Goncharov's 'Oblomov'." Do not complete space 6a for compilations.

Material Added to This Work (space 6b): Give a brief, general statement of the new material covered by the copyright claim for which registration is sought. **Derivative work** examples include: "Foreword, editing, critical annotations"; "Translation"; "Chapters 11-17." If the work is a **compilation**, describe both the compilation itself and the material that has been compiled. Example: "Compilation of certain 1917 Speeches by Woodrow Wilson." A work may be both a derivative work and compilation, in which case a sample statement might be: "Compilation and additional new material."

7 SPACE 7: Manufacturing Provisions

Due to the expiration of the Manufacturing Clause of the copyright law on June 30, 1986, this space has been deleted.

8 SPACE 8: Reproduction for Use of Blind or Physically Handicapped Individuals

General Instructions: One of the major programs of the Library of Congress is to provide Braille editions and special recordings of works for the exclusive use of the blind and physically handicapped. In an effort to simplify and speed up the copyright licensing procedures that are a necessary part of this program, section 710 of the copyright statute provides for the establishment of a voluntary licensing system to be tied in with copyright registration. Copyright Office regulations provide that you may grant a license for such reproduction and distribution solely for the use of persons who are certified by competent authority as unable to read normal printed material as a result of physical limitations. The license is entirely voluntary, nonexclusive, and may be terminated upon 90 days notice.

How to Grant the License: If you wish to grant it, check one of the three boxes in space 8. Your check in one of these boxes together with your signature in space 10 will mean that the Library of Congress can proceed to reproduce and distribute under the license without further paperwork. For further information, write for Circular 63.

9,10,11 SPACE 9,10,11: Fee, Correspondence, Certification, Return Address

Deposit Account: If you maintain a Deposit Account in the Copyright Office, identify it in space 9. Otherwise leave the space blank and send the fee of $20 with your application and deposit.

Correspondence (space 9) This space should contain the name, address, area code, and telephone number of the person to be consulted if correspondence about this application becomes necessary.

Certification (space 10): The application can not be accepted unless it bears the date and the **handwritten signature** of the author or other copyright claimant, or of the owner of exclusive right(s), or of the duly authorized agent of author, claimant, or owner of exclusive right(s).

Address for Return of Certificate (space 11): The address box must be completed legibly since the certificate will be returned in a window envelope.

FORM TX

For a Literary Work
UNITED STATES COPYRIGHT OFFICE

REGISTRATION NUMBER

TX TXU

EFFECTIVE DATE OF REGISTRATION

Month Day Year

DO NOT WRITE ABOVE THIS LINE. IF YOU NEED MORE SPACE, USE A SEPARATE CONTINUATION SHEET.

1

TITLE OF THIS WORK ▼

PREVIOUS OR ALTERNATIVE TITLES ▼

PUBLICATION AS A CONTRIBUTION If this work was published as a contribution to a periodical, serial, or collection, give information about the collective work in which the contribution appeared. **Title of Collective Work ▼**

If published in a periodical or serial give: **Volume ▼** **Number ▼** **Issue Date ▼** **On Pages ▼**

2

a

NAME OF AUTHOR ▼

DATES OF BIRTH AND DEATH
Year Born ▼ Year Died ▼

Was this contribution to the work a "work made for hire"?
☐ Yes
☐ No

AUTHOR'S NATIONALITY OR DOMICILE
Name of Country
OR { Citizen of ▶
Domiciled in ▶

WAS THIS AUTHOR'S CONTRIBUTION TO THE WORK
Anonymous? ☐ Yes ☐ No
Pseudonymous? ☐ Yes ☐ No
If the answer to either of these questions is "Yes," see detailed instructions.

NATURE OF AUTHORSHIP Briefly describe nature of material created by this author in which copyright is claimed. ▼

b

NAME OF AUTHOR ▼

DATES OF BIRTH AND DEATH
Year Born ▼ Year Died ▼

Was this contribution to the work a "work made for hire"?
☐ Yes
☐ No

AUTHOR'S NATIONALITY OR DOMICILE
Name of Country
OR { Citizen of ▶
Domiciled in ▶

WAS THIS AUTHOR'S CONTRIBUTION TO THE WORK
Anonymous? ☐ Yes ☐ No
Pseudonymous? ☐ Yes ☐ No
If the answer to either of these questions is "Yes," see detailed instructions.

NATURE OF AUTHORSHIP Briefly describe nature of material created by this author in which copyright is claimed. ▼

c

NAME OF AUTHOR ▼

DATES OF BIRTH AND DEATH
Year Born ▼ Year Died ▼

Was this contribution to the work a "work made for hire"?
☐ Yes
☐ No

AUTHOR'S NATIONALITY OR DOMICILE
Name of Country
OR { Citizen of ▶
Domiciled in ▶

WAS THIS AUTHOR'S CONTRIBUTION TO THE WORK
Anonymous? ☐ Yes ☐ No
Pseudonymous? ☐ Yes ☐ No
If the answer to either of these questions is "Yes," see detailed instructions.

NATURE OF AUTHORSHIP Briefly describe nature of material created by this author in which copyright is claimed. ▼

NOTE

Under the law, the "author" of a "work made for hire" is generally the employer, not the employee (see instructions). For any part of this work that was "made for hire" check "Yes" in the space provided, give the employer (or other person for whom the work was prepared) as "Author" of that part, and leave the space for dates of birth and death blank.

3

a **YEAR IN WHICH CREATION OF THIS WORK WAS COMPLETED** **This information must be given in all cases.** ◀ Year

b **DATE AND NATION OF FIRST PUBLICATION OF THIS PARTICULAR WORK** **Complete this information ONLY if this work has been published.** Month ▶ Day ▶ Year ▶ ◀ Nation

4

See instructions before completing this space.

COPYRIGHT CLAIMANT(S) Name and address must be given even if the claimant is the same as the author given in space 2. ▼

TRANSFER If the claimant(s) named here in space 4 is (are) different from the author(s) named in space 2, give a brief statement of how the claimant(s) obtained ownership of the copyright. ▼

DO NOT WRITE HERE
OFFICE USE ONLY

APPLICATION RECEIVED

ONE DEPOSIT RECEIVED

TWO DEPOSITS RECEIVED

FUNDS RECEIVED

MORE ON BACK ▶ • Complete all applicable spaces (numbers 5-11) on the reverse side of this page.
• See detailed instructions. • Sign the form at line 10.

DO NOT WRITE HERE

Page 1 of ____ pages

EXAMINED BY

CHECKED BY

☐ CORRESPONDENCE Yes

FORM TX

FOR COPYRIGHT OFFICE USE ONLY

DO NOT WRITE ABOVE THIS LINE. IF YOU NEED MORE SPACE, USE A SEPARATE CONTINUATION SHEET.

5

PREVIOUS REGISTRATION Has registration for this work, or for an earlier version of this work, already been made in the Copyright Office?

☐ **Yes** ☐ **No** If your answer is "Yes," why is another registration being sought? (Check appropriate box) ▼

a. ☐ This is the first published edition of a work previously registered in unpublished form.

b. ☐ This is the first application submitted by this author as copyright claimant.

c. ☐ This is a changed version of the work, as shown by space 6 on this application.

If your answer is "Yes," give: **Previous Registration Number** ▼ **Year of Registration** ▼

6

DERIVATIVE WORK OR COMPILATION Complete both space 6a and 6b for a derivative work; complete only 6b for a compilation.

a. Preexisting Material Identify any preexisting work or works that this work is based on or incorporates. ▼

b. Material Added to This Work Give a brief, general statement of the material that has been added to this work and in which copyright is claimed. ▼

See instructions before completing this space.

7

—space deleted—

8

REPRODUCTION FOR USE OF BLIND OR PHYSICALLY HANDICAPPED INDIVIDUALS A signature on this form at space 10 and a check in one of the boxes here in space 8 constitutes a non-exclusive grant of permission to the Library of Congress to reproduce and distribute solely for the blind and physically handicapped and under the conditions and limitations prescribed by the regulations of the Copyright Office: (1) copies of the work identified in space 1 of this application in Braille (or similar tactile symbols); or (2) phonorecords embodying a fixation of a reading of that work; or (3) both.

a ☐ Copies and Phonorecords b ☐ Copies Only c ☐ Phonorecords Only

See instructions.

9

DEPOSIT ACCOUNT If the registration fee is to be charged to a Deposit Account established in the Copyright Office, give name and number of Account.

Name ▼ **Account Number** ▼

CORRESPONDENCE Give name and address to which correspondence about this application should be sent. Name/Address/Apt/City/State/ZIP ▼

Area Code and Telephone Number ▶

Be sure to give your daytime phone ◀ number

10

CERTIFICATION* I, the undersigned, hereby certify that I am the

Check only one ▶
- ☐ author
- ☐ other copyright claimant
- ☐ owner of exclusive right(s)
- ☐ authorized agent of ______

Name of author or other copyright claimant, or owner of exclusive right(s) ▲

of the work identified in this application and that the statements made by me in this application are correct to the best of my knowledge.

Typed or printed name and date ▼ If this application gives a date of publication in space 3, do not sign and submit it before that date.

Date ▶

Handwritten signature (X) ▼

11

MAIL CERTIFICATE TO

Name ▼

Number/Street/Apt ▼

City/State/ZIP ▼

Certificate will be mailed in window envelope

YOU MUST:
- Complete all necessary spaces
- Sign your application in space 10

SEND ALL 3 ELEMENTS IN THE SAME PACKAGE:
1. Application form
2. Nonrefundable $20 filing fee in check or money order payable to *Register of Copyrights*
3. Deposit material

MAIL TO:
Register of Copyrights
Library of Congress
Washington, D.C. 20559-6000

*17 U.S.C. § 506(e): Any person who knowingly makes a false representation of a material fact in the application for copyright registration provided for by section 409, or in any written statement filed in connection with the application, shall be fined not more than $2,500.

May 1995—300,000 PRINTED ON RECYCLED PAPER ☆U.S. GOVERNMENT PRINTING OFFICE: 1995-387-237/47

Filling Out Application Form PA

Detach and read these instructions before completing this form.
Make sure all applicable spaces have been filled in before you return this form.

BASIC INFORMATION

When to Use This Form: Use Form PA for registration of published or unpublished works of the performing arts. This class includes works prepared for the purpose of being "performed" directly before an audience or indirectly "by means of any device or process." Works of the performing arts include: (1) musical works, including any accompanying words; (2) dramatic works, including any accompanying music; (3) pantomimes and choreographic works; and (4) motion pictures and other audiovisual works.

Deposit to Accompany Application: An application for copyright registration must be accompanied by a deposit consisting of copies or phonorecords representing the entire work for which registration is made. The following are the general deposit requirements as set forth in the statute:

Unpublished Work: Deposit one complete copy (or phonorecord).

Published Work: Deposit two complete copies (or one phonorecord) of the best edition.

Work First Published Outside the United States: Deposit one complete copy (or phonorecord) of the first foreign edition.

Contribution to a Collective Work: Deposit one complete copy (or phonorecord) of the best edition of the collective work.

Motion Pictures: Deposit *both* of the following: (1) a separate written description of the contents of the motion picture; and (2) for a published work, one complete copy of the best edition of the motion picture; or, for an unpublished work, one complete copy of the motion picture or identifying material. Identifying material may be either an audiorecording of the entire soundtrack or one frame enlargement or similar visual print from each 10-minute segment.

The Copyright Notice: For works first published on or after March 1, 1989, the law provides that a copyright notice in a specified form "may be placed on all publicly distributed copies from which the work can be visually perceived." Use of the copyright notice is the responsibility of the copyright owner and does not require advance permission from the Copyright Office. The required form of the notice for copies generally consists of three elements: (1) the symbol "©", or the word "Copyright," or the abbreviation "Copr."; (2) the year of first publication; and (3) the name of the owner of copyright. For example: "© 1995 Jane Cole." The notice is to be affixed to the copies "in such manner and location as to give reasonable notice of the claim of copyright." Works first published prior to March 1, 1989, **must** carry the notice or risk loss of copyright protection.

For information about requirements for works published before March 1, 1989, or other copyright information, write: Information Section, LM-401, Copyright Office, Library of Congress, Washington, D.C. 20559-6000.

PRIVACY ACT ADVISORY STATEMENT Required by the Privacy Act of 1974 (P.L. 93-579)
The authority for requesting this information is title 17, U.S.C., secs. 409 and 410. Furnishing the requested information is voluntary. But if the information is not furnished, it may be necessary to delay or refuse registration and you may not be entitled to certain relief, remedies, and benefits provided in chapters 4 and 5 of title 17, U.S.C.
The principal uses of the requested information are the establishment and maintenance of a public record and the examination of the application for compliance with legal requirements.
Other routine uses include public inspection and copying, preparation of public indexes, preparation of public catalogs of copyright registrations, and preparation of search reports upon request.
NOTE: No other advisory statement will be given in connection with this application. Please keep this statement and refer to it if we communicate with you regarding this application.

LINE-BY-LINE INSTRUCTIONS

Please type or print using black ink.

1 SPACE 1: Title

Title of This Work: Every work submitted for copyright registration must be given a title to identify that particular work. If the copies or phonorecords of the work bear a title (or an identifying phrase that could serve as a title), transcribe that wording *completely* and *exactly* on the application. Indexing of the registration and future identification of the work will depend on the information you give here. If the work you are registering is an entire "collective work" (such as a collection of plays or songs), give the overall title of the collection. If you are registering one or more individual contributions to a collective work, give the title of each contribution, followed by the title of the collection. For an unpublished collection, you may give the titles of the individual works after the collection title.

Previous or Alternative Titles: Complete this space if there are any additional titles for the work under which someone searching for the registration might be likely to look, or under which a document pertaining to the work might be recorded.

Nature of This Work: Briefly describe the general nature or character of the work being registered for copyright. Examples: "Music"; "Song Lyrics"; "Words and Music"; "Drama"; "Musical Play"; "Choreography"; "Pantomime"; "Motion Picture"; "Audiovisual Work."

2 SPACE 2: Author(s)

General Instructions: After reading these instructions, decide who are the "authors" of this work for copyright purposes. Then, unless the work is a "collective work," give the requested information about every "author" who contributed any appreciable amount of copyrightable matter to this version of the work. If you need further space, request additional Continuation Sheets. In the case of a collective work, such as a songbook or a collection of plays, give the information about the author of the collective work as a whole.

Name of Author: The fullest form of the author's name should be given. Unless the work was "made for hire," the individual who actually created the work is its "author." In the case of a work made for hire, the statute provides that "the employer or other person for whom the work was prepared is considered the author."

What is a "Work Made for Hire"? A "work made for hire" is defined as: (1) "a work prepared by an employee within the scope of his or her employment"; or (2) "a work specially ordered or commissioned for use as a contribution to a collective work, as a part of a motion picture or other audiovisual work, as a translation, as a supplementary work, as a compilation, as an instructional text, as a test, as answer material for a test, or as an atlas, if the parties expressly agree in a written instrument signed by them that the work shall be considered a work made for hire." If you have checked "Yes" to indicate that the work was "made for hire," you must give the full legal name of the employer (or other person for whom the work was prepared). You may also include the name of the employee along with the name of the employer (for example: "Elster Music Co., employer for hire of John Ferguson").

"Anonymous" or "Pseudonymous" Work: An author's contribution to a work is "anonymous" if that author is not identified on the copies or phonorecords of the work. An author's contribution to a work is "pseudonymous" if that author is identified on the copies or phonorecords under a fictitious name. If the work is "anonymous" you may: (1) leave the line blank; or (2) state "anonymous" on the line; or (3) reveal the author's identity. If the work is "pseudonymous" you may: (1) leave the line blank; or (2) give the pseudonym and identify it as such (example: "Huntley Haverstock, pseudonym"); or (3) reveal the author's name, making clear which is the real name and which is the pseudonym (for example: "Judith Barton, whose pseudonym is Madeline Elster"). However, the citizenship or domicile of the author **must** be given in all cases.

Dates of Birth and Death: If the author is dead, the statute requires that the year of death be included in the application unless the work is anonymous or pseudonymous. The author's birth date is optional, but is useful as a form of identification. Leave this space blank if the author's contribution was a "work made for hire."

Author's Nationality or Domicile: Give the country of which the author is a citizen, or the country in which the author is domiciled. Nationality or domicile **must** be given in all cases.

Nature of Authorship: Give a brief general statement of the nature of this particular author's contribution to the work. Examples: "Words"; "Coauthor of Music"; "Words and Music"; "Arrangement"; "Coauthor of Book and Lyrics"; "Dramatization"; "Screen Play"; "Compilation and English Translation"; "Editorial Revisions."

3 SPACE 3: Creation and Publication

General Instructions: Do not confuse "creation" with "publication." Every application for copyright registration must state "the year in which creation of the work was completed." Give the date and nation of first publication only if the work has been published.

Creation: Under the statute, a work is "created" when it is fixed in a copy or phonorecord for the first time. Where a work has been prepared over a period of time, the part of the work existing in fixed form on a particular date constitutes the created work on that date. The date you give here should be the year in which the author completed the particular version for which registration is now being sought, even if other versions exist or if further changes or additions are planned.

Publication: The statute defines "publication" as "the distribution of copies or phonorecords of a work to the public by sale or other transfer of ownership, or by rental, lease, or lending"; a work is also "published" if there has been an "offering to distribute copies or phonorecords to a group of persons for purposes of further distribution, public performance, or public display." Give the full date (month, day, year) when, and the country where, publication first occurred. If first publication took place simultaneously in the United States and other countries, it is sufficient to state "U.S.A."

4 SPACE 4: Claimant(s)

Name(s) and Address(es) of Copyright Claimant(s): Give the name(s) and address(es) of the copyright claimant(s) in this work even if the claimant is the same as the author. Copyright in a work belongs initially to the author of the work (including, in the case of a work made for hire, the employer or other person for whom the work was prepared). The copyright claimant is either the author of the work or a person or organization to whom the copyright initially belonging to the author has been transferred.

Transfer: The statute provides that, if the copyright claimant is not the author, the application for registration must contain "a brief statement of how the claimant obtained ownership of the copyright." If any copyright claimant named in space 4 is not an author named in space 2, give a brief statement explaining how the claimant(s) obtained ownership of the copyright. Examples: "By written contract"; "Transfer of all rights by author"; "Assignment"; "By will." Do not attach transfer documents or other attachments or riders.

5 SPACE 5: Previous Registration

General Instructions: The questions in space 5 are intended to show whether an earlier registration has been made for this work and, if so, whether there is any basis for a new registration. As a general rule, only one basic copyright registration can be made for the same version of a particular work.

Same Version: If this version is substantially the same as the work covered by a previous registration, a second registration is not generally possible unless: (1) the work has been registered in unpublished form and a second registration is now being sought to cover this first published edition; or (2) someone other than the author is identified as copyright claimant in the earlier registration, and the author is now seeking registration in his or her own name. If either of these two exceptions apply, check the appropriate box and give the earlier registration number and date. Otherwise, do not submit Form PA; instead, write the Copyright Office for information about supplementary registration or recordation of transfers of copyright ownership.

Changed Version: If the work has been changed, and you are now seeking registration to cover the additions or revisions, check the last box in space 5, give the earlier registration number and date, and complete both parts of space 6 in accordance with the instructions below.

Previous Registration Number and Date: If more than one previous registration has been made for the work, give the number and date of the latest registration.

6 SPACE 6: Derivative Work or Compilation

General Instructions: Complete space 6 if this work is a "changed version," "compilation," or "derivative work," and if it incorporates one or more earlier works that have already been published or registered for copyright or that have fallen into the public domain. A "compilation" is defined as "a work formed by the collection and assembling of preexisting materials or of data that are selected, coordinated, or arranged in such a way that the resulting work as a whole constitutes an original work of authorship." A "derivative work" is "a work based on one or more preexisting works." Examples of derivative works include musical arrangements, dramatizations, translations, abridgments, condensations, motion picture versions, or "any other form in which a work may be recast, transformed, or adapted." Derivative works also include works "consisting of editorial revisions, annotations, or other modifications" if these changes, as a whole, represent an original work of authorship.

Preexisting Material (space 6a): Complete this space and space 6b for derivative works. In this space identify the preexisting work that has been recast, transformed, or adapted. For example, the preexisting material might be: "French version of Hugo's 'Le Roi s'amuse'." Do not complete this space for compilations.

Material Added to This Work (space 6b): Give a brief, general statement of the **additional** new material covered by the copyright claim for which registration is sought. In the case of a derivative work, identify this new material. Examples: "Arrangement for piano and orchestra"; "Dramatization for television"; "New film version"; "Revisions throughout; Act III completely new." If the work is a compilation, give a brief, general statement describing both the material that has been compiled **and** the compilation itself. Example: "Compilation of 19th Century Military Songs."

7,8,9 SPACE 7, 8, 9: Fee, Correspondence, Certification, Return Address

Deposit Account: If you maintain a Deposit Account in the Copyright Office, identify it in space 7. Otherwise leave the space blank and send the fee of $20 with your application and deposit.

Correspondence (space 7): This space should contain the name, address, area code, and telephone number of the person to be consulted if correspondence about this application becomes necessary.

Certification (space 8): The application cannot be accepted unless it bears the date and the **handwritten signature** of the author or other copyright claimant, or of the owner of exclusive right(s), or of the duly authorized agent of the author, claimant, or owner of exclusive right(s).

Address for Return of Certificate (space 9): The address box must be completed legibly since the certificate will be returned in a window envelope.

MORE INFORMATION

How to Register a Recorded Work: If the musical or dramatic work that you are registering has been recorded (as a tape, disk, or cassette), you may choose either copyright application Form PA (Performing Arts) or Form SR (Sound Recordings), depending on the purpose of the registration.

Form PA should be used to register the underlying musical composition or dramatic work. Form SR has been developed specifically to register a "sound recording" as defined by the Copyright Act—a work resulting from the "fixation of a series of sounds," separate and distinct from the underlying musical or dramatic work. Form SR should be used when the copyright claim is limited to the sound recording itself. (In one instance, Form SR may also be used to file for a copyright registration for both kinds of works—see (4) below.) Therefore:

(1) File Form PA if you are seeking to register the musical or dramatic work, not the "sound recording," even though what you deposit for copyright purposes may be in the form of a phonorecord.

(2) File Form PA if you are seeking to register the audio portion of an audiovisual work, such as a motion picture soundtrack; these are considered integral parts of the audiovisual work.

(3) File Form SR if you are seeking to register the "sound recording" itself, that is, the work that results from the fixation of a series of musical, spoken, or other sounds, but not the underlying musical or dramatic work.

(4) File Form SR if you are the copyright claimant for both the underlying musical or dramatic work and the sound recording, *and* you prefer to register both on the same form.

(5) File both forms PA and SR if the copyright claimant for the underlying work and sound recording differ, or you prefer to have separate registration for them.

"Copies" and "Phonorecords": To register for copyright, you are required to deposit "copies" or "phonorecords." These are defined as follows:

Musical compositions may be embodied (fixed) in "copies," objects from which a work can be read or visually perceived, directly or with the aid of a machine or device, such as manuscripts, books, sheet music, film, and videotape. They may also be fixed in "phonorecords," objects embodying fixations of sounds, such as tapes and phonograph disks, commonly known as phonograph records. For example, a song (the work to be registered) can be reproduced in sheet music ("copies") or phonograph records ("phonorecords"), or both.

FORM PA

For a Work of the Performing Arts
UNITED STATES COPYRIGHT OFFICE

REGISTRATION NUMBER

PA PAU

EFFECTIVE DATE OF REGISTRATION

Month Day Year

DO NOT WRITE ABOVE THIS LINE. IF YOU NEED MORE SPACE, USE A SEPARATE CONTINUATION SHEET.

1

TITLE OF THIS WORK ▼

PREVIOUS OR ALTERNATIVE TITLES ▼

NATURE OF THIS WORK ▼ See instructions

2

a

NAME OF AUTHOR ▼

DATES OF BIRTH AND DEATH
Year Born ▼ Year Died ▼

Was this contribution to the work a "work made for hire"?
☐ Yes
☐ No

AUTHOR'S NATIONALITY OR DOMICILE
Name of Country
OR { Citizen of ▶ / Domiciled in ▶

WAS THIS AUTHOR'S CONTRIBUTION TO THE WORK
Anonymous? ☐ Yes ☐ No
Pseudonymous? ☐ Yes ☐ No
If the answer to either of these questions is "Yes," see detailed instructions.

NATURE OF AUTHORSHIP Briefly describe nature of material created by this author in which copyright is claimed. ▼

NOTE

Under the law, the "author" of a "work made for hire" is generally the employer, not the employee (see instructions). For any part of this work that was "made for hire" check "Yes" in the space provided, give the employer (or other person for whom the work was prepared) as "Author" of that part, and leave the space for dates of birth and death blank.

b

NAME OF AUTHOR ▼

DATES OF BIRTH AND DEATH
Year Born ▼ Year Died ▼

Was this contribution to the work a "work made for hire"?
☐ Yes
☐ No

AUTHOR'S NATIONALITY OR DOMICILE
Name of Country
OR { Citizen of ▶ / Domiciled in ▶

WAS THIS AUTHOR'S CONTRIBUTION TO THE WORK
Anonymous? ☐ Yes ☐ No
Pseudonymous? ☐ Yes ☐ No
If the answer to either of these questions is "Yes," see detailed instructions.

NATURE OF AUTHORSHIP Briefly describe nature of material created by this author in which copyright is claimed. ▼

c

NAME OF AUTHOR ▼

DATES OF BIRTH AND DEATH
Year Born ▼ Year Died ▼

Was this contribution to the work a "work made for hire"?
☐ Yes
☐ No

AUTHOR'S NATIONALITY OR DOMICILE
Name of Country
OR { Citizen of ▶ / Domiciled in ▶

WAS THIS AUTHOR'S CONTRIBUTION TO THE WORK
Anonymous? ☐ Yes ☐ No
Pseudonymous? ☐ Yes ☐ No
If the answer to either of these questions is "Yes," see detailed instructions.

NATURE OF AUTHORSHIP Briefly describe nature of material created by this author in which copyright is claimed. ▼

3

a **YEAR IN WHICH CREATION OF THIS WORK WAS COMPLETED** **This information must be given in all cases.**
◀ Year

b **DATE AND NATION OF FIRST PUBLICATION OF THIS PARTICULAR WORK**
Complete this information ONLY if this work has been published.
Month ▶ Day ▶ Year ▶
◀ Nation

4

See instructions before completing this space.

COPYRIGHT CLAIMANT(S) Name and address must be given even if the claimant is the same as the author given in space 2. ▼

TRANSFER If the claimant(s) named here in space 4 is (are) different from the author(s) named in space 2, give a brief statement of how the claimant(s) obtained ownership of the copyright. ▼

DO NOT WRITE HERE
OFFICE USE ONLY

APPLICATION RECEIVED

ONE DEPOSIT RECEIVED

TWO DEPOSITS RECEIVED

FUNDS RECEIVED

MORE ON BACK ▶
• Complete all applicable spaces (numbers 5-9) on the reverse side of this page.
• See detailed instructions.
• Sign the form at line 8.

DO NOT WRITE HERE

Page 1 of ______ pages

EXAMINED BY

CHECKED BY

☐ CORRESPONDENCE Yes

FORM PA

FOR COPYRIGHT OFFICE USE ONLY

DO NOT WRITE ABOVE THIS LINE. IF YOU NEED MORE SPACE, USE A SEPARATE CONTINUATION SHEET.

5

PREVIOUS REGISTRATION Has registration for this work, or for an earlier version of this work, already been made in the Copyright Office?

☐ Yes ☐ No If your answer is "Yes," why is another registration being sought? (Check appropriate box) ▼

a. ☐ This is the first published edition of a work previously registered in unpublished form.

b. ☐ This is the first application submitted by this author as copyright claimant.

c. ☐ This is a changed version of the work, as shown by space 6 on this application.

If your answer is "Yes," give: **Previous Registration Number** ▼ **Year of Registration** ▼

6

DERIVATIVE WORK OR COMPILATION Complete both space 6a and 6b for a derivative work; complete only 6b for a compilation.

a. Preexisting Material Identify any preexisting work or works that this work is based on or incorporates. ▼

See instructions before completing this space.

b. Material Added to This Work Give a brief, general statement of the material that has been added to this work and in which copyright is claimed. ▼

7

DEPOSIT ACCOUNT If the registration fee is to be charged to a Deposit Account established in the Copyright Office, give name and number of Account.

Name ▼ **Account Number** ▼

CORRESPONDENCE Give name and address to which correspondence about this application should be sent. Name/Address/Apt/City/State/ZIP ▼

Area Code and Telephone Number ▶

Be sure to give your daytime phone ◀ number

8

CERTIFICATION* I, the undersigned, hereby certify that I am the

Check only one ▼

☐ author

☐ other copyright claimant

☐ owner of exclusive right(s)

☐ authorized agent of ______________________

Name of author or other copyright claimant, or owner of exclusive right(s) ▲

of the work identified in this application and that the statements made by me in this application are correct to the best of my knowledge.

Typed or printed name and date ▼ If this application gives a date of publication in space 3, do not sign and submit it before that date.

Date ▶

Handwritten signature (X) ▼

9

MAIL CERTIFICATE TO

Name ▼

Number/Street/Apt ▼

City/State/ZIP ▼

Certificate will be mailed in window envelope

YOU MUST:
- Complete all necessary spaces
- Sign your application in space 8

SEND ALL 3 ELEMENTS IN THE SAME PACKAGE:
1. Application form
2. Nonrefundable $20 filing fee in check or money order payable to *Register of Copyrights*
3. Deposit material

MAIL TO:
Register of Copyrights
Library of Congress
Washington, D.C. 20559-6000

*17 U.S.C. § 506(e): Any person who knowingly makes a false representation of a material fact in the application for copyright registration provided for by section 409, or in any written statement filed in connection with the application, shall be fined not more than $2,500.

May 1995—300,000 PRINTED ON RECYCLED PAPER ☆U.S. GOVERNMENT PRINTING OFFICE: 1995-387-237/46

Filling Out Application Form SR

Detach and read these instructions before completing this form.
Make sure all applicable spaces have been filled in before you return this form.

BASIC INFORMATION

When to Use This Form: Use Form SR for copyright registration of published or unpublished sound recordings. It should be used when the copyright claim is limited to the sound recording itself, and it may also be used where the same copyright claimant is seeking simultaneous registration of the underlying musical, dramatic, or literary work embodied in the phonorecord.

With one exception, "sound recordings" are works that result from the fixation of a series of musical, spoken, or other sounds. The exception is for the audio portions of audiovisual works, such as a motion picture soundtrack or an audio cassette accompanying a filmstrip; these are considered a part of the audiovisual work as a whole.

Deposit to Accompany Application: An application for copyright registration of a sound recording must be accompanied by a deposit consisting of phonorecords representing the entire work for which registration is to be made.

Unpublished Work: Deposit one complete phonorecord.

Published Work: Deposit two complete phonorecords of the best edition, together with "any printed or other visually perceptible material" published with the phonorecords.

Work First Published Outside the United States: Deposit one complete phonorecord of the first foreign edition.

Contribution to a Collective Work: Deposit one complete phonorecord of the best edition of the collective work.

The Copyright Notice: For sound recordings first published on or after March 1, 1989, the law provides that a copyright notice in a specified form "may be placed on all publicly distributed phonorecords of the sound recording." Use of the copyright notice is the responsibility of the copyright owner and does not require advance permission from the Copyright Office. The required form of the notice for phonorecords of sound recordings consists of three elements: (1) the symbol "℗" (the letter "P" in a circle); (2) the year of first publication of the sound recording; and (3) the name of the owner of copyright. For example "℗ 1993 XYZ Record Co." The notice is to be "placed on the surface of the phonorecord, or on the label or container, in such manner and location as to give reasonable notice of the claim of copyright." Works first published prior to March 1, 1989, **must** carry the notice or risk loss of copyright protection.

For information about notice requirements for works published before March 1, 1989, or other copyright information, write: Information Section, LM-401, Copyright Office, Library of Congress, Washington, D.C. 20559.

PRIVACY ACT ADVISORY STATEMENT Required by the Privacy Act of 1974 (P.L. 93-579)

The authority for requesting this information is title 17, U.S.C., secs. 409 and 410. Furnishing the requested information is voluntary. But if the information is not furnished, it may be necessary to delay or refuse registration and you may not be entitled to certain relief, remedies, and benefits provided in chapters 4 and 5 of title 17, U.S.C.

The principal uses of the requested information are the establishment and maintenance of a public record and the examination of the application for compliance with legal requirements.

Other routine uses include public inspection and copying, preparation of public indexes, preparation of public catalogs of copyright registrations, and preparation of search reports upon request.

NOTE: No other advisory statement will be given in connection with this application. Please keep this statement and refer to it if we communicate with you regarding this application.

LINE-BY-LINE INSTRUCTIONS

Please type or print using black ink.

1 SPACE 1: Title

Title of This Work: Every work submitted for copyright registration must be given a title to identify that particular work. If the phonorecords or any accompanying printed material bear a title (or an identifying phrase that could serve as a title), transcribe that wording completely and exactly on the application. Indexing of the registration and future identification of the work may depend on the information you give here.

Nature of Material Recorded: Indicate the general type or character of the works or other material embodied in the recording. The box marked "Literary" should be checked for nondramatic spoken material of all sorts, including narration, interviews, panel discussions, and training material. If the material recorded is not musical, dramatic, or literary in nature, check "Other" and briefly describe the type of sounds fixed in the recording. For example: "Sound Effects"; "Bird Calls"; "Crowd Noises."

Previous or Alternative Titles: Complete this space if there are any additional titles for the work under which someone searching for the registration might be likely to look or under which a document pertaining to the work might be recorded.

2 SPACE 2: Author(s)

General Instructions: After reading these instructions, decide who are the "authors" of this work for copyright purposes. Then, unless the work is a "collective work," give the requested information about every "author" who contributed any appreciable amount of copyrightable matter to this version of the work. If you need further space, request additional Continuation Sheets. In the case of a collective work such as a collection of previously published or registered sound recordings, give information about the author of the collective work as a whole. If you are submitting this Form SR to cover the recorded musical, dramatic, or literary work as well as the sound recording itself, it is important for space 2 to include full information about the various authors of all of the material covered by the copyright claim, making clear the nature of each author's contribution.

Name of Author: The fullest form of the author's name should be given. Unless the work was "made for hire," the individual who actually created the work is its "author." In the case of a work made for hire, the statute provides that "the employer or other person for whom the work was prepared is considered the author."

What is a "Work Made for Hire"? A "work made for hire" is defined as: (1) "a work prepared by an employee within the scope of his or her employment"; or (2) "a work specially ordered or commissioned for use as a contribution to a collective work, as a part of a motion picture or other audiovisual work, as a translation, as a supplementary work, as a compilation, as an instructional text, as a test, as answer material for a test, or as an atlas, if the parties expressly agree in a written instrument signed by them that the work shall be considered a work made for hire." If you have checked "Yes" to indicate that the work was "made for hire," you must give the full legal name of the employer (or other person for whom the work was prepared). You may also include the name of the employee along with the name of the employer (for example: "Elster Record Co., employer for hire of John Ferguson").

"Anonymous" or "Pseudonymous" Work: An author's contribution to a work is "anonymous" if that author is not identified on the copies or phonorecords of the work. An author's contribution to a work is "pseudonymous" if that author is identified on the copies or phonorecords under a fictitious name. If the work is "anonymous" you may: (1) leave the line blank; or (2) state "anonymous" on the line; or (3) reveal the author's identity. If the work is "pseudonymous" you may: (1) leave the line blank; or (2) give the pseudonym and identify it as such (for example: "Huntley Haverstock, pseudonym"); or (3) reveal the author's name, making clear which is the real name and which is the pseudonym (for example: "Judith Barton, whose pseudonym is Madeline Elster"). However, the citizenship or domicile of the author **must** be given in all cases.

Dates of Birth and Death: If the author is dead, the statute requires that the year of death be included in the application unless the work is anonymous or pseudonymous. The author's birth date is optional, but is useful as a form of identification. Leave this space blank if the author's contribution was a "work made for hire."

Author's Nationality or Domicile: Give the country in which the author is a citizen, or the country in which the author is domiciled. Nationality or domicile **must** be given in all cases.

Nature of Authorship: Give a brief general statement of the nature of this particular author's contribution to the work. If you are submitting this Form SR to cover both the sound recording and the underlying musical, dramatic, or literary work, make sure that the precise nature of each author's contribution is reflected here. Examples where the authorship pertains to the recording: "Sound Recording"; "Performance and Recording"; "Compilation and Remixing of Sounds." Examples where the authorship pertains to both the recording and the underlying work: "Words, Music, Performance, Recording"; "Arrangement of Music and Recording"; "Compilation of Poems and Reading."

3 SPACE 3: Creation and Publication

General Instructions: Do not confuse "creation" with "publication." Every application for copyright registration must state "the year in which creation of the work was completed." Give the date and nation of first publication only if the work has been published.

Creation: Under the statute, a work is "created" when it is fixed in a copy or phonorecord for the first time. Where a work has been prepared over a period of time, the part of the work existing in fixed form on a particular date constitutes the created work on that date. The date you give here should be the year in which the author completed the particular version for which registration is now being sought, even if other versions exist or if further changes or additions are planned.

Publication: The statute defines "publication" as "the distribution of copies or phonorecords of a work to the public by sale or other transfer of ownership, or by rental, lease, or lending"; a work is also "published" if there has been an "offering to distribute copies or phonorecords to a group of persons for purposes of further distribution, public performance, or public display." Give the full date (month, date, year) when, and the country where, publication first occurred. If first publication took place simultaneously in the United States and other countries, it is sufficient to state "U.S.A."

4 SPACE 4: Claimant(s)

Name(s) and Address(es) of Copyright Claimant(s): Give the name(s) and address(es) of the copyright claimant(s) in the work even if the claimant is the same as the author. Copyright in a work belongs initially to the author of the work (including, in the case of a work made for hire, the employer or other person for whom the work was prepared). The copyright claimant is either the author of the work or a person or organization to whom the copyright initially belonging to the author has been transferred.

Transfer: The statute provides that, if the copyright claimant is not the author, the application for registration must contain "a brief statement of how the claimant obtained ownership of the copyright." If any copyright claimant named in space 4 is not an author named in space 2, give a brief statement explaining how the claimant(s) obtained ownership of the copyright. Examples: "By written contract"; "Transfer of all rights by author"; "Assignment"; "By will." Do not attach transfer documents or other attachments or riders.

5 SPACE 5: Previous Registration

General Instructions: The questions in space 5 are intended to show whether an earlier registration has been made for this work and, if so, whether there is any basis for a new registration. As a rule, only one basic copyright registration can be made for the same version of a particular work.

Same Version: If this version is substantially the same as the work covered by a previous registration, a second registration is not generally possible unless: (1) the work has been registered in unpublished form and a second registration is now being sought to cover this first published edition; or (2) someone other than the author is identified as copyright claimant in the earlier registration and the author is now seeking registration in his or her own name. If either of these two exceptions apply, check the appropriate box and give the earlier registration number and date. Otherwise, do not submit Form SR; instead, write the Copyright Office for information about supplementary registration or recordation of transfers of copyright ownership.

Changed Version: If the work has been changed, and you are now seeking registration to cover the additions or revisions, check the last box in space 5, give the earlier registration number and date, and complete both parts of space 6 in accordance with the instructions below.

Previous Registration Number and Date: If more than one previous registration has been made for the work, give the number and date of the latest registration.

6 SPACE 6: Derivative Work or Compilation

General Instructions: Complete space 6 if this work is a "changed version," "compilation," or "derivative work," and if it incorporates one or more earlier works that have already been published or registered for copyright, or that have fallen into the public domain, or sound recordings that were fixed before February 15, 1972. A "compilation" is defined as "a work formed by the collection and assembling of preexisting materials or of data that are selected, coordinated, or arranged in such a way that the resulting work as a whole constitutes an original work of authorship." A "derivative work" is "a work based on one or more preexisting works." Examples of derivative works include recordings reissued with substantial editorial revisions or abridgments of the recorded sounds, and recordings republished with new recorded material, or "any other form in which a work may be recast, transformed, or adapted." Derivative works also include works "consisting of editorial revisions, annotations, or other modifications" if these changes, as a whole, represent an original work of authorship.

Preexisting Material (space 6a): Complete this space and space 6b for derivative works. In this space identify the preexisting work that has been recast, transformed, or adapted. For example, the preexisting material might be: "1970 recording by Sperryville Symphony of Bach Double Concerto." Do not complete this space for compilations.

Material Added to This Work (space 6b): Give a brief, general statement of the **additional** new material covered by the copyright claim for which registration is sought. In the case of a derivative work, identify this new material. Examples: "Recorded performances on bands 1 and 3"; "Remixed sounds from original multitrack sound sources"; "New words, arrangement, and additional sounds." If the work is a compilation, give a brief, general statement describing both the material that has been compiled **and** the compilation itself. Example: "Compilation of 1938 Recordings by various swing bands."

7,8,9 SPACE 7,8,9: Fee, Correspondence, Certification, Return Address

Fee: The Copyright Office has the authority to adjust fees at 5-year intervals, based on changes in the Consumer Price Index. The next adjustment is due in 1996. Please contact the Copyright Office after July 1995 to determine the actual fee schedule.

Deposit Account: If you maintain a Deposit Account in the Copyright Office, identify it in space 7. Otherwise leave the space blank and send the fee of $20 with your application and deposit.

Correspondence (space 7): This space should contain the name, address, area code, and telephone number of the person to be consulted if correspondence about this application become necessary.

Certification (space 8): This application cannot be accepted unless it bears the date and the **handwritten signature** of the author or other copyright claimant, or of the owner of exclusive right(s), or of the duly authorized agent of the author, claimant, or owner of exclusive right(s).

Address for Return of Certificate (space 9): The address box must be completed legibly since the certificate will be returned in a window envelope.

MORE INFORMATION

"Works": "Works" are the basic subject matter of copyright; they are what authors create and copyright protects. The statute draws a sharp distinction between the "work" and "any material object in which the work is embodied."

"Copies" and "Phonorecords": These are the two types of material objects in which "works" are embodied. In general, **"copies"** are objects from which a work can be read or visually perceived, directly or with the aid of a machine or device, such as manuscripts, books, sheet music, film, and videotape. **"Phonorecords"** are objects embodying fixations of sounds, such as audio tapes and phonograph disks. For example, a song (the "work") can be reproduced in sheet music ("copies") or phonograph disks ("phonorecords"), or both.

"Sound Recordings": These are "works," not "copies" or "phonorecords." "Sound recordings" are "works that result from the fixation of a series of musical, spoken, or other sounds, but not including the sounds accompanying a motion picture or other audiovisual work." Example: When a record company issues a new release, the release will typically involve two distinct "works": the "musical work" that has been recorded, and the "sound recording" as a separate work in itself. The material objects that the recorded company sends out are "phonorecords": physical reproductions of both the "musical work" and the "sound recording."

Should You File More Than One Application? If your work consists of a recorded musical, dramatic, or literary work and if both that "work" and the sound recording as a separate "work" are eligible for registration, the application form you should file depends on the following:

File Only Form SR if: The copyright claimant is the same for both the musical, dramatic, or literary work and for the sound recording, and you are seeking a single registration to cover both of these "works."

File Only Form PA (or Form TX) if: You are seeking to register only the musical, dramatic, or literary work, not the sound recording. Form PA is appropriate for works of the performing arts; Form TX is for nondramatic literary works.

Separate Applications Should Be Filed on Form PA (or Form TX) and on Form SR if: (1) The copyright claimant for the musical, dramatic, or literary work is different from the copyright claimant for the sound recording; or (2) You prefer to have separate registrations for the musical, dramatic, or literary work and for the sound recording.

FORM SR
For a Sound Recording
UNITED STATES COPYRIGHT OFFICE

REGISTRATION NUMBER

SR SRU

EFFECTIVE DATE OF REGISTRATION

Month Day Year

DO NOT WRITE ABOVE THIS LINE. IF YOU NEED MORE SPACE, USE A SEPARATE CONTINUATION SHEET.

1

TITLE OF THIS WORK ▼

PREVIOUS OR ALTERNATIVE TITLES ▼

NATURE OF MATERIAL RECORDED ▼ See instructions
☐ Musical ☐ Musical-Dramatic
☐ Dramatic ☐ Literary
☐ Other ______

2

a NAME OF AUTHOR ▼

DATES OF BIRTH AND DEATH
Year Born ▼ Year Died ▼

Was this contribution to the work a "work made for hire"?
☐ Yes
☐ No

AUTHOR'S NATIONALITY OR DOMICILE
Name of Country
OR { Citizen of ▶ ______
Domiciled in ▶ ______

WAS THIS AUTHOR'S CONTRIBUTION TO THE WORK
Anonymous? ☐ Yes ☐ No
Pseudonymous? ☐ Yes ☐ No
If the answer to either of these questions is "Yes," see detailed instructions.

NATURE OF AUTHORSHIP Briefly describe nature of material created by this author in which copyright is claimed. ▼

b NAME OF AUTHOR ▼

DATES OF BIRTH AND DEATH
Year Born ▼ Year Died ▼

Was this contribution to the work a "work made for hire"?
☐ Yes
☐ No

AUTHOR'S NATIONALITY OR DOMICILE
Name of Country
OR { Citizen of ▶ ______
Domiciled in ▶ ______

WAS THIS AUTHOR'S CONTRIBUTION TO THE WORK
Anonymous? ☐ Yes ☐ No
Pseudonymous? ☐ Yes ☐ No
If the answer to either of these questions is "Yes," see detailed instructions.

NATURE OF AUTHORSHIP Briefly describe nature of material created by this author in which copyright is claimed. ▼

c NAME OF AUTHOR ▼

DATES OF BIRTH AND DEATH
Year Born ▼ Year Died ▼

Was this contribution to the work a "work made for hire"?
☐ Yes
☐ No

AUTHOR'S NATIONALITY OR DOMICILE
Name of Country
OR { Citizen of ▶ ______
Domiciled in ▶ ______

WAS THIS AUTHOR'S CONTRIBUTION TO THE WORK
Anonymous? ☐ Yes ☐ No
Pseudonymous? ☐ Yes ☐ No
If the answer to either of these questions is "Yes," see detailed instructions.

NATURE OF AUTHORSHIP Briefly describe nature of material created by this author in which copyright is claimed. ▼

NOTE

Under the law, the "author" of a "work made for hire" is generally the employer, not the employee (see instructions). For any part of this work that was "made for hire," check "Yes" in the space provided, give the employer (or other person for whom the work was prepared) as "Author" of that part, and leave the space for dates of birth and death blank.

3

a YEAR IN WHICH CREATION OF THIS WORK WAS COMPLETED This information must be given in all cases.
______ ◀ Year

b DATE AND NATION OF FIRST PUBLICATION OF THIS PARTICULAR WORK
Complete this information ONLY if this work has been published.
Month ▶ ______ Day ▶ ______ Year ▶ ______
______ ◀ Nation

4

COPYRIGHT CLAIMANT(S) Name and address must be given even if the claimant is the same as the author given in space 2. ▼

See instructions before completing this space.

TRANSFER If the claimant(s) named here in space 4 is (are) different from the author(s) named in space 2, give a brief statement of how the claimant(s) obtained ownership of the copyright. ▼

DO NOT WRITE HERE OFFICE USE ONLY

APPLICATION RECEIVED

ONE DEPOSIT RECEIVED

TWO DEPOSITS RECEIVED

REMITTANCE NUMBER AND DATE

MORE ON BACK ▶ • Complete all applicable spaces (numbers 5-9) on the reverse side of this page.
• See detailed instructions. • Sign the form at line 8.

DO NOT WRITE HERE

Page 1 of ______ pages

EXAMINED BY

CHECKED BY

☐ CORRESPONDENCE Yes

FORM SR

FOR COPYRIGHT OFFICE USE ONLY

DO NOT WRITE ABOVE THIS LINE. IF YOU NEED MORE SPACE, USE A SEPARATE CONTINUATION SHEET.

5

PREVIOUS REGISTRATION Has registration for this work, or for an earlier version of this work, already been made in the Copyright Office?

☐ **Yes** ☐ **No** If your answer is "Yes," why is another registration being sought? (Check appropriate box) ▼

a. ☐ This is the first published edition of a work previously registered in unpublished form.

b. ☐ This is the first application submitted by this author as copyright claimant.

c. ☐ This is a changed version of the work, as shown by space 6 on this application.

If your answer is "Yes," give: **Previous Registration Number** ▼ **Year of Registration** ▼

6

DERIVATIVE WORK OR COMPILATION Complete both space 6a and 6b for a derivative work; complete only 6b for a compilation.

a. Preexisting Material Identify any preexisting work or works that this work is based on or incorporates. ▼

See instructions before completing this space.

b. Material Added to This Work Give a brief, general statement of the material that has been added to this work and in which copyright is claimed. ▼

7

DEPOSIT ACCOUNT If the registration fee is to be charged to a Deposit Account established in the Copyright Office, give name and number of Account.

Name ▼ **Account Number** ▼

CORRESPONDENCE Give name and address to which correspondence about this application should be sent. Name/Address/Apt/City/State/ZIP ▼

Area Code and Telephone Number ▶

Be sure to give your daytime phone ◀ number

8

CERTIFICATION* I, the undersigned, hereby certify that I am the

Check only one ▼

☐ author

☐ other copyright claimant

☐ owner of exclusive right(s)

☐ authorized agent of ______

Name of author or other copyright claimant, or owner of exclusive right(s) ▲

of the work identified in this application and that the statements made by me in this application are correct to the best of my knowledge.

Typed or printed name and date ▼ If this application gives a date of publication in space 3, do not sign and submit it before that date.

date ▶

Handwritten signature (X) ▼

9

MAIL CERTIFICATE TO

Name ▼

Number/Street/Apartment Number ▼

City/State/ZIP ▼

Certificate will be mailed in window envelope

YOU MUST:
- Complete all necessary spaces
- Sign your application in space 8

SEND ALL 3 ELEMENTS IN THE SAME PACKAGE:
1. Application form
2. Nonrefundable $20 filing fee in check or money order payable to *Register of Copyrights*
3. Deposit material

MAIL TO:
Register of Copyrights
Library of Congress
Washington, D.C. 20559

The Copyright Office has the authority to adjust fees at 5-year intervals, based on changes in the Consumer Price Index. The next adjustment is due in 1996. Please contact the Copyright Office after July 1995 to determine the actual fee schedule.

*17 U.S.C. § 506(e): Any person who knowingly makes a false representation of a material fact in the application for copyright registration provided for by section 409, or in any written statement filed in connection with the application, shall be fined not more than $2,500.

December 1993—75,000

☆U.S. GOVERNMENT PRINTING OFFICE: 1993-301-241/80,051

Filling Out Application Form VA

Detach and read these instructions before completing this form.
Make sure all applicable spaces have been filled in before you return this form.

BASIC INFORMATION

When to Use This Form: Use Form VA for copyright registration of published or unpublished works of the visual arts. This category consists of "pictorial, graphic, or sculptural works," including two-dimensional and three-dimensional works of fine, graphic, and applied art, photographs, prints and art reproductions, maps, globes, charts, technical drawings, diagrams, and models.

What Does Copyright Protect? Copyright in a work of the visual arts protects those pictorial, graphic, or sculptural elements that, either alone or in combination, represent an "original work of authorship." The statute declares: "In no case does copyright protection for an original work of authorship extend to any idea, procedure, process, system, method of operation, concept, principle, or discovery, regardless of the form in which it is described, explained, illustrated, or embodied in such work."

Works of Artistic Craftsmanship and Designs: "Works of artistic craftsmanship" are registrable on Form VA, but the statute makes clear that protection extends to "their form" and not to "their mechanical or utilitarian aspects." The "design of a useful article" is considered copyrightable "only if, and only to the extent that, such design incorporates pictorial, graphic, or sculptural features that can be identified separately from, and are capable of existing independently of, the utilitarian aspects of the article."

Labels and Advertisements: Works prepared for use in connection with the sale or advertisement of goods and services are registrable if they contain "original work of authorship." Use Form VA if the copyrightable material in the work you are registering is mainly pictorial or graphic; use Form TX if it consists mainly of text. NOTE: Words and short phrases such as names, titles, and slogans cannot be protected by copyright, and the same is true of standard symbols, emblems, and other commonly used graphic designs that are in the public domain. When used commercially, material of that sort can sometimes be protected under state laws of unfair competition or under the Federal trademark laws. For information about trademark registration, write to the Commissioner of Patents and Trademarks, Washington, D.C. 20231.

Architectural Works: Copyright protection extends to the design of buildings created for the use of human beings. Architectural works created on or after December 1, 1990, or that on December 1, 1990, were unconstructed and embodied only in unpublished plans or drawings are eligible. Request Circular 41 for more information.

Deposit to Accompany Application: An application for copyright registration must be accompanied by a deposit consisting of copies representing the entire work for which registration is to be made.

Unpublished Work: Deposit one complete copy.

Published Work: Deposit two complete copies of the best edition.

Work First Published Outside the United States: Deposit one complete copy of the first foreign edition.

Contribution to a Collective Work: Deposit one complete copy of the best edition of the collective work.

The Copyright Notice: For works first published on or after March 1, 1989, the law provides that a copyright notice in a specified form "may be placed on all publicly distributed copies from which the work can be visually perceived." Use of the copyright notice is the responsibility of the copyright owner and does not require advance permission from the Copyright Office. The required form of the notice for copies generally consists of three elements: (1) the symbol "©", or the word "Copyright," or the abbreviation "Copr."; (2) the year of first publication; and (3) the name of the owner of copyright. For example: "© 1995 Jane Cole." The notice is to be affixed to the copies "in such manner and location as to give reasonable notice of the claim of copyright." Works first published prior to March 1, 1989, must carry the notice or risk loss of copyright protection.

For information about notice requirements for works published before March 1, 1989, or other copyright information, write: Information Section, LM-401, Copyright Office, Library of Congress, Washington, D.C. 20559-6000.

LINE-BY-LINE INSTRUCTIONS

Please type or print using black ink.

1 SPACE 1: Title

Title of This Work: Every work submitted for copyright registration must be given a title to identify that particular work. If the copies of the work bear a title (or an identifying phrase that could serve as a title), transcribe that wording *completely* and *exactly* on the application. Indexing of the registration and future identification of the work will depend on the information you give here. For an architectural work that has been constructed, add the date of construction after the title; if unconstructed at this time, add "not yet constructed."

Previous or Alternative Titles: Complete this space if there are any additional titles for the work under which someone searching for the registration might be likely to look, or under which a document pertaining to the work might be recorded.

Publication as a Contribution: If the work being registered is a contribution to a periodical, serial, or collection, give the title of the contribution in the "Title of This Work" space. Then, in the line headed "Publication as a Contribution," give information about the collective work in which the contribution appeared.

Nature of This Work: Briefly describe the general nature or character of the pictorial, graphic, or sculptural work being registered for copyright. Examples: "Oil Painting"; "Charcoal Drawing"; "Etching"; "Sculpture"; "Map"; "Photograph"; "Scale Model"; "Lithographic Print"; "Jewelry Design"; "Fabric Design."

2 SPACE 2: Author(s)

General Instruction: After reading these instructions, decide who are the "authors" of this work for copyright purposes. Then, unless the work is a "collective work," give the requested information about every "author" who contributed any appreciable amount of copyrightable matter to this version of the work. If you need further space, request Continuation Sheets. In the case of a collective work, such as a catalog of paintings or collection of cartoons by various authors, give information about the author of the collective work as a whole.

Name of Author: The fullest form of the author's name should be given. Unless the work was "made for hire," the individual who actually created the work is its "author." In the case of a work made for hire, the statute provides that "the employer or other person for whom the work was prepared is considered the author."

What is a "Work Made for Hire"? A "work made for hire" is defined as: (1) "a work prepared by an employee within the scope of his or her employment"; or (2) "a work specially ordered or commissioned for use as a contribution to a collective work, as a part of a motion picture or other audiovisual work, as a translation, as a supplementary work, as a compilation, as an instructional text, as a test, as answer material for a test, or as an atlas, if the parties expressly agree in a written instrument signed by them that the work shall be considered a work made for hire." If you have checked "Yes" to indicate that the work was "made for hire," you must give the full legal name of the employer (or other person for whom the work was prepared). You may also include the name of the employee along with the name of the employer (for example: "Elster Publishing Co., employer for hire of John Ferguson").

"Anonymous" or "Pseudonymous" Work: An author's contribution to a work is "anonymous" if that author is not identified on the copies or phonorecords of the work. An author's contribution to a work is "pseudonymous" if that author is identified on the copies or phonorecords under a fictitious name. If the work is "anonymous" you may: (1) leave the line blank; or (2) state "anonymous" on the line; or (3) reveal the author's identity. If the work is "pseudonymous" you may: (1) leave the line blank; or (2) give the pseudonym and identify it as such (for example: "Huntley Haverstock, pseudonym"); or (3) reveal the author's name, making clear which is the real name and which is the pseudonym (for example: "Henry Leek, whose pseudonym is Priam Farrel"). However, the citizenship or domicile of the author **must** be given in all cases.

Dates of Birth and Death: If the author is dead, the statute requires that the year of death be included in the application unless the work is anonymous or pseudonymous. The author's birth date is optional but is useful as a form of identification. Leave this space blank if the author's contribution was a "work made for hire."

Author's Nationality or Domicile: Give the country of which the author is a citizen or the country in which the author is domiciled. Nationality or domicile **must** be given in all cases.

Nature of Authorship: Catagories of pictorial, graphic, and sculptural authorship are listed below. Check the box(es) that best describe(s) each author's contribution to the work.

3-Dimensional sculptures: fine art sculptures, toys, dolls, scale models, and sculptural designs applied to useful articles.

2-Dimensional artwork: watercolor and oil paintings; pen and ink drawings; logo illustrations; greeting cards; collages; stencils; patterns; computer graphics; graphics appearing in screen displays; artwork appearing on posters, calendars, games, commercial prints and labels, and packaging, as well as 2-dimensional artwork applied to useful articles.

Reproductions of works of art: reproductions of preexisting artwork made by, for example, lithography, photoengraving, or etching.

Maps: cartographic representations of an area such as state and county maps, atlases, marine charts, relief maps, and globes.

Photographs: pictorial photographic prints and slides and holograms.

Jewelry designs: 3-dimensional designs applied to rings, pendants, earrings, necklaces, and the like.

Designs on sheetlike materials: designs reproduced on textiles, lace, and other fabrics; wallpaper; carpeting; floor tile; wrapping paper; and clothing.

Technical drawings: diagrams illustrating scientific or technical information in linear form such as architectural blueprints or mechanical drawings.

Text: textual material that accompanies pictorial, graphic, or sculptural works such as comic strips, greeting cards, games rules, commercial prints or labels, and maps.

Architectural works: designs of buildings, including the overall form as well as the arrangement and composition of spaces and elements of the design. NOTE: Any registration for the underlying architectural plans must be applied for on a separate Form VA, checking the box "Technical drawing."

3 SPACE 3: Creation and Publication

General Instructions: Do not confuse "creation" with "publication." Every application for copyright registration must state "the year in which creation of the work was completed." Give the date and nation of first publication only if the work has been published.

Creation: Under the statute, a work is "created" when it is fixed in a copy or phonorecord for the first time. Where a work has been prepared over a period of time, the part of the work existing in fixed form on a particular date constitutes the created work on that date. The date you give here should be the year in which the author completed the particular version for which registration is now being sought, even if other versions exist or if further changes or additions are planned.

Publication: The statute defines "publication" as "the distribution of copies or phonorecords of a work to the public by sale or other transfer of ownership, or by rental, lease, or lending"; a work is also "published" if there has been an "offering to distribute copies or phonorecords to a group of persons for purposes of further distribution, public performance, or public display." Give the full date (month, day, year) when, and the country where, publication first occurred. If first publication took place simultaneously in the United States and other countries, it is sufficient to state "U.S.A."

4 SPACE 4: Claimant(s)

Name(s) and Address(es) of Copyright Claimant(s): Give the name(s) and address(es) of the copyright claimant(s) in this work even if the claimant is the same as the author. Copyright in a work belongs initially to the author of the work (including, in the case of a work make for hire, the employer or other person for whom the work was prepared). The copyright claimant is either the author of the work or a person or organization to whom the copyright initially belonging to the author has been transferred.

Transfer: The statute provides that, if the copyright claimant is not the author, the application for registration must contain "a brief statement of how the claimant obtained ownership of the copyright." If any copyright claimant named in space 4 is not an author named in space 2, give a brief statement explaining how the claimant(s) obtained ownership of the copyright. Examples: "By written contract"; "Transfer of all rights by author"; "Assignment"; "By will." Do not attach transfer documents or other attachments or riders.

5 SPACE 5: Previous Registration

General Instructions: The questions in space 5 are intended to find out whether an earlier registration has been made for this work and, if so, whether there is any basis for a new registration. As a rule, only one basic copyright registration can be made for the same version of a particular work.

Same Version: If this version is substantially the same as the work covered by a previous registration, a second registration is not generally possible unless: (1) the work has been registered in unpublished form and a second registration is now being sought to cover this first published edition; or (2) someone other than the author is identified as a copyright claimant in the earlier registration, and the author is now seeking registration in his or her own name. If either of these two exceptions apply, check the appropriate box and give the earlier registration number and date. Otherwise, do not submit Form VA; instead, write the Copyright Office for information about supplementary registration or recordation of transfers of copyright ownership.

Changed Version: If the work has been changed and you are now seeking registration to cover the additions or revisions, check the last box in space 5, give the earlier registration number and date, and complete both parts of space 6 in accordance with the instruction below.

Previous Registration Number and Date: If more than one previous registration has been made for the work, give the number and date of the latest registration.

6 SPACE 6: Derivative Work or Compilation

General Instructions: Complete space 6 if this work is a "changed version," "compilation," or "derivative work," and if it incorporates one or more earlier works that have already been published or registered for copyright, or that have fallen into the public domain. A "compilation" is defined as "a work formed by the collection and assembling of preexisting materials or of data that are selected, coordinated, or arranged in such a way that the resulting work as a whole constitutes an original work of authorship." A "derivative work" is "a work based on one or more preexisting works." Examples of derivative works include reproductions of works of art, sculptures based on drawings, lithographs based on paintings, maps based on previously published sources, or "any other form in which a work may be recast, transformed, or adapted." Derivative works also include works "consisting of editorial revisions, annotations, or other modifications" if these changes, as a whole, represent an original work of authorship.

Preexisting Material (space 6a): Complete this space and space 6b for derivative works. In this space identify the preexisting work that has been recast, transformed, or adapted. Examples of preexisting material might be "Grunewald Altarpiece" or "19th century quilt design." Do not complete this space for compilations.

Material Added to This Work (space 6b): Give a brief, general statement of the additional new material covered by the copyright claim for which registration is sought. In the case of a derivative work, identify this new material. Examples: "Adaptation of design and additional artistic work"; "Reproduction of painting by photolithography"; "Additional cartographic material"; "Compilation of photographs." If the work is a compilation, give a brief, general statement describing both the material that has been compiled and the compilation itself. Example: "Compilation of 19th century political cartoons."

7,8,9 SPACE 7,8,9: Fee, Correspondence, Certification, Return Address

Deposit Account: If you maintain a Deposit Account in the Copyright Office, identify it in space 7. Otherwise leave the space blank and send the fee of $20 with your application and deposit.

Correspondence (space 7): This space should contain the name, address, area code, and telephone number of the person to be consulted if correspondence about this application becomes necessary.

Certification (space 8): The application cannot be accepted unless it bears the date and the **handwritten signature** of the author or other copyright claimant, or of the owner of exclusive right(s), or of the duly authorized agent of the author, claimant, or owner of exclusive right(s).

Address for Return of Certificate (space 9): The address box must be completed legibly since the certificate will be returned in a window envelope.

PRIVACY ACT ADVISORY STATEMENT Required by the Privacy Act of 1974 (P.L. 93 - 579)
The authority for requesting this information is title 17, U.S.C., secs. 409 and 410. Furnishing the requested information is voluntary. But if the information is not furnished, it may be necessary to delay or refuse registration and you may not be entitled to certain relief, remedies, and benefits provided in chapters 4 and 5 of title 17, U.S.C.
The principal uses of the requested information are the establishment and maintenance of a public record and the examination of the application for compliance with legal requirements.
Other routine uses include public inspection and copying, preparation of public indexes, preparation of public catalogs of copyright registrations, and preparation of search reports upon request.
NOTE: No other advisory statement will be given in connection with this application. Please keep this statement and refer to it if we communicate with you regarding this application.

FORM VA

For a Work of the Visual Arts
UNITED STATES COPYRIGHT OFFICE

REGISTRATION NUMBER

VA VAU

EFFECTIVE DATE OF REGISTRATION

Month Day Year

DO NOT WRITE ABOVE THIS LINE. IF YOU NEED MORE SPACE, USE A SEPARATE CONTINUATION SHEET.

1

TITLE OF THIS WORK ▼

NATURE OF THIS WORK ▼ See instructions

PREVIOUS OR ALTERNATIVE TITLES ▼

PUBLICATION AS A CONTRIBUTION If this work was published as a contribution to a periodical, serial, or collection, give information about the collective work in which the contribution appeared. **Title of Collective Work ▼**

If published in a periodical or serial give: **Volume ▼** **Number ▼** **Issue Date ▼** **On Pages ▼**

2

a **NAME OF AUTHOR ▼**

DATES OF BIRTH AND DEATH
Year Born ▼ Year Died ▼

Was this contribution to the work a "work made for hire"?
☐ Yes
☐ No

AUTHOR'S NATIONALITY OR DOMICILE
Name of Country
OR { Citizen of ▶ ____
Domiciled in ▶ ____

WAS THIS AUTHOR'S CONTRIBUTION TO THE WORK
Anonymous? ☐ Yes ☐ No
Pseudonymous? ☐ Yes ☐ No
If the answer to either of these questions is "Yes," see detailed instructions.

NATURE OF AUTHORSHIP Check appropriate box(es). **See instructions**
☐ 3-Dimensional sculpture ☐ Map ☐ Technical drawing
☐ 2-Dimensional artwork ☐ Photograph ☐ Text
☐ Reproduction of work of art ☐ Jewelry design ☐ Architectural work
☐ Design on sheetlike material

NOTE

Under the law, the "author" of a "work made for hire" is generally the employer, not the employee (see instructions). For any part of this work that was "made for hire" check "Yes" in the space provided, give the employer (or other person for whom the work was prepared) as "Author" of that part, and leave the space for dates of birth and death blank.

b **NAME OF AUTHOR ▼**

DATES OF BIRTH AND DEATH
Year Born ▼ Year Died ▼

Was this contribution to the work a "work made for hire"?
☐ Yes
☐ No

AUTHOR'S NATIONALITY OR DOMICILE
Name of Country
OR { Citizen of ▶ ____
Domiciled in ▶ ____

WAS THIS AUTHOR'S CONTRIBUTION TO THE WORK
Anonymous? ☐ Yes ☐ No
Pseudonymous? ☐ Yes ☐ No
If the answer to either of these questions is "Yes," see detailed instructions.

NATURE OF AUTHORSHIP Check appropriate box(es). **See instructions**
☐ 3-Dimensional sculpture ☐ Map ☐ Technical drawing
☐ 2-Dimensional artwork ☐ Photograph ☐ Text
☐ Reproduction of work of art ☐ Jewelry design ☐ Architectural work
☐ Design on sheetlike material

3

a **YEAR IN WHICH CREATION OF THIS WORK WAS COMPLETED** This information must be given in all cases. ◀ Year

b **DATE AND NATION OF FIRST PUBLICATION OF THIS PARTICULAR WORK** Complete this information ONLY if this work has been published. Month ▶ ____ Day ▶ ____ Year ▶ ____ ◀ Nation

4

See instructions before completing this space.

COPYRIGHT CLAIMANT(S) Name and address must be given even if the claimant is the same as the author given in space 2. ▼

TRANSFER If the claimant(s) named here in space 4 is (are) different from the author(s) named in space 2, give a brief statement of how the claimant(s) obtained ownership of the copyright. ▼

DO NOT WRITE HERE
OFFICE USE ONLY

APPLICATION RECEIVED

ONE DEPOSIT RECEIVED

TWO DEPOSITS RECEIVED

FUNDS RECEIVED

MORE ON BACK ▶ • Complete all applicable spaces (numbers 5-9) on the reverse side of this page.
• See detailed instructions. • Sign the form at line 8.

DO NOT WRITE HERE

Page 1 of ____ pages

EXAMINED BY

FORM VA

CHECKED BY

☐ CORRESPONDENCE
Yes

FOR COPYRIGHT OFFICE USE ONLY

DO NOT WRITE ABOVE THIS LINE. IF YOU NEED MORE SPACE, USE A SEPARATE CONTINUATION SHEET.

5

PREVIOUS REGISTRATION Has registration for this work, or for an earlier version of this work, already been made in the Copyright Office?

☐ **Yes** ☐ **No** If your answer is "Yes," why is another registration being sought? (Check appropriate box) ▼

a. ☐ This is the first published edition of a work previously registered in unpublished form.

b. ☐ This is the first application submitted by this author as copyright claimant.

c. ☐ This is a changed version of the work, as shown by space 6 on this application.

If your answer is "Yes," give: **Previous Registration Number** ▼ **Year of Registration** ▼

6

DERIVATIVE WORK OR COMPILATION Complete both space 6a and 6b for a derivative work; complete only 6b for a compilation.

a. Preexisting Material Identify any preexisting work or works that this work is based on or incorporates. ▼

See instructions before completing this space.

b. Material Added to This Work Give a brief, general statement of the material that has been added to this work and in which copyright is claimed. ▼

7

DEPOSIT ACCOUNT If the registration fee is to be charged to a Deposit Account established in the Copyright Office, give name and number of Account.

Name ▼ **Account Number** ▼

CORRESPONDENCE Give name and address to which correspondence about this application should be sent. Name/Address/Apt/City/State/ZIP ▼

Area Code and Telephone Number ▶

Be sure to give your daytime phone ◀ number

8

CERTIFICATION* I, the undersigned, hereby certify that I am the

check only one ▼

☐ author

☐ other copyright claimant

☐ owner of exclusive right(s)

☐ authorized agent of ______________________

Name of author or other copyright claimant, or owner of exclusive right(s) ▲

of the work identified in this application and that the statements made by me in this application are correct to the best of my knowledge.

Typed or printed name and date ▼ If this application gives a date of publication in space 3, do not sign and submit it before that date.

Date▶

Handwritten signature (X) ▼

9

Mail certificate to:

Certificate will be mailed in window envelope

Name ▼

Number/Street/Apt ▼

City/State/ZIP ▼

YOU MUST:
- Complete all necessary spaces
- Sign your application in space 8

SEND ALL 3 ELEMENTS IN THE SAME PACKAGE:
1. Application form
2. Nonrefundable $20 filing fee in check or money order payable to *Register of Copyrights*
3. Deposit material

MAIL TO:
Register of Copyrights
Library of Congress
Washington, D.C. 20559-6000

*17 U.S.C. § 506(e): Any person who knowingly makes a false representation of a material fact in the application for copyright registration provided for by section 409, or in any written statement filed in connection with the application, shall be fined not more than $2,500.

March 1995—300,000 PRINTED ON RECYCLED PAPER

☆U.S. GOVERNMENT PRINTING OFFICE: 1995-387-237/41

TRADEMARK/SERVICE MARK APPLICATION, PRINCIPAL REGISTER, WITH DECLARATION	MARK (Word(s) and/or Design)	CLASS NO. (If known)

TO THE ASSISTANT COMMISSIONER FOR TRADEMARKS:

APPLICANT'S NAME:

APPLICANT'S BUSINESS ADDRESS: ______

(Display address exactly as it should appear on registration)

APPLICANT'S ENTITY TYPE: (Check one and supply requested information)

	Individual - Citizen of (Country):
	Partnership - State where organized (Country, if appropriate): ______ Names and Citizenship (Country) of General Partners: ______
	Corporation - State (Country, if appropriate) of Incorporation:
	Other (Specific Nature of Entity and Domicile):

GOODS AND/OR SERVICES:

Applicant requests registration of the trademark/service mark shown in the accompanying drawing in the United States Patent and Trademark Office on the Principal Register established by the Act of July 5, 1946 (15 U.S.C. 1051 et. seq., as amended) for the following goods/services (**SPECIFIC GOODS AND/OR SERVICES MUST BE INSERTED HERE**):

______

BASIS FOR APPLICATION: (Check boxes which apply, but never both the first AND second boxes, and supply requested information related to each box checked.)

[ ] Applicant is using mark in commerce on or in connection with the above identified goods/services. (15 U.S.C. 1051(a), as amended.) Three specimens showing the mark as used in commerce are submitted with this application.
- Date of first use of the mark in commerce which the U.S. Congress may regulate (for example, interstate or between the U.S. and a foreign country): ______
- Specify the type of commerce: ______
  (for example, interstate or between the U.S. and a specified foreign country)
- Date of first use anywhere (the same as or before use in commerce date): ______
- Specify intended manner or mode of use of mark on or in connection with the goods/services: ______
  (for example, trademark is applied to labels, service mark is used in advertisements)

[ ] Applicant has a bona fide intention to use the mark in commerce on or in connection with the above identified goods/services. (15 U.S.C. 1051(b), as amended.)
- Specify manner or mode of use of mark on or in connection with the goods/services: ______
  (for example, trademark will be applied to labels, service mark will be used in advertisements)

[ ] Applicant has a bona fide intention to use the mark in commerce on or in connection with the above identified goods/services and asserts a claim of priority based upon a foreign application in accordance with 15 U.S.C. 1126(d), as amended.
- Country of foreign filing: ______
- Date of foreign filing: ______

[ ] Applicant has a bona fide intention to use the mark in commerce or in connection with the above identified goods/services, and, accompanying this application, submits a certification or certified copy of a foreign registration in accordance with 15 U.S.C 1126(e), as amended.
- Country of registration: ______
- Registration number: ______

NOTE: Declaration, on Reverse Side, MUST be Signed

PTO Form 1478 (REV 10/94)
OMB No. 0651-0009 (Exp. 6/30/95)

U.S. DEPARTMENT OF COMMERCE/Patent and Trademark Office

If submitted on one page, side two of the form should be Upside Down" in relation to page 1.

DECLARATION

The undersigned being hereby warned that willful false statements and the like so made are punishable by fine or imprisonment, or both, under 18 U.S.C. 1001, and that such willful false statements may jeopardize the validity of the application or any resulting registration, declares that he/she is properly authorized to execute this application this application on behalf of the applicant; he/she believes the applicant to be owner of the trademark/service mark sought to be registered, or if the application is being files under 15 U.S.C. 1051(b), he/she believes applicant to be entitled to use such mark in commerce; to the best of his/her knowledge and belief no other person, firm, corporation, or association has the right to use the above identified mark in commerce, either in the identical form thereof or in such near resemblance thereto as to be likely, when used on or in connection with the goods/services of such other person, to cause confusion, or to cause mistake, or to deceive; and that all statements made of his/her own knowledge are true and that all statements made on information and belief are believed to be true.

____________________ DATE	____________________ SIGNATURE
____________________ TELEPHONE NUMBER	____________________ PRINT OR TYPE NAME

INSTRUCTIONS AND INFORMATION FOR APPLICANT

TO RECEIVE A FILING DATE, THE APPLICATION MUST BE COMPLETED AND SIGNED BY THE APPLICANT AND SUBMITTED ALONG WITH:

1. The prescribed **FEE of $245.00*** for each class of goods/services listed in the application;
2. A **DRAWING PAGE** displaying the mark in conformance with 37 CFR 2.52;
3. If the application is based on use of the mark in commerce, **THREE (3) SPECIMENS** (evidence) of the mark as used in commerce for each class of goods/services listed in the application. All three specimens may be in the nature of: (a) labels showing the mark which are placed on the goods; (b) photographs of the mark as it appears on the goods, (c) brochures or advertisements showing the mark as used in connection with the services.
4. An **APPLICATION WITH DECLARATION** (this form) - The application must be signed in order for the application to receive a filing date. Only the following person may sign the declaration, depending on the applicant's legal entity: (a) the individual applicant; (b) an officer of the corporate applicant; (c) one general partner of a partnership applicant; (d) all joint applicants.

SEND APPLICATION FORM, DRAWING PAGE, FEE AND SPECIMENS (IF APPROPRIATE) TO:

Assistant Commissioner for Trademarks
Box New App / Fee
2900 Crystal Drive
Arlington, VA 22202-3513

Additional information concerning the requirements for filing an application is available in a booklet entitled **Basic Facts About Registering a Trademark,** which may be obtained by writing to the above address or by calling: (703) 308-9000.

* Fees are subject to change; changes usually take effect on October 1. If filing on or after October 1, 1995, please call the PTO to confirm the correct fee.

This form is estimated to take an average of 1 hour to complete, including time required for reading and understanding instructions, gathering necessary information, recordkeeping, and actually providing the information. Any comments on this form, including the amount of time required to complete this form, should be sent to the Office of Management and Organizations, U.S. Patent and Trademark Office, U.S. Department of Commerce, Washington, D.C. 20231, and Paper Reduction Project 0651-0009, Office of Information and Regulatory Affairs, Office of Management and Budget, Washington, D.C. 20503. Do NOT send completed forms to either of these addresses.

International schedule of classes of goods and services

Goods

1 Chemicals used in industry, science and photography, as well as in agriculture, horticulture and forestry; unprocessed artificial resins, unprocessed plastics; manures; fire extinguishing compositions; tempering and soldering preparations; chemical substances for preserving foodstuffs; tanning substances; adhesives used in industry.

2 Paints, varnishes, lacquers; preservatives against rust and against deterioration of wood; colorants; mordants; raw natural resins; metals in foil and powder form for painters, decorators, printers and artists.

3 Bleaching preparations and other substances for laundry use; cleaning polishing, scouring and abrasive preparations; soaps; perfumery, essential oils, cosmetics, hair lotions; dentifrices.

4 Industrial oils and greases; lubricants; dust absorbing, wetting and binding compositions; fuels (including motor spirit) and illuminants; candles, wicks.

5 Pharmaceutical, veterinary and sanitary preparations; dietetic substances adapted for medical use, food for babies; plasters, materials for dressings; material for stopping teeth, dental wax; disinfectants; preparations for destroying vermin; fungicides, herbicides.

6 Common metals and their alloys; metal building materials; transportable buildings of metal; materials of metal for railway tracks; non-electric cables and wires of common metal; ironmongery, small items of metal hardware; pipes and tubes of metal; safes; goods of common metal not included in other classes; ores.

7 Machines and machine tools; motors and engines (except for land vehicles); machine coupling and transmission components (except for land vehicles); agricultural implements; incubators for eggs.

8 Hand tools and implements (hand operated); cutlery; side arms; razors.

9 Scientific, nautical, surveying, electric, photographic, cinematographic, optical, weighing, measuring, signalling, checking (supervision), life-saving and teaching apparatus and instruments; apparatus for recording, transmission or reproduction of sound or images; magnetic data carriers, recording discs; automatic vending machines and mechanisms for coin operated apparatus; cash registers, calculating machines, data processing equipment and computers; fire-extinguishing apparatus.

10 Surgical, medical, dental and veterinary apparatus and instruments, artificial limbs, eyes and teeth; orthopedic articles; suture materials.

11 Apparatus for lighting, heating, steam generating, cooking, refrigerating, drying, ventilating, water supply and sanitary purposes.

12 Vehicles; apparatus for locomotion by land, air or water.

13 Firearms; ammunition and projectiles; explosives; fireworks.

14 Precious metals and their alloys and goods in precious metals or coated therewith, not included in other classes; jewellery, precious stones; horological and chronometric instruments.

15 Musical instruments.

16 Paper, cardboard and goods made from these materials, not included in other classes; printed matter; bookbinding material; photographs; stationery; adhesives for stationery or household purposes; artists' materials; paint brushes; typewriters and office requisites (except furniture); instructional and teaching material (except apparatus); playing cards; printers' type; printing blocks.

17 Rubber, gutta-percha, gum asbestos, mica and goods made from these materials and not included in other classes; plastics in extruded form for use in manufacture; packing, stopping and insulating materials; flexible pipes, not of metal.

18 Leather and imitations of leather, and goods made of these materials and not included in other classes; animal skins, hides; trunks and travelling bags; umbrellas, parasols and walking sticks; whips, harness and saddlery.

19 Building materials (non-metallic); non-metallic rigid pipes for building; asphalt, pitch and bitumen; non-metallic transportable buildings; monuments, not of metal.

20 Furniture, mirrors, picture frames; goods (not included in other classes) of wood, cork, reed, cane, wicker, horn, bone, ivory, whalebone, shell, amber, mother-of-pearl, meerschaum and substitutes for all these materials, or of plastics

21 Household or kitchen utensils and containers (not of precious metal or coated therewith); combs and sponges; brushes (except paint brushes); brush-making materials; articles for cleaning purposes; steelwool; unworked or semi-worked glass (except glass used in building); glassware, porcelain and earthenware not included in other classes.

22 Ropes, string, nets, tents, awnings, tarpaulins, sails, sacks and bags (not included in other classes); padding and stuffing materials (except of rubber or plastics); raw fibrous textile materials.

23 Yarns and threads, for textile use.

24 Textiles and textile goods, not included in other classes; bed and table covers.

25 Clothing, footwear, headgear.

26 Lace and embroidery, ribbons and braid; buttons, hooks and eyes, pins and needles; artificial flowers.

27 Carpets, rugs, mates and matting, linoleum and other materials for covering existing floors; wall hangings (non-textile).

28 Games and playthings; gymnastic and sporting articles not included in other classes; decorations for Christmas trees.

29 Meat, fish, poultry and game; meat extracts; preserved, dried and cooked fruits and vegetables; jellies, james, fruit sauces; eggs, milk and milk products; edible oils and fats.

30 Coffee, tea, cocoa, sugar, rice, tapioca, sago, artificial coffee; flour and preparations made from cereals, bread, pastry and confectionery, honey, treacle; yeast, baking-powder; salt, mustard; vinegar, sauces (condiments); spices; ice.

31 Agricultural, horticultural and forestry products and grains not included in other classes; live animals; fresh fruits and vegetables; seeds, natural plants and flowers; foodstuffs for animals, malt.

32 Beers; mineral and aerated waters and other non-alcoholic drinks; fruit drinks and fruit juices; syrups and other preparations for making beverages.

33 Alcoholic beverages (except beers).

34 Tobacco; smokers' articles; matches.

Services

35 Advertising; business management; business administration; office functions.

36 Insurance; financial affairs; monetary affairs; real estate affairs.

37 Building construction; repair; installation services.

38 Telecommunications.

39 Transport; packaging and storage of goods; travel arrangement.

40 Treatment of materials.

41 Education; providing of training; entertainment; sporting and cultural activities.

42 Providing of food and drink; temporary accommodation; medical, hygienic and beauty care; veterinary and agricultural services; legal services; scientific and industrial research; computer programming; services that cannot be placed in other classes.

STATE OF ILLINOIS
TRADE-MARK OR SERVICE MARK APPLICATION
Complete and Return with $10 fee

1. Name of Applicant ______________________________

2. Address ______________________________
Street
____
City State Zip Code

3. State whether applicant is an individual, partnership, corporation, union or association: ______________

4. If a corporation, what is state of incorporation? ______________________________

5. Name or description of mark ______________________________
____
____

6. Describe the specific goods or services in connection with which mark is used ______________
____

7. Class No. ______________ *(one classification number only)*

8. (a) If a trade-mark, check how the mark is used. By applying it: directly to the goods ______, directly to the containers for the goods ______, to tags or labels affixed to the goods ______, to tags or labels affixed to the containers for the goods ______, or by displaying it: in physical association with the goods in the sale or distribution thereof ______.
(b) If a service mark, by displaying it: in advertisements of the service ______, on documents, wrappers, or articles delivered in connection with the service rendered ______, in other fashion ______, if so, *(Specify)*: ______________

9. Date of first use of mark by applicant or predecessor. Mark must be used prior to registration. *(If first use of mark was in Illinois use same date in both (a) and (b))*
(a) Anywhere ______________________________
(b) In Illinois ______________________________

10. If either of the above first uses was by a predecessor of applicant, state which use or uses were by a predecessor and identify predecessor ______________________________

Applicant hereby appoints the Secretary of State of Illinois as agent for service of process in any action relating only to the registration which may be issued pursuant to this application, if the applicant be, or shall become, a non-resident individual, partnership, or association, or foreign corporation not licensed to do business in this State, or cannot be found in this State.

X ______________________________
Signature of Applicant

STATE OF ______________ }
 } ss.
COUNTY OF ______________ }

____
Official Capacity

______________, being duly sworn, deposes and says that he is ______________ ______________ the above named applicant, that the statements contained in the foregoing statement are true and that he verily believes that said applicant is the owner of the mark sought to be registered and that no other person has the right in the State of Illinois to use such mark either in the identical form thereof, or in such near resemblance thereto, as to be likely, when applied to the goods or services of such person, to cause confusion or to cause mistake or to deceive.

X ______________________________
Signature of Applicant

SUBSCRIBED to before me this ______ day of ______________, 19 ______

(SEAL)

____
Notary Public

NOTE

The application must be accompanied by three specimens or facsimiles of the mark and by a filing fee of $10.00 payable to the Secretary of State. Staple or clip specimens or facsimiles to application. DO NOT GLUE. In a few instances, for example, where the mark is a word spoken over radio, no specimens are possible. In such event, explain the absence of specimens in connection with your answer to paragraph 5.

Specimens larger than 3" x 3" will not be accepted. If the specimens are larger than that, send facsimiles such as photostats reduced in size of the actual specimens.

Send a separate check for each application. This will prevent return of multiple applications for correction.

The following general classes of goods and services are established for convenience of administration of this Act but not to limit or extend the applicant's or registrant's rights. A single application for registration of a mark may include any or all goods or services upon which the mark is actually being used and which are comprised in a single class. In no event shall a single application include goods or services upon which the mark is being used and which fall within different classes.

CLASSIFICATION OF GOODS FOR TRADE-MARKS

(1) Raw or partly prepared materials. (2) Receptacles. (3) Baggage, animal equipments, portfolios, and pocketbooks. (4) Abrasives and polishing materials. (5) Adhesives. (6) Chemicals and chemical compositions. (7) Cordage. (8) Smoker's articles, not including tobacco products. (9) Explosives, firearms, equipments and projectiles. (10) Fertilizers. (11) Inks and inking materials. (12) Construction materials. (13) Hardware and plumbing and steam-fitting supplies. (14) Metals and metal castings and forgings. (15) Oils and greases. (16) Protective and decorative coatings. (17) Tobacco products. (18) Medicines and pharmaceutical preparations. (19) Vehicles. (20) Linoleum and oiled cloth. (21) Electrical apparatus, machines, and supplies. (22) Games, toys and sporting goods. (23) Cutlery, machinery, and tools, and parts thereof. (24) Laundry appliances and machines. (25) Locks and safes. (26) Measuring and scientific appliances. (27) Horological instruments. (28) Jewelry and precious-metal ware. (29) Brooms, brushes, and dusters. (30) Crockery, earthenware, and porcelain. (31) Filters and refrigerators. (32) Furniture and upholstery. (33) Glassware. (34) Heating, lighting, and ventilating apparatus. (35) Belting, hose, machinery packing, and non-metallic tires. (36) Musical instruments and supplies. (37) Paper and stationery. (38) Printing and publications. (39) Clothing. (40) Fancy goods, furnishings, and notions. (41) Canes, parasols, and umbrellas. (42) Knitted, netted and textile fabrics, and substitutes therefor. (43) Thread and yarn. (44) Dental, medical, and surgical appliances. (45) Soft drinks and carbonated waters. (46) Foods and ingredients of foods. (47) Wines. (48) Malt beverages and liquors. (49) Distilled alcoholic liquors. (50) Merchandise not otherwise classified. (51) Cosmetics and toilet preparations. (52) Detergents and soaps.

CLASSIFICATION OF SERVICES FOR SERVICE MARKS

(100) Miscellaneous. (101) Advertising and business. (102) Insurance and financial. (103) Construction and repair. (104) Communication. (105) Transportation and storage. (106) Material treatment. (107) Education and entertainment.

The Secretary of State will fill in the answer to this question *(#7)* if no answer is given, and has the right to change the classification if that furnished by applicant is not correct. ***Each classification requires a separate application, set of three specimens and fee.***

APPLICATION FOR REGISTRATION OF TRADE-MARK OR SERVICE MARK

Filed by

Secretary of State's Office
Department of Business Services Trademarks
Room 328, Centennial Building
Springfield, Illinois 62756
(217) 524-0400

FEE

For filing $10.00

C-246

DECLARATION FOR PATENT APPLICATION Docket No. ____________

As a below named inventor, I hereby declare that:

My residence, post office address and citizenship are as stated below next to my name.

I believe I am the original, first and sole inventor (if only one name is listed below) or an original, first and joint inventor (if plural names are listed below) of the subject matter which is claimed and for which a patent is sought on the invention entitled ________________________________, the specification of which

(check one) ☐ is attached hereto.
☐ was filed on ________________________________ as
Application Serial No. ________________________________
and was amended on ________________________________ (if applicable).

I hereby state that I have reviewed and understand the contents of the above identified specification, including the claims, as amended by any amendment referred to above.

I acknowledge the duty to disclose information which is material to the examination of this application in accordance with Title 37, Code of Federal Regulations, §1.56(a).

I hereby claim foreign priority benefits under Title 35, United States Code, §119 of any foreign application(s) for patent or inventor's certificate listed below and have also identified below any foreign application for patent or inventor's certificate having a filing date before that of the application on which priority is claimed:

Prior Foreign Application(s) Priority Claimed

(Number)	(Country)	(Day/Month/Year Filed)	Yes	No
(Number)	(Country)	(Day/Month/Year Filed)	Yes	No
(Number)	(Country)	(Day/Month/Year Filed)	Yes	No

I hereby claim the benefit under Title 35, United States Code, §120 of any United States application(s) listed below and, insofar as the subject matter of each of the claims of this application is not disclosed in the prior United States application in the manner provided by the first paragraph of Title 35, United States Code, §112, I acknowledge the duty to disclose material information as defined in Title 37, Code of Federal Regulations, §1.56(a) which occurred between the filing date of the prior application and the national or PCT international filing date of this application:

(Application Serial No.)	(Filing Date)	(Status—patented, pending, abandoned)
(Application Serial No.)	(Filing Date)	(Status—patented, pending, abandoned)

I hereby appoint the following attorney(s) and/or agent(s) to prosecute this application and to transact all business in the Patent and Trademark Office connected therewith:

________________________________.

Address all telephone calls to ________________ at telephone no. ________________.

Address all correspondence to ________________________________
____
____
________________________________.

I hereby declare that all statements made herein of my own knowledge are true and that all statements made on information and belief are believed to be true; and further that these statements were made with the knowledge that willful false statements and the like so made are punishable by fine or imprisonment, or both, under Section 1001 of Title 18 of the United States Code and that such willful false statements may jeopardize the validity of the application or any patent issued thereon.

Full name of sole or first inventor ________________________________
Inventor's signature ________________ Date ________________
Residence ________________ Citizenship ________________
Post Office Address ________________________________
____

Full name of second joint inventor, if any ________________________________
Second Inventor's signature ________________ Date ________________
Residence ________________ Citizenship ________________
Post Office Address ________________________________
____

(Supply similar information and signature for third and subsequent joint inventors.)

Form PTO-FB-A110

Applicant or Patentee: ______________________ Attorney's
Serial or Patent No.: ______________________ Docket No.: ________
Filed or Issued: ______________________
For: ______________________

VERIFIED STATEMENT (DECLARATION) CLAIMING SMALL ENTITY STATUS (37 CFR 1.9 (f) and 1.27 (b)) — INDEPENDENT INVENTOR

As a below named inventor, I hereby declare that I qualify as an independent inventor as defined in 37 CFR 1.9 (c) for purposes of paying reduced fees under section 41 (a) and (b) of Title 35, United States Code, to the Patent and Trademark Office with regard to the invention entitled ______________________ described in

- [ ] the specification filed herewith
- [ ] application serial no. ______________, filed ______________.
- [ ] patent no. ______________, issued ______________.

I have not assigned, granted, conveyed or licensed and am under no obligation under contract or law to assign, grant, convey or license, any rights in the invention to any person who could not be classified as an independent inventor under 37 CFR 1.9 (c) if that person had made the invention, or to any concern which would not qualify as a small business concern under 37 CFR 1.9 (d) or a nonprofit organization under 37 CFR 1.9 (e).

Each person, concern or organization to which I have assigned, granted, conveyed, or licensed or am under an obligation under contract or law to assign, grant, convey, or license any rights in the invention is listed below:

- [ ] no such person, concern, or organization
- [ ] persons, concerns or organizations listed below*

*NOTE: Separate verified statements are required from each named person, concern or organization having rights to the invention averring to their status as small entities. (37 CFR 1.27)

FULL NAME ______________________
ADDRESS ______________________
[ ] INDIVIDUAL [ ] SMALL BUSINESS CONCERN [ ] NONPROFIT ORGANIZATION

FULL NAME ______________________
ADDRESS ______________________
[ ] INDIVIDUAL [ ] SMALL BUSINESS CONCERN [ ] NONPROFIT ORGANIZATION

FULL NAME ______________________
ADDRESS ______________________
[ ] INDIVIDUAL [ ] SMALL BUSINESS CONCERN [ ] NONPROFIT ORGANIZATION

I acknowledge the duty to file, in this application or patent, notification of any change in status resulting in loss of entitlement to small entity status prior to paying, or at the time of paying, the earliest of the issue fee or any maintenance fee due after the date on which status as a small entity is no longer appropriate. (37 CFR 1.28 (b))

I hereby declare that all statements made herein of my own knowledge are true and that all statements made on information and belief are believed to be true; and further that these statements were made with the knowledge that willful false statements and the like so made are punishable by fine or imprisonment, or both, under section 1001 of Title 18 of the United States Code, and that such willful false statements may jeopardize the validity of the application, any patent issuing thereon, or any patent to which this verified statement is directed.

NAME OF INVENTOR	NAME OF INVENTOR	NAME OF INVENTOR
Signature of Inventor	Signature of Inventor	Signature of Inventor
Date	Date	Date

Form PTO-FB-A410

AMENDMENT TRANSMITTAL LETTER			ATTORNEY'S DOCKET NO.
SERIAL NO.	FILING DATE	EXAMINER	GROUP ART UNIT
INVENTION			

TO THE COMMISSIONER OF PATENTS AND TRADEMARKS:

Transmitted herewith is an amendment in the above-identified application.

Small entity status of this application under 37 CFR 1.27 has been established by a verified statement previously submitted.

A verified statement to establish small entity status under 37 CFR 1.9 and 1.27 is enclosed.

No additional fee is required.

The fee has been calculated as shown below:

	(1) CLAIMS REMAINING AFTER AMENDMENT		(2) HIGHEST NO PREVIOUSLY PAID FOR	(3) PRESENT EXTRA	SMALL ENTITY RATE	SMALL ENTITY ADDIT FEE		OTHER THAN A SMALL ENTITY RATE	OTHER THAN A SMALL ENTITY ADDIT FEE
TOTAL	*	MINUS	**	=	x $ 6=	$	OR	x $ 12=	$
INDEP	*	MINUS	***	=	x $ 18=	$	OR	x $ 36=	$
FIRST PRESENTATION OF MULTIPLE DEP CLAIM					+$ 60=	$	OR	+ $120=	$
					TOTAL ADDIT. FEE	$	OR	TOTAL	$

* If the entry in Col. 1 is less than the entry in Col. 2, write "0" in Col. 3.

** If the "Highest No. Previously Paid For" IN THIS SPACE is less than 20, enter "20".

*** If the "Highest No. Previously Paid For" IN THIS SPACE is less than 3, enter "3".

The "Highest No. Previously Paid For" (Total or Indep.) is the highest number found in the appropriate box in Col. 1

Please charge my Deposit Account No. ______________ in the amount of $ __________ .
A duplicate copy of this sheet is enclosed.

A check in the amount of $ ________ to cover the filing fee is enclosed.

The Commissioner is hereby authorized to charge payment of the following fees associated with this communication or credit any overpayment to Deposit Account No. ________________. A Duplicate copy of this sheet is enclosed.

Any additional filing fees required under 37 CFR 1.16.

Any patent application processing fees under 37 CFR 1.17

______________________ (date)

______________________ (signature)

Form PTO-FB-A520
(also form PTO-1083)

Patent and Trademark Office - U.S. DEPARTMENT of COMMERCE

PATENT APPLICATION TRANSMITTAL LETTER

ATTORNEY'S DOCKET NO.

TO THE COMMISSIONER OF PATENTS AND TRADEMARKS:

Transmitted herewith for filing is the patent application of ____________________

____

for ____________________

____

Enclosed are:

- ☐ ________ sheets of drawing.
- ☐ an assignment of the invention to ____________________
- ☐ a certified copy of a ____________________ application.
- ☐ associate power of attorney.
- ☐ verified statement to establish small entity status under 37 CFR 1.9 and 1.27. ____

CLAIMS AS FILED

FOR	NO. FILED	NO. EXTRA	SMALL ENTITY RATE	SMALL ENTITY FEE		OTHER THAN A SMALL ENTITY RATE	OTHER THAN A SMALL ENTITY FEE
BASIC FEE				$185	OR		$370
TOTAL CLAIMS	—20 -	*	x $ 6=	$	OR	x $ 12=	$
INDEP. CLAIMS	—3 -	*	x $ 18=	$	OR	x $ 36=	$
MULTIPLE DEPENDENT CLAIM PRESENT			+ $120=	$	OR	+ $120=	$
			TOTAL	$	OR	TOTAL	$

* If the difference in col. 1 is less than zero, enter "0" in col. 2

- ☐ Please charge my Deposit Account No. __________ in the amount of $ ________ .
- ☐ A duplicate copy of this sheet is enclosed.
- ☐ A check in the amount of $ ________ to cover the filing fee is enclosed.
- ☐ The Commissioner is hereby authorized to charge payment of the following fees associated with this communication or credit any overpayment to Deposit Account No. __________. A Duplicate copy of this sheet is enclosed.
  - ☐ Any additional filing fees required under 37 CFR 1.16.
  - ☐ Any patent application processing fees under 37 CFR 1.17
- ☐ The Commissioner is hereby authorized to charge payment of the following fees during the pendency of this application or credit any overpayment to Deposit Account No. __________. A duplicate copy of this sheet is enclosed.
  - ☐ Any filing fees under 37 CFR 1.16 for presentation of extra claims.
  - ☐ Any patent application processing fees under 37 CFR 1.17.
  - ☐ The issue fee set in 37 CFR 1.18 at or before mailing of the Notice of Allowance, pursuant to 37 CFR 1.311(b).

__________ date

__________ signature

Form PTO-FB-A510
(also form PTO-1082)

Patent and Trademark Office - U.S. DEPARTMENT of COMMERCE

GREGORY J. SMITH
RECORDER/COUNTY CLERK
1600 Pacific Highway, Room 260
P.O. Box 1750
San Diego, California 92112-4147
(619) 237-0502

This Space For Use of County Clerk

PLEASE PRINT OR TYPE FIRMLY. YOU ARE MAKING MULTIPLE COPIES.

SEE REVERSE SIDE FOR INSTRUCTIONS

FILING FEE

- $13.00 - FOR FIRST BUSINESS NAME ON STATEMENT
- $ 2.00 - FOR EACH ADDITIONAL BUSINESS NAME FILED ON SAME STATEMENT AND DOING BUSINESS AT THE SAME LOCATION
- $ 2.00 - FOR EACH ADDITIONAL OWNER IN EXCESS OF ONE OWNER

FICTITIOUS BUSINESS NAME STATEMENT

THE NAME[S] OF THE BUSINESS[ES] :

(1) ....
(Print Fictitious Business Name[s] on Line Above)

(2) LOCATED AT: ....
(Street Address of Business — If No Street Address Assigned — Give Exact Location of Business Plus P.O. Box or Rural Route)

IN: ....
(City and Zip)

IS (ARE) HEREBY REGISTERED BY THE FOLLOWING OWNER(S):

(3) #1 ....
(Corporate or Owner's Full Name — Type/Print)

....
(Residence address if not incorporated)
(State of incorporation if incorporated)

....
(City and Zip)

#2 ....
(Corporate or Owner's Full Name — Type/Print)

....
(Residence address if not incorporated)
(State of incorporation if incorporated)

....
(City and Zip)

#3 ....
(Corporate or Owner's Full Name — Type/Print)

....
(Residence address if not incorporated)
(State of incorporation if incorporated)

....
(City and Zip)

#4 ....
(Corporate or Owner's Full Name — Type/Print)

....
(Residence address if not incorporated)
(State of incorporation if incorporated)

....
(City and Zip)

(4) **This business is conducted by:** ☐ an Individual ☐ Individuals – Husband and Wife ☐ a General Partnership ☐ a Limited Partnership ☐ a Corporation ☐ a Business Trust ☐ Co-Partners ☐ a Joint Venture ☐ an Unincorporated Association – other than a Partnership ☐ Other *(Specify)* ....

(5) **THE TRANSACTION OF BUSINESS BEGAN ON:** ....

SIGNATURE OF REGISTRANT: ....

....
(Print name of person signing and, if a Corporate Officer, also state title)

THIS STATEMENT WAS FILED WITH GREGORY J. SMITH, RECORDER/COUNTY CLERK OF SAN DIEGO COUNTY ON DATE INDICATED BY FILE STAMP ABOVE.

THE FILING OF THIS STATEMENT DOES NOT OF ITSELF AUTHORIZE THE USE IN THE STATE OF A FICTITIOUS BUSINESS NAME IN VIOLATION OF THE RIGHTS OF ANOTHER UNDER FEDERAL, STATE, OR COMMON LAW (see section 14400 et seq., Business and Professions Code). THIS FICTITIOUS BUSINESS STATEMENT NAME EXPIRES FIVE (5) YEARS FROM THE DATE IT WAS FILED IN THE OFFICE OF THE RECORDER/COUNTY CLERK, IF YOU INTEND TO CONTINUE BUSINESS UNDER THIS NAME A NEW FICTITIOUS BUSINESS NAME STATEMENT MUST BE FILED PRIOR TO:

....

ASSIGNED FILE NO. ....

Form 231 Co. CLK (REV. 11-91)

RECORDER/COUNTY CLERK

Form 9. IRS SS-4—Federal Employer Identification Number

Form **SS-4**
(Rev. December 1993)
Department of the Treasury
Internal Revenue Service

Application for Employer Identification Number

(For use by employers, corporations, partnerships, trusts, estates, churches, government agencies, certain individuals, and others. See instructions.)

EIN

OMB No. 1545-0003
Expires 12-31-96

Please type or print clearly.

1 Name of applicant (Legal name) (See instructions.)

2 Trade name of business, if different from name in line 1

3 Executor, trustee, "care of" name

4a Mailing address (street address) (room, apt., or suite no.)

5a Business address, if different from address in lines 4a and 4b

4b City, state, and ZIP code

5b City, state, and ZIP code

6 County and state where principal business is located

7 Name of principal officer, general partner, grantor, owner, or trustor—SSN required (See instructions.) ▶

8a Type of entity (Check only one box.) (See instructions.)
- ☐ Sole Proprietor (SSN)
- ☐ REMIC
- ☐ State/local government
- ☐ Other nonprofit organization (specify) ____ (enter GEN if applicable) ____
- ☐ Other (specify) ▶
- ☐ Personal service corp.
- ☐ National guard
- ☐ Estate (SSN of decedent)
- ☐ Plan administrator-SSN
- ☐ Other corporation (specify)
- ☐ Federal government/military
- ☐ Church or church controlled organization
- ☐ Trust
- ☐ Partnership
- ☐ Farmers' cooperative

8b If a corporation, name the state or foreign country (if applicable) where incorporated ▶ | State | Foreign country

9 Reason for applying (Check only one box.)
- ☐ Started new business (specify) ▶
- ☐ Hired employees
- ☐ Created a pension plan (specify type) ▶
- ☐ Banking purpose (specify) ▶
- ☐ Changed type of organization (specify) ▶
- ☐ Purchased going business
- ☐ Created a trust (specify) ▶
- ☐ Other (specify) ▶

10 Date business started or acquired (Mo., day, year) (See instructions.)

11 Enter closing month of accounting year. (See instructions.)

12 First date wages or annuities were paid or will be paid (Mo., day, year). **Note:** *If applicant is a withholding agent, enter date income will first be paid to nonresident alien. (Mo., day, year)* . . . . ▶

13 Enter highest number of employees expected in the next 12 months. **Note:** *If the applicant does not expect to have any employees during the period, enter "0."* . . . . ▶

Nonagricultural	Agricultural	Household

14 Principal activity (See instructions.) ▶

15 Is the principal business activity manufacturing? . . . . ☐ Yes ☐ No
If "Yes," principal product and raw material used ▶

16 To whom are most of the products or services sold? Please check the appropriate box. ☐ Business (wholesale)
☐ Public (retail) ☐ Other (specify) ▶ ☐ N/A

17a Has the applicant ever applied for an identification number for this or any other business? . . . . ☐ Yes ☐ No
Note: *If "Yes," please complete lines 17b and 17c.*

17b If you checked the "Yes" box in line 17a, give applicant's legal name and trade name, if different than name shown on prior application.

Legal name ▶ Trade name ▶

17c Enter approximate date, city, and state where the application was filed and the previous employer identification number if known.

Approximate date when filed (Mo., day, year)	City and state where filed	Previous EIN

Under penalties of perjury, I declare that I have examined this application, and to the best of my knowledge and belief, it is true, correct, and complete.

Business telephone number (include area code)

Name and title (Please type or print clearly.) ▶

Signature ▶ Date ▶

Note: *Do not write below this line. For official use only.*

Please leave blank ▶	Geo.	Ind.	Class	Size	Reason for applying

For Paperwork Reduction Act Notice, see attached instructions. Cat. No. 16055N Form **SS-4** (Rev. 12-93)

General Instructions

(Section references are to the Internal Revenue Code unless otherwise noted.)

Purpose

Use Form SS-4 to apply for an employer identification number (EIN). An EIN is a nine-digit number (for example, 12-3456789) assigned to sole proprietors, corporations, partnerships, estates, trusts, and other entities for filing and reporting purposes. The information you provide on this form will establish your filing and reporting requirements.

Who Must File

You must file this form if you have not obtained an EIN before and

- You pay wages to one or more employees.
- You are required to have an EIN to use on any return, statement, or other document, even if you are not an employer.
- You are a withholding agent required to withhold taxes on income, other than wages, paid to a nonresident alien (individual, corporation, partnership, etc.). A withholding agent may be an agent, broker, fiduciary, manager, tenant, or spouse, and is required to file **Form 1042,** Annual Withholding Tax Return for U.S. Source Income of Foreign Persons.
- You file **Schedule C,** Profit or Loss From Business, or **Schedule F,** Profit or Loss From Farming, of **Form 1040,** U.S. Individual Income Tax Return, and have a Keogh plan or are required to file excise, employment, or alcohol, tobacco, or firearms returns.

The following must use EINs even if they do not have any employees:

- Trusts, except the following:

  1. Certain grantor-owned revocable trusts (see the Instructions for Form 1040).

  2. Individual Retirment Arrangement (IRA) trusts, unless the trust has to file **Form 990-T,** Exempt Organization Business Income Tax Return (See the Instructions for Form 990-T.)
- Estates
- Partnerships
- REMICS (real estate mortgage investment conduits) (See the instructions for **Form 1066,** U.S. Real Estate Mortgage Investment Conduit Income Tax Return.)
- Corporations
- Nonprofit organizations (churches, clubs, etc.)
- Farmers' cooperatives
- Plan administrators (A plan administrator is the person or group of persons specified as the administrator by the instrument under which the plan is operated.)

Note: *Household employers are not required to file Form SS-4 to get an EIN. An EIN may be assigned to you without filing Form SS-4 if your only employees are household employees (domestic workers) in your private home. To have an EIN assigned to you, write "NONE" in the space for the EIN on* ***Form 942,*** *Employer's Quarterly Tax Return for Household Employees, when you file it.*

When To Apply for A New EIN

New Business.—If you become the new owner of an existing business, **DO NOT** use the EIN of the former owner. If you already have an EIN, use that number. If you do not have an EIN, apply for one on this form. If you become the "owner" of a corporation by acquiring its stock, use the corporation's EIN.

Changes in Organization or Ownership.—If you already have an EIN, you may need to get a new one if either the organization or ownership of your business changes. If you incorporate a sole proprietorship or form a partnership, you must get a new EIN. However, **DO NOT** apply for a new EIN if you change only the name of your business.

File Only One Form SS-4.—File only one Form SS-4, regardless of the number of businesses operated or trade names under which a business operates. However, each corporation in an affiliated group must file a separate application.

EIN Applied For, But Not Received.—If you do not have an EIN by the time a return is due, write "Applied for" and the date you applied in the space shown for the number. **DO NOT** show your social security number as an EIN on returns.

If you do not have an EIN by the time a tax deposit is due, send your payment to the Internal Revenue service center for your filing area. (See **Where To Apply** below.) Make your check or money order payable to Internal Revenue Service and show your name (as shown on Form SS-4), address, kind of tax, period covered, and date you applied for an EIN.

For more information about EINs, see **Pub. 583,** Taxpayers Starting a Business and **Pub. 1635,** EINs Made Easy.

How To Apply

You can apply for an EIN either by mail or by telephone. You can get an EIN immediately by calling the Tele-TIN phone number for the service center for your state, or you can send the completed Form SS-4 directly to the service center to receive your EIN in the mail.

Application by Tele-TIN.—Under the Tele-TIN program, you can receive your EIN over the telephone and use it immediately to file a return or make a payment. To receive an EIN by phone, complete Form SS-4, then call the Tele-TIN phone number listed for your state under **Where To Apply.** The person making the call must be authorized to sign the form (see **Signature block** on page 3).

An IRS representative will use the information from the Form SS-4 to establish your account and assign you an EIN. Write the number you are given on the upper right-hand corner of the form, sign and date it.

You should mail or FAX the signed SS-4 ***within 24 hours*** *to the Tele-TIN Unit at the service center address for your state.* The IRS representative will give you the FAX number. The FAX numbers are also listed in Pub. 1635.

Taxpayer representatives can receive their client's EIN by phone if they first send a facsimile (FAX) of a completed **Form 2848,** Power of Attorney and Declaration of Representative, or **Form 8821,** Tax Information Authorization, to the Tele-TIN unit. The Form 2848 or Form 8821 will be used solely to release the EIN to the representative authorized on the form.

Application by Mail.—Complete Form SS-4 at least 4 to 5 weeks before you will need an EIN. Sign and date the application and mail it to the service center address for your state. You will receive your EIN in the mail in approximately 4 weeks.

Where To Apply

The Tele-TIN phone numbers listed below will involve a long-distance charge to callers outside of the local calling area, and should be used only to apply for an EIN. THE NUMBERS MAY CHANGE WITHOUT NOTICE. Use 1-800-829-1040 to verify a number or to ask about an application by mail or other Federal tax matters.

If your principal business, office or agency, or legal residence in the case of an individual, is located in:	Call the Tele-TIN phone number shown or file with the Internal Revenue Service center at:
Florida, Georgia, South Carolina	Attn. Entity Control Atlanta, GA 39901 (404) 455-2360
New Jersey, New York City and counties of Nassau, Rockland, Suffolk, and Westchester	Attn: Entity Control Holtsville, NY 00501 (516) 447-4955
New York (all other counties), Connecticut, Maine, Massachusetts, New Hampshire, Rhode Island, Vermont	Attn: Entity Control Andover, MA 05501 (508) 474-9717
Illinois, Iowa, Minnesota, Missouri, Wisconsin	Attn: Entity Control Stop 57A 2306 E. Bannister Rd. Kansas City, MO 64131 (816) 926-5999
Delaware, District of Columbia, Maryland, Pennsylvania, Virginia	Attn: Entity Control Philadelphia, PA 19255 (215) 574-2400

Indiana, Kentucky, Michigan, Ohio, West Virginia	Attn: Entity Control Cincinnati, OH 45999 (606) 292-5467
Kansas, New Mexico, Oklahoma, Texas	Attn: Entity Control Austin, TX 73301 (512) 462-7843
Alaska, Arizona, California (counties of Alpine, Amador, Butte, Calaveras, Colusa, Contra Costa, Del Norte, El Dorado, Glenn, Humboldt, Lake, Lassen, Marin, Mendocino, Modoc, Napa, Nevada, Placer, Plumas, Sacramento, San Joaquin, Shasta, Sierra, Siskiyou, Solano, Sonoma, Sutter, Tehama, Trinity, Yolo, and Yuba), Colorado, Idaho, Montana, Nebraska, Nevada, North Dakota, Oregon, South Dakota, Utah, Washington, Wyoming	Attn: Entity Control Mail Stop 6271-T P.O. Box 9950 Ogden, UT 84409 (801) 620-7645
California (all other counties), Hawaii	Attn: Entity Control Fresno, CA 93888 (209) 452-4010
Alabama, Arkansas, Louisiana, Mississippi, North Carolina, Tennessee	Attn: Entity Control Memphis, TN 37501 (901) 365-5970

If you have no legal residence, principal place of business, or principal office or agency in any state, file your form with the Internal Revenue Service Center, Philadelphia, PA 19255 or call (215) 574-2400.

Specific Instructions

The instructions that follow are for those items that are not self-explanatory. Enter N/A (nonapplicable) on the lines that do not apply.

Line 1.—Enter the legal name of the entity applying for the EIN exactly as it appears on the social security card, charter, or other applicable legal document.

Individuals.—Enter the first name, middle initial, and last name.

Trusts.—Enter the name of the trust.

Estate of a decedent.—Enter the name of the estate.

Partnerships.—Enter the legal name of the partnership as it appears in the partnership agreement.

Corporations.—Enter the corporate name as set forth in the corporation charter or other legal document creating it.

Plan administrators.—Enter the name of the plan administrator. A plan administrator who already has an EIN should use that number.

Line 2.—Enter the trade name of the business if different from the legal name. The trade name is the "doing business as" name.

Note: *Use the full legal name on line 1 on all tax returns filed for the entity. However, if you enter a trade name on line 2 and choose to use the trade name instead of the legal name, enter the trade name on all returns you file. To prevent processing delays and errors,* ***always*** *use either the legal name only or the trade name only on all tax returns.*

Line 3.—Trusts enter the name of the trustee. Estates enter the name of the executor, administrator, or other fiduciary. If the entity applying has a designated person to receive tax information, enter that person's name as the "care of" person. Print or type the first name, middle initial, and last name.

Line 7.—Enter the first name, middle initial, last name, and social security number (SSN) of a principal officer if the business is a corporation; of a general partner if a partnership; and of a grantor owner, or trustor if a trust.

Line 8a.—Check the box that best describes the type of entity applying for the EIN. If not specifically mentioned, check the "other" box and enter the type of entity. Do not enter N/A.

Sole proprietor.—Check this box if you file Schedule C or F (Form 1040) and have a Keogh plan, or are required to file excise, employment, or alcohol, tobacco, or firearms returns. Enter your SSN (social security number) in the space provided.

Plan administrator.—If the plan administrator is an individual, enter the plan administrator's SSN in the space provided.

Withholding agent.—If you are a withholding agent required to file Form 1042, check the "other" box and enter "withholding agent."

REMICs.—Check this box if the entity has elected to be treated as a real estate mortgage investment conduit (REMIC). See the Instructions for Form 1066 for more information.

Personal service corporations.—Check this box if the entity is a personal service corporation. An entity is a personal service corporation for a tax year only if:

- The principal activity of the entity during the testing period (prior tax year) for the tax year is the performance of personal services substantially by employee-owners.
- The employee-owners own 10 percent of the fair market value of the outstanding stock in the entity on the last day of the testing period.

Personal services include performance of services in such fields as health, law, accounting, consulting, etc. For more information about personal service corporations, see the instructions to **Form 1120,** U.S. Corporation Income Tax Return, and **Pub. 542,** Tax Information on Corporations.

Other corporations.—This box is for any corporation other than a personal service corporation. If you check this box, enter the type of corporation (such as insurance company) in the space provided.

Other nonprofit organizations.—Check this box if the nonprofit organization is other than a church or church-controlled organization and specify the type of nonprofit organization (for example, an educational organization.)

If the organization also seeks tax-exempt status, you must file either **Package 1023** or **Package 1024,** Application for Recognition of Exemption. Get **Pub. 557,** Tax-Exempt Status for Your Organization, for more information.

Group exemption number (GEN).—If the organization is covered by a group exemption letter, enter the four-digit GEN. (Do not confuse the GEN with the nine-digit EIN.) If you do not know the GEN, contact the parent organization. Get Pub. 557 for more information about group exemption numbers.

Line 9.—Check only **one** box. Do not enter N/A.

Started new business.—Check this box if you are starting a new business that requires an EIN. If you check this box, enter the type of business being started. **DO NOT** apply if you already have an EIN and are only adding another place of business.

Changed type of organization.—Check this box if the business is changing its type of organization, for example, if the business was a sole proprietorship and has been incorporated or has become a partnership. If you check this box, specify in the space provided the type of change made, for example, "from sole proprietorship to partnership."

Purchased going business.—Check this box if you purchased an existing business. DO NOT use the former owner's EIN. Use your own EIN if you already have one.

Hired employees.—Check this box if the existing business is requesting an EIN because it has hired or is hiring employees and is therefore required to file employment tax returns. **DO NOT** apply if you already have an EIN and are only hiring employees. If you are hiring household employees, see **Note** under **Who Must File** on page 2.

Created a trust.—Check this box if you created a trust, and enter the type of trust created.

Note: *DO NOT file this form if you are the individual-grantor/owner of a revocable trust. You must use your SSN for the trust. See the instructions for Form 1040.*

Created a pension plan.—Check this box if you have created a pension plan and need this number for reporting purposes. Also, enter the type of plan created.

Banking purpose.—Check this box if you are requesting an EIN for banking purposes only and enter the banking purpose (for example, a bowling league for depositing dues, an investment club for dividend and interest reporting, etc.).

Other (specify).—Check this box if you are requesting an EIN for any reason other than those for which there are checkboxes, and enter the reason.

Line 10.—If you are starting a new business, enter the starting date of the business. If the business you acquired is already operating, enter the date you acquired the business. Trusts should enter the date the trust was legally created. Estates should enter the date of death of the decedent whose name appears on line 1 or the date when the estate was legally funded.

Line 11.—Enter the last month of your accounting year or tax year. An accounting or tax year is usually 12 consecutive months, either a calendar year or a fiscal year (including a period of 52 or 53 weeks). A calendar year is 12 consecutive months ending on December 31. A fiscal year is either 12 consecutive months ending on the last day of any month other than December or a 52-53 week year. For more information on accounting periods, see **Pub. 538,** Accounting Periods and Methods.

Individuals.—Your tax year generally will be a calendar year.

Partnerships.—Partnerships generally must adopt the tax year of either (1) the majority partners; (2) the principal partners; (3) the tax year that results in the least aggregate (total) deferral of income; or (4) some other tax year. (See the Instructions for **Form 1065,** U.S. Partnership Return of Income, for more information.)

REMICs.—Remics must have a calendar year as their tax year.

Personal service corporations.—A personal service corporation generally must adopt a calendar year unless:

- It can establish a business purpose for having a different tax year, or
- It elects under section 444 to have a tax year other than a calendar year.

Trusts.—Generally, a trust must adopt a calendar year except for the following:

- Tax-exempt trusts,
- Charitable trusts, and
- Grantor-owned trusts.

Line 12.—If the business has or will have employees, enter the date on which the business began or will begin to pay wages. If the business does not plan to have employees, enter N/A.

Withholding agent.—Enter the date you began or will begin to pay income to a nonresident alien. This also applies to individuals who are required to file Form 1042 to report alimony paid to a nonresident alien.

Line 14.—Generally, enter the exact type of business being operated (for example, advertising agency, farm, food or beverage establishment, labor union, real estate agency, steam laundry, rental of coin-operated vending machine, investment club, etc.). Also state if the business will involve the sale or distribution of alcoholic beverages.

Governmental.—Enter the type of organization (state, county, school district, or municipality, etc.).

Nonprofit organization (other than governmental).—Enter whether organized for religious, educational, or humane purposes, and the principal activity (for example, religious organization—hospital, charitable).

Mining and quarrying.—Specify the process and the principal product (for example, mining bituminous coal, contract drilling for oil, quarrying dimension stone, etc.).

Contract construction.—Specify whether general contracting or special trade contracting. Also, show the type of work normally performed (for example, general contractor for residential buildings, electrical subcontractor, etc.).

Food or beverage establishments.—Specify the type of establishment and state whether you employ workers who receive tips (for example, lounge—yes).

Trade.—Specify the type of sales and the principal line of goods sold (for example, wholesale dairy products, manufacturer's representative for mining machinery, retail hardware, etc.).

Manufacturing.—Specify the type of establishment operated (for example, sawmill, vegetable cannery, etc.).

Signature block.—The application must be signed by: (1) the individual, if the applicant is an individual, (2) the president, vice president, or other principal officer, if the applicant is a corporation, (3) a responsible and duly authorized member or officer having knowledge of its affairs, if the applicant is a partnership or other unincorporated organization, or (4) the fiduciary, if the applicant is a trust or estate.

Some Useful Publications

You may get the following publications for additional information on the subjects covered on this form. To get these and other free forms and publications, call 1-800-TAX-FORM (1-800-829-3676).

Pub. 1635, EINs Made Easy

Pub. 538, Accounting Periods and Methods

Pub. 541, Tax Information on Partnerships

Pub. 542, Tax Information on Corporations

Pub. 557, Tax-Exempt Status for Your Organization

Pub. 583, Taxpayers Starting A Business

Pub. 937, Employment Taxes and Information Returns

Package 1023, Application for Recognition of Exemption

Package 1024, Application for Recognition of Exemption Under Section 501(a) or for Determination Under Section 120

Paperwork Reduction Act Notice

We ask for the information on this form to carry out the Internal Revenue laws of the United States. You are required to give us the information. We need it to ensure that you are complying with these laws and to allow us to figure and collect the right amount of tax.

The time needed to complete and file this form will vary depending on individual circumstances. The estimated average time is:

Recordkeeping	7 min.
Learning about the law or the form	18 min.
Preparing the form	44 min.
Copying, assembling, and sending the form to the IRS	20 min.

If you have comments concerning the accuracy of these time estimates or suggestions for making this form more simple, we would be happy to hear from you. You can write to both the **Internal Revenue Service,** Attention: Reports Clearance Officer, PC:FP, Washington, DC 20224; and the **Office of Management and Budget,** Paperwork Reduction Project (1545-0003), Washington, DC 20503. **DO NOT** send this form to either of these offices. Instead, see **Where To Apply** on page 2.

Printed on recycled paper

*U.S. Government Printing Office: 1993 — 363-331/99125

Form **SS-8**
(Rev. July 1993)
Department of the Treasury
Internal Revenue Service

Determination of Employee Work Status for Purposes of Federal Employment Taxes and Income Tax Withholding

OMB No. 1545-0004
Expires 7-31-96

Paperwork Reduction Act Notice

We ask for the information on this form to carry out the Internal Revenue laws of the United States. You are required to give us this information. We need it to ensure that you are complying with these laws and to allow us to figure and collect the right amount of tax.

The time needed to complete and file this form will vary depending on individual circumstances. The estimated average time is: **recordkeeping,** 34 hr., 55 min., **learning about the law or the form,** 6 min. and **preparing and sending the form to IRS,** 40 min. If you have comments concerning the accuracy of these time estimates or suggestions for making this form more simple, we would be happy to hear from you. You can write to both the **Internal Revenue Service,** Attention: Reports Clearance Officer, T:FP, Washington, DC 20224; and the **Office of Management and Budget,** Paperwork Reduction Project (1545-0004), Washington, DC 20503. **DO NOT** send the tax form to either of these offices. Instead, see **General Information** for where to file.

Purpose

Employers and workers file Form SS-8 to get a determination as to whether a worker is an employee for purposes of Federal employment taxes and income tax withholding.

General Information

This form should be completed carefully. If the firm is completing the form, it should be completed for **ONE** individual who is representative of the class of workers whose status is in question. If a written determination is desired for more than one class of workers, a separate Form SS-8 should be completed for one worker from each class whose status is typical of that class. A written determination for any worker will apply to other workers of the same class if the facts are not materially different from those of the worker whose status was ruled upon.

Please return Form SS-8 to the Internal Revenue Service office that provided the form. If the Internal Revenue Service did not ask you to complete this form but you wish a determination on whether a worker is an employee, file Form SS-8 with your District Director.

***Caution:** Form SS-8 is **not** a claim for refund of social security and Medicare taxes or Federal income tax withholding. Also, a determination that an individual is an employee does not necessarily reduce any current or prior tax liability. A worker must file his or her income tax return even if a determination has not been made by the due date of the return.*

Name of firm (or person) for whom the worker performed services		Name of worker
Address of firm (include street address, apt. or suite no., city, state, and ZIP code)		Address of worker (include street address, apt. or suite no., city, state, and ZIP code)
Trade name		Telephone number (include area code) ( ) / Worker's social security number – –
Telephone number (include area code) ( )	Firm's taxpayer identification number –	

Check type of firm for which the work relationship is in question:
☐ **Individual** ☐ **Partnership** ☐ **Corporation** ☐ **Other** (specify) ▶

Important Information Needed to Process Your Request

This form is being completed by: ☐ Firm ☐ Worker

If this form is being completed by the worker, the IRS **must** have your permission to disclose your name to the firm.

Do you object to disclosing your name and the information on this form to the firm? . . . . ☐ **Yes** ☐ **No**

If you answer "Yes," the IRS cannot act on your request. **DO NOT complete the rest of this form unless the IRS asks for it.**

Under section 6110 of the Internal Revenue Code, the information on this form and related file documents will be open to the public if any ruling or determination is made. However, names, addresses, and taxpayer identification numbers must be removed before the information can be made public.

Is there any other information you want removed? . . . . ☐ **Yes** ☐ **No**

If you check "Yes," we cannot process your request unless you submit a copy of this form and copies of all supporting documents showing, in brackets, the information you want removed. Attach a separate statement telling which specific exemption of section 6110(c) applies to each bracketed part.

*This form is designed to cover many work activities, so some of the questions may not apply to you. **You must answer ALL items or mark them "Unknown" or "Does not apply."** If you need more space, attach another sheet.*

Total number of workers in this class. (Attach names and addresses. If more than 10 workers, attach only 10.) ▶ ____________

This information is about services performed by the worker from ____________ (month, day, year) to ____________ (month, day, year)

Is the worker still performing services for the firm? . . . . ☐ **Yes** ☐ **No**

If "No," what was the date of termination? ▶ ____________ (month, day, year)

Cat. No. 16106T

Form **SS-8** (Rev. 7-93)

Published by Tax Management Inc., a Subsidiary of The Bureau of National Affairs, Inc.

SS-8.1

Form SS-8 (Rev. 7-93) Page 2

1a Describe the firm's business

b Describe the work done by the worker

2a If the work is done under a written agreement between the firm and the worker, attach a copy.

b If the agreement is not in writing, describe the terms and conditions of the work arrangement

c If the actual working arrangement differs in any way from the agreement, explain the differences and why they occur

3a Is the worker given training by the firm? ☐ Yes ☐ No

If "Yes": What kind?

How often?

b Is the worker given instructions in the way the work is to be done (exclusive of actual training in 3a)? ☐ Yes ☐ No

If "Yes," give specific examples.

c Attach samples of any written instructions or procedures.

d Does the firm have the right to change the methods used by the worker or direct that person on how to do the work? ☐ Yes ☐ No

Explain your answer

e Does the operation of the firm's business require that the worker be supervised or controlled in the performance of the service? ☐ Yes ☐ No

Explain your answer

4a The firm engages the worker:

☐ To perform and complete a particular job only

☐ To work at a job for an indefinite period of time

☐ Other (explain)

b Is the worker required to follow a routine or a schedule established by the firm? ☐ Yes ☐ No

If "Yes," what is the routine or schedule?

c Does the worker report to the firm or its representative?. ☐ Yes ☐ No

If "Yes": How often?

For what purpose?

In what manner (in person, in writing, by telephone, etc.)?

Attach copies of report forms used in reporting to the firm.

d Does the worker furnish a time record to the firm?. ☐ Yes ☐ No

If "Yes," attach copies of time records.

5a State the kind and value of tools, equipment, supplies, and materials furnished by:

The firm

The worker

b What expenses are incurred by the worker in the performance of services for the firm?

c Does the firm reimburse the worker for any expenses? ☐ Yes ☐ No

If "Yes," specify the reimbursed expenses

6a Will the worker perform the services personally? ☐ Yes ☐ No

b Does the worker have helpers? ☐ Yes ☐ No

If "Yes": Who hires the helpers? ☐ Firm ☐ Worker

If hired by the worker, is the firm's approval necessary? ☐ Yes ☐ No

Who pays the helpers? ☐ Firm ☐ Worker

Are social security and Medicare taxes and Federal income tax withheld from the helpers' wages? ☐ Yes ☐ No

If "Yes": Who reports and pays these taxes? ☐ Firm ☐ Worker

Who reports the helpers' incomes to the Internal Revenue Service? ☐ Firm ☐ Worker

If the worker pays the helpers, does the firm repay the worker? ☐ Yes ☐ No

What services do the helpers perform?

Published by Tax Management Inc., a Subsidiary of The Bureau of National Affairs, Inc.

Form SS-8 (Rev. 7-93) Page **3**

7 At what location are the services performed? ☐ Firm's ☐ Worker's ☐ Other (specify) ....

8a Type of pay worker receives:
☐ Salary ☐ Commission ☐ Hourly wage ☐ Piecework ☐ Lump sum ☐ Other (specify) ....

b Does the firm guarantee a minimum amount of pay to the worker? ☐ Yes ☐ No

c Does the firm allow the worker a drawing account or advances against pay? ☐ Yes ☐ No
If "Yes": Is the worker paid such advances on a regular basis? ☐ Yes ☐ No

d How does the worker repay such advances? ....

9a Is the worker eligible for a pension, bonus, paid vacations, sick pay, etc.? ☐ Yes ☐ No
If "Yes," specify ....

b Does the firm carry workmen's compensation insurance on the worker? ☐ Yes ☐ No

c Does the firm deduct social security and Medicare taxes from amounts paid the worker? ☐ Yes ☐ No

d Does the firm deduct Federal income taxes from amounts paid the worker? ☐ Yes ☐ No

e How does the firm report the worker's income to the Internal Revenue Service?
☐ Form W-2 ☐ Form 1099-MISC ☐ Does not report ☐ Other (specify) ....
Attach a copy.

f Does the firm bond the worker? ☐ Yes ☐ No

10a Approximately how many hours a day does the worker perform services for the firm? ....
Does the firm set hours of work for the worker? ☐ Yes ☐ No
If "Yes," what are the worker's set hours? ______ am/pm to ______ am/pm (Circle whether am or pm)

b Does the worker perform similar services for others? ☐ Yes ☐ No ☐ Unknown
If "Yes": Are these services performed on a daily basis for other firms? ☐ Yes ☐ No ☐ Unknown
Percentage of time spent in performing these services for:
This firm .... % Other firms .... % ☐ **Unknown**
Does the firm have priority on the worker's time? ☐ Yes ☐ No
If "No," explain ....

c Is the worker prohibited from competing with the firm either while performing services or during any later period? ☐ Yes ☐ No

11a Can the firm discharge the worker at any time without incurring a liability? ☐ Yes ☐ No
If "No," explain ....

b Can the worker terminate the services at any time without incurring a liability? ☐ Yes ☐ No
If "No," explain ....

12a Does the worker perform services for the firm under:
☐ The firm's business name ☐ The worker's own business name ☐ Other (specify) ....

b Does the worker advertise or maintain a business listing in the telephone directory, a trade journal, etc.? ☐ Yes ☐ No ☐ Unknown
If "Yes," specify ....

c Does the worker represent himself or herself to the public as being in business to perform the same or similar services? ☐ Yes ☐ No ☐ Unknown
If "Yes," how? ....

d Does the worker have his or her own shop or office? ☐ Yes ☐ No ☐ Unknown
If "Yes," where? ....

e Does the firm represent the worker as an employee of the firm to its customers? ☐ Yes ☐ No
If "No," how is the worker represented? ....

f How did the firm learn of the worker's services? ....

13 Is a license necessary for the work? ☐ Yes ☐ No ☐ Unknown
If "Yes," what kind of license is required? ....
By whom is it issued? ....
By whom is the license fee paid? ....

14 Does the worker have a financial investment in a business related to the services performed? ☐ Yes ☐ No ☐ Unknown
If "Yes," specify and give amounts of the investment ....

15 Can the worker incur a loss in the performance of the service for the firm? ☐ Yes ☐ No
If "Yes," how? ....

16a Has any other government agency ruled on the status of the firm's workers? ☐ Yes ☐ No
If "Yes," attach a copy of the ruling.

b Is the same issue being considered by any IRS office in connection with the audit of the worker's tax return or the firm's tax return, or has it recently been considered? ☐ Yes ☐ No
If "Yes," for which year(s)?

Published by Tax Management Inc., a Subsidiary of The Bureau of National Affairs, Inc.

Form SS-8 (Rev. 7-93) Page 4

17 Does the worker assemble or process a product at home or away from the firm's place of business? ☐ Yes ☐ No

If "Yes":

Who furnishes materials or goods used by the worker? ☐ Firm ☐ Worker

Is the worker furnished a pattern or given instructions to follow in making the product? ☐ Yes ☐ No

Is the worker required to return the finished product to the firm or to someone designated by the firm? ☐ Yes ☐ No

Answer items 18a through n only if the worker is a salesperson or provides a service directly to customers.

18a Are leads to prospective customers furnished by the firm? ☐ Yes ☐ No ☐ Does not apply

b Is the worker required to pursue or report on leads? ☐ Yes ☐ No ☐ Does not apply

c Is the worker required to adhere to prices, terms, and conditions of sale established by the firm? ☐ Yes ☐ No

d Are orders submitted to and subject to approval by the firm? ☐ Yes ☐ No

e Is the worker expected to attend sales meetings? ☐ Yes ☐ No

If "Yes": Is the worker subject to any kind of penalty for failing to attend? ☐ Yes ☐ No

f Does the firm assign a specific territory to the worker? ☐ Yes ☐ No ☐ Does not apply

g Who does the customer pay? ☐ Firm ☐ Worker

If worker, does the worker remit the total amount to the firm? ☐ Yes ☐ No

h Does the worker sell a consumer product in a home or establishment other than a permanent retail establishment? ☐ Yes ☐ No

i List the products and/or services distributed by the worker, such as meat, vegetables, fruit, bakery products, beverages (other than milk), or laundry or dry cleaning services. If more than one type of product and/or service is distributed, specify the principal one. ....

j Did the firm or another person assign the route or territory and a list of customers to the worker? ☐ Yes ☐ No

If "Yes," enter the name and job title of the person who made the assignment. ....

....

k Did the worker pay the firm or person for the privilege of serving customers on the route or in the territory? ☐ Yes ☐ No

If "Yes," how much did the worker pay (not including any amount paid for a truck or racks, etc.)? $ ....

What factors were considered in determining the value of the route or territory? ....

l How are new customers obtained by the worker? Explain fully, showing whether the new customers called the firm for service, were solicited by the worker, or both. ....

m Does the worker sell life insurance? ☐ Yes ☐ No

If "Yes":

Is the selling of life insurance or annuity contracts for the firm the worker's entire business activity? ☐ Yes ☐ No

If "No," list the other business activities and the amount of time spent on them ....

Does the worker sell other types of insurance for the firm? ☐ Yes ☐ No

If "Yes," state the percentage of the worker's total working time spent in selling other types of insurance .... %

At the time the contract was entered into between the firm and the worker, was it their intention that the worker sell life insurance for the firm: ☐ on a full-time basis ☐ on a part-time basis

State the manner in which the intention was expressed. ....

n Is the worker a traveling or city salesperson? ☐ Yes ☐ No

If "Yes": From whom does worker principally solicit orders for the firm? ....

If the worker solicits orders from wholesalers, retailers, contractors, or operators of hotels, restaurants, or other similar establishments, specify the percentage of the worker's time spent in this solicitation. .... %

Is the merchandise purchased by the customers for resale or for use in their business operations? If used by the customers in their business operations, describe the merchandise and state whether it is equipment installed on their premises or a consumable supply. ....

....

19 Attach a detailed explanation of any other reason why you believe the worker is an independent contractor or is an employee of the firm.

Under penalties of perjury, I declare that I have examined this request, including accompanying documents, and to the best of my knowledge and belief, the facts presented are true, correct, and complete.

Signature ► Title ► Date ►

If this form is used by the firm in requesting a written determination, the form must be signed by an officer or member of the firm.
If this form is used by the worker in requesting a written determination, the form must be signed by the worker. If the worker wants a written determination about services performed for two or more firms, a separate form must be completed and signed for each firm.
Additional copies of this form may be obtained from any Internal Revenue Service office or by calling 1-800-TAX-FORM (1-800-829-3676).

Department of the Treasury
Internal Revenue Service

Instructions for Form 2553

(Revised September 1993)

Election by a Small Business Corporation

Section references are to the Internal Revenue Code unless otherwise noted.

Paperwork Reduction Act Notice.—We ask for the information on this form to carry out the Internal Revenue laws of the United States. You are required to give us the information. We need it to ensure that you are complying with these laws and to allow us to figure and collect the right amount of tax.

The time needed to complete and file this form will vary depending on individual circumstances. The estimated average time is:

Recordkeeping . . . . . . 6 hr., 13 min.
Learning about the law or the form . . . . . . 2 hr., 59 min.
Preparing, copying, assembling, and sending the form to the IRS . . . . 3 hr., 13 min.

If you have comments concerning the accuracy of these time estimates or suggestions for making this form more simple, we would be happy to hear from you. You can write to both the **Internal Revenue Service,** Attention: Reports Clearance Officer, T:FP, Washington, DC 20224; and the **Office of Management and Budget,** Paperwork Reduction Project (1545-0146), Washington, DC 20503. **DO NOT** send the tax form to either of these offices. Instead, see **Where To File** below.

General Instructions

Purpose.—To elect to be an "S corporation," a corporation must file Form 2553. The election permits the income of the S corporation to be taxed to the shareholders of the corporation rather than to the corporation itself, except as provided in Subchapter S of the Code. For more information, get **Pub. 589,** Tax Information on S Corporations.

Who May Elect.—A corporation may elect to be an S corporation only if it meets **all** of the following tests:

1. It is a domestic corporation.

2. It has no more than 35 shareholders. A husband and wife (and their estates) are treated as one shareholder for this requirement. All other persons are treated as separate shareholders.

3. It has only individuals, estates, or certain trusts as shareholders. See the instructions for Part III regarding qualified subchapter S trusts.

4. It has no nonresident alien shareholders.

5. It has only one class of stock (disregarding differences in voting rights). Generally, a corporation is treated as having only one class of stock if all outstanding shares of the corporation's stock confer identical rights to distribution and liquidation proceeds. See Regulations section 1.1361-1(l) for more details.

6. It is not one of the following ineligible corporations:

a. A corporation that owns 80% or more of the stock of another corporation, unless the other corporation has not begun business and has no gross income;

b. A bank or thrift institution;

c. An insurance company subject to tax under the special rules of Subchapter L of the Code;

d. A corporation that has elected to be treated as a possessions corporation under section 936; or

e. A domestic international sales corporation (DISC) or former DISC.

7. It has a permitted tax year as required by section 1378 or makes a section 444 election to have a tax year other than a permitted tax year. Section 1378 defines a permitted tax year as a tax year ending December 31, or any other tax year for which the corporation establishes a business purpose to the satisfaction of the IRS. See Part II for details on requesting a fiscal tax year based on a business purpose or on making a section 444 election.

8. Each shareholder consents as explained in the instructions for Column K.

See sections 1361, 1362, and 1378 for additional information on the above tests.

Where To File.—File this election with the Internal Revenue Service Center listed below.

If the corporation's principal business, office, or agency is located in	Use the following Internal Revenue Service Center address
New Jersey, New York (New York City and counties of Nassau, Rockland, Suffolk, and Westchester)	Holtsville, NY 00501
New York (all other counties), Connecticut, Maine, Massachusetts, New Hampshire, Rhode Island, Vermont	Andover, MA 05501
Illinois, Iowa, Minnesota, Missouri, Wisconsin	Kansas City, MO 64999
Delaware, District of Columbia, Maryland, Pennsylvania, Virginia	Philadelphia, PA 19255
Florida, Georgia, South Carolina	Atlanta, GA 39901
Indiana, Kentucky, Michigan, Ohio, West Virginia	Cincinnati, OH 45999
Kansas, New Mexico, Oklahoma, Texas	Austin, TX 73301
Alaska, Arizona, California (counties of Alpine, Amador, Butte, Calaveras, Colusa, Contra Costa, Del Norte, El Dorado, Glenn, Humboldt, Lake, Lassen, Marin, Mendocino, Modoc, Napa, Nevada, Placer, Plumas, Sacramento, San Joaquin, Shasta, Sierra, Siskiyou, Solano, Sonoma, Sutter, Tehama, Trinity, Yolo, and Yuba), Colorado, Idaho, Montana, Nebraska, Nevada, North Dakota, Oregon, South Dakota, Utah, Washington, Wyoming	Ogden, UT 84201
California (all other counties), Hawaii	Fresno, CA 93888
Alabama, Arkansas, Louisiana, Mississippi, North Carolina, Tennessee	Memphis, TN 37501

When To Make the Election.—Complete and file Form 2553 **(a)** at any time before the 16th day of the third month of the tax year, if filed during the tax year the election is to take effect, or **(b)** at any time during the preceding tax year. An election made no later than 2 months and 15 days after the beginning of a tax year that is less than 2½ months long is treated as timely made for that tax year. An election made after the 15th day of the third month but before the end of the tax year is effective for the next year. For example, if a calendar tax year corporation makes the election in April 1994, it is effective for the corporation's 1995 calendar tax year. See section 1362(b) for more information.

Acceptance or Nonacceptance of Election.—The Service Center will notify the corporation if its election is accepted and when it will take effect. The corporation will also be notified if its election is not accepted. The corporation should generally receive a determination on its election within 60 days after it has filed Form 2553. If box Q1 in Part II is checked on page 2, the corporation will receive a ruling letter from the IRS in Washington, DC, that either approves or denies the selected tax year. When box Q1 is checked, it will generally take an additional 90 days for the Form 2553 to be accepted.

Do not file Form 1120S until the corporation is notified that its election has been accepted. If the corporation is now required to file **Form 1120,** U.S. Corporation Income Tax Return, or any other applicable tax return, continue filing it until the election takes effect.

Care should be exercised to ensure that the IRS receives the election. If the corporation is not notified of acceptance or nonacceptance of its election within 3 months

Cat. No. 49978N

of date of filing (date mailed), or within 6 months if box Q1 is checked, please take follow-up action by corresponding with the Service Center where the corporation filed the election. If the IRS questions whether Form 2553 was filed, an acceptable proof of filing is: **(a)** certified or registered mail receipt (timely filed); **(b)** Form 2553 with accepted stamp; **(c)** Form 2553 with stamped IRS received date; or **(d)** IRS letter stating that Form 2553 has been accepted.

End of Election.— Once the election is made, it stays in effect for all years until it is terminated. During the 5 years after the election is terminated under section 1362(d), the corporation (or a successor corporation) can make another election on Form 2553 only with IRS consent. See Regulations section 1.1362-5 for more details.

Specific Instructions

Part I

Part I must be completed by all corporations.

Name and Address of Corporation.—Enter the true corporate name as set forth in the corporate charter or other legal document creating it. If the corporation's mailing address is the same as someone else's, such as a shareholder's, please enter "c/o" and this person's name following the name of the corporation. Include the suite, room, or other unit number after the street address. If the Post Office does not deliver to the street address and the corporation has a P.O. box, show the box number instead of the street address. If the corporation changed its name or address after applying for its EIN, be sure to check the box in item G of Part I.

Item A. Employer Identification Number.—If the corporation has applied for an employer identification number (EIN) but has not received it, enter "applied for." If the corporation does not have an EIN, it should apply for one on **Form SS-4,** Application for Employer Identification Number, available from most IRS and Social Security Administration offices.

Item D. Effective Date of Election.—Enter the beginning effective date (month, day, year) of the tax year requested for the S corporation. Generally, this will be the beginning date of the tax year for which the ending effective date is required to be shown in item I, Part I. For a new corporation (first year the corporation exists) it will generally be the date required to be shown in item H, Part I. The tax year of a new corporation starts on the date that it has shareholders, acquires assets, or begins doing business, whichever happens first. If the effective date for item D for a newly formed corporation is later than the date in item H, the corporation should file Form 1120 or Form 1120-A, for the tax period between these dates.

Column K. Shareholders' Consent Statement.—Each shareholder who owns (or is deemed to own) stock at the time the election is made must consent to the election. If the election is made during the corporation's tax year for which it first takes effect, any person who held stock at any time during the part of that year that occurs before the election is made, must consent to the election, even though the person may have sold or transferred his or her stock before the election is made. Each shareholder consents by signing and dating in column K or signing and dating a separate consent statement described below.

An election made during the first 2½ months of the tax year is effective for the following tax year if any person who held stock in the corporation during the part of the tax year before the election was made, and who did not hold stock at the time the election was made, did not consent to the election.

If a husband and wife have a community interest in the stock or in the income from it, both must consent. Each tenant in common, joint tenant, and tenant by the entirety also must consent.

A minor's consent is made by the minor or the legal representative of the minor, or by a natural or adoptive parent of the minor if no legal representative has been appointed.

The consent of an estate is made by an executor or administrator.

If stock is owned by a trust that is a qualified shareholder, the deemed owner of the trust must consent. See section 1361(c)(2) for details regarding qualified trusts that may be shareholders and rules on determining who is the deemed owner of the trust.

Continuation sheet or separate consent statement.—If you need a continuation sheet or use a separate consent statement, attach it to Form 2553. The separate consent statement must contain the name, address, and employer identification number of the corporation and the shareholder information requested in columns J through N of Part I.

If you want, you may combine all the shareholders' consents in one statement.

Column L.—Enter the number of shares of stock each shareholder owns and the dates the stock was acquired. If the election is made during the corporation's tax year for which it first takes effect, do not list the shares of stock for those shareholders who sold or transferred all of their stock before the election was made. However, these shareholders must still consent to the election for it to be effective for the tax year.

Column M.—Enter the social security number of each shareholder who is an individual. Enter the employer identification number of each shareholder that is an estate or a qualified trust.

Column N.—Enter the month and day that each shareholder's tax year ends. If a shareholder is changing his or her tax year, enter the tax year the shareholder is changing to, and attach an explanation indicating the present tax year and the basis for the change (e.g., automatic revenue procedure or letter ruling request).

If the election is made during the corporation's tax year for which it first takes effect, you do not have to enter the tax year of any shareholder who sold or transferred all of his or her stock before the election was made.

Signature.—Form 2553 must be signed by the president, treasurer, assistant treasurer, chief accounting officer, or other corporate officer (such as tax officer) authorized to sign.

Part II

Complete Part II if you selected a tax year ending on any date other than December 31 (other than a 52-53-week tax year ending with reference to the month of December).

Box P1.—Attach a statement showing separately for each month the amount of gross receipts for the most recent 47 months as required by section 4.03(3) of Revenue Procedure 87-32, 1987-2 C.B. 396. A corporation that does not have a 47-month period of gross receipts cannot establish a natural business year under section 4.01(1).

Box Q1.—For examples of an acceptable business purpose for requesting a fiscal tax year, see Revenue Ruling 87-57, 1987-2 C.B. 117.

In addition to a statement showing the business purpose for the requested fiscal year, you must attach the other information necessary to meet the ruling request requirements of Revenue Procedure 93-1, 1993-1 I.R.B. 10 (updated annually). Also attach a statement that shows separately the amount of gross receipts from sales or services (and inventory costs, if applicable) for each of the 36 months preceding the effective date of the election to be an S corporation. If the corporation has been in existence for fewer than 36 months, submit figures for the period of existence.

If you check box Q1, you must also pay a user fee of $200 (subject to change). Do not pay the fee when filing Form 2553. The Service Center will send Form 2553 to the IRS in Washington, DC, who, in turn, will notify the corporation that the fee is due. See Revenue Procedure 93-23, 1993-19 I.R.B. 6.

Box Q2.—If the corporation makes a back-up section 444 election for which it is qualified, then the election must be exercised in the event the business purpose request is not approved. Under certain circumstances, the tax year requested under the back-up section 444 election may be different than the tax year requested under business purpose. See **Form 8716,** Election To Have a Tax Year Other Than a Required Tax Year, for details on making a back-up section 444 election.

Boxes Q2 and R2.—If the corporation is not qualified to make the section 444 election after making the item Q2 back-up section 444 election or indicating its intention to make the election in item R1, and therefore it later files a calendar year return, it should write "Section 444 Election Not Made" in the top left corner of the 1st calendar year Form 1120S it files.

Part III

Certain Qualified Subchapter S Trusts (QSSTs) may make the QSST election required by section 1361(d)(2) in Part III. Part III may be used to make the QSST election only if corporate stock has been transferred to the trust on or before the date on which the corporation makes its election to be an S corporation. However, a statement can be used in lieu of Part III to make the election.

Note: *Part III may be used only in conjunction with making the Part I election (i.e., Form 2553 cannot be filed with only Part III completed).*

The deemed owner of the QSST must also consent to the S corporation election in column K, page 1, of Form 2553. See section 1361(c)(2).

Printed on recycled paper

*U.S. Government Printing Office: 1993 — 301-628/80221

Form **2553**
(Rev. September 1993)
Department of the Treasury
Internal Revenue Service

Election by a Small Business Corporation

(Under section 1362 of the Internal Revenue Code)
▶ For Paperwork Reduction Act Notice, see page 1 of instructions.
▶ See separate instructions.

OMB No. 1545-0146
Expires 8-31-96

Notes: 1. *This election, to be an "S corporation," can be accepted only if all the tests are met under* ***Who May Elect*** *on page 1 of the instructions; all signatures in Parts I and III are originals (no photocopies); and the exact name and address of the corporation and other required form information are provided.*

2. *Do not file Form 1120S, U.S. Income Tax Return for an S Corporation, until you are notified that your election is accepted.*

Part I — Election Information

Please Type or Print	Name of corporation (see instructions)	**A** Employer identification number (EIN)
	Number, street, and room or suite no. (If a P.O. box, see instructions.)	**B** Date incorporated
	City or town, state, and ZIP code	**C** State of incorporation

D Election is to be effective for tax year beginning (month, day, year) . . . . ▶ / /

E Name and title of officer or legal representative who the IRS may call for more information

F Telephone number of officer or legal representative ( )

G If the corporation changed its name or address after applying for the EIN shown in **A**, check this box . . . . ▶ ☐

H If this election takes effect for the first tax year the corporation exists, enter month, day, and year of the **earliest** of the following: (1) date the corporation first had shareholders, (2) date the corporation first had assets, or (3) date the corporation began doing business . . . . ▶ / /

I Selected tax year: Annual return will be filed for tax year ending (month and day) ▶ ....

If the tax year ends on any date other than December 31, except for an automatic 52-53-week tax year ending with reference to the month of December, you **must** complete Part II on the back. If the date you enter is the ending date of an automatic 52-53-week tax year, write "52-53-week year" to the right of the date. See Temporary Regulations section 1.441-2T(e)(3).

J Name and address of each shareholder, shareholder's spouse having a community property interest in the corporation's stock, and each tenant in common, joint tenant, and tenant by the entirety. (A husband and wife (and their estates) are counted as one shareholder in determining the number of shareholders without regard to the manner in which the stock is owned.)	K Shareholders' Consent Statement. Under penalties of perjury, we declare that we consent to the election of the above-named corporation to be an "S corporation" under section 1362(a) and that we have examined this consent statement, including accompanying schedules and statements, and to the best of our knowledge and belief, it is true, correct, and complete. (Shareholders sign and date below.)*		L Stock owned		M Social security number or employer identification number (see instructions)	N Share-holder's tax year ends (month and day)
	Signature	Date	Number of shares	Dates acquired		

*For this election to be valid, the consent of each shareholder, shareholder's spouse having a community property interest in the corporation's stock, and each tenant in common, joint tenant, and tenant by the entirety must either appear above or be attached to this form. (See instructions for Column K if a continuation sheet or a separate consent statement is needed.)

Under penalties of perjury, I declare that I have examined this election, including accompanying schedules and statements, and to the best of my knowledge and belief, it is true, correct, and complete.

Signature of officer ▶ **Title ▶** **Date ▶**

See Parts II and III on back. Cat. No. 18629R Form **2553** (Rev. 9-93)

Form 2553 (Rev. 9-93) Page 2

Part II **Selection of Fiscal Tax Year (All corporations using this part must complete item O and one of items P, Q, or R.)**

O Check the applicable box below to indicate whether the corporation is:

1. ☐ A new corporation adopting the tax year entered in item I, Part I.
2. ☐ An existing corporation retaining the tax year entered in item I, Part I.
3. ☐ An existing corporation changing to the tax year entered in item I, Part I.

P Complete item P if the corporation is using the expeditious approval provisions of Revenue Procedure 87-32, 1987-2 C.B. 396, to request: (1) a natural business year (as defined in section 4.01(1) of Rev. Proc. 87-32), or (2) a year that satisfies the ownership tax year test in section 4.01(2) of Rev. Proc. 87-32. Check the applicable box below to indicate the representation statement the corporation is making as required under section 4 of Rev. Proc. 87-32.

1. Natural Business Year ▶ ☐ I represent that the corporation is retaining or changing to a tax year that coincides with its natural business year as defined in section 4.01(1) of Rev. Proc. 87-32 and as verified by its satisfaction of the requirements of section 4.02(1) of Rev. Proc. 87-32. In addition, if the corporation is changing to a natural business year as defined in section 4.01(1), I further represent that such tax year results in less deferral of income to the owners than the corporation's present tax year. I also represent that the corporation is not described in section 3.01(2) of Rev. Proc. 87-32. (See instructions for additional information that must be attached.)

2. Ownership Tax Year ▶ ☐ I represent that shareholders holding more than half of the shares of the stock (as of the first day of the tax year to which the request relates) of the corporation have the same tax year or are concurrently changing to the tax year that the corporation adopts, retains, or changes to per item I, Part I. I also represent that the corporation is not described in section 3.01(2) of Rev. Proc. 87-32.

Note: *If you do not use item P and the corporation wants a fiscal tax year, complete either item Q or R below. Item Q is used to request a fiscal tax year based on a business purpose and to make a back-up section 444 election. Item R is used to make a regular section 444 election.*

Q Business Purpose—To request a fiscal tax year based on a business purpose, you must check box Q1 and pay a user fee. See instructions for details. You may also check box Q2 and/or box Q3.

1. Check here ▶ ☐ if the fiscal year entered in item I, Part I, is requested under the provisions of section 6.03 of Rev. Proc. 87-32. Attach to Form 2553 a statement showing the business purpose for the requested fiscal year. See instructions for additional information that must be attached.

2. Check here ▶ ☐ to show that the corporation intends to make a back-up section 444 election in the event the corporation's business purpose request is not approved by the IRS. (See instructions for more information.)

3. Check here ▶ ☐ to show that the corporation agrees to adopt or change to a tax year ending December 31 if necessary for the IRS to accept this election for S corporation status in the event: (1) the corporation's business purpose request is not approved and the corporation makes a back-up section 444 election, but is ultimately not qualified to make a section 444 election, or (2) the corporation's business purpose request is not approved and the corporation did not make a back-up section 444 election.

R Section 444 Election—To make a section 444 election, you must check box R1 and you may also check box R2.

1. Check here ▶ ☐ to show the corporation will make, if qualified, a section 444 election to have the fiscal tax year shown in item I, Part I. To make the election, you must complete **Form 8716,** Election To Have a Tax Year Other Than a Required Tax Year, and either attach it to Form 2553 or file it separately.

2. Check here ▶ ☐ to show that the corporation agrees to adopt or change to a tax year ending December 31 if necessary for the IRS to accept this election for S corporation status in the event the corporation is ultimately not qualified to make a section 444 election.

Part III **Qualified Subchapter S Trust (QSST) Election Under Section 1361(d)(2)****

Income beneficiary's name and address	Social security number
Trust's name and address	Employer identification number

Date on which stock of the corporation was transferred to the trust (month, day, year) . . . . ▶ / /

In order for the trust named above to be a QSST and thus a qualifying shareholder of the S corporation for which this Form 2553 is filed, I hereby make the election under section 1361(d)(2). Under penalties of perjury, I certify that the trust meets the definitional requirements of section 1361(d)(3) and that all other information provided in Part III is true, correct, and complete.

Signature of income beneficiary or signature and title of legal representative or other qualified person making the election — Date

**Use of Part III to make the QSST election may be made only if stock of the corporation has been transferred to the trust on or before the date on which the corporation makes its election to be an S corporation. The QSST election must be made and filed separately if stock of the corporation is transferred to the trust after the date on which the corporation makes the S election.

Printed on recycled paper *U.S. Government Printing Office: 1993 — 301-628/80216

Form 12. UCC-1—Standard Financing Statement

STATE OF CALIFORNIA   WOLCOTTS FORM UCCCAØ1 (formerly UCC-1CA) (price class 13C)
UNIFORM COMMERCIAL CODE--FINANCING STATEMENT--FORM UCC-1
IMPORTANT--Read Instructions on back before completing form

7 67775 82901 3

This **FINANCING STATEMENT** is presented for filing and will remain effective, with certain exceptions, for five years from the date of filing, pursuant to Section 9403 of the California Uniform Commercial Code.

1. DEBTOR (LAST NAME FIRST—IF AN INDIVIDUAL) | 1A. SOCIAL SECURITY OR FEDERAL TAX NO.

1B. MAILING ADDRESS | 1C. CITY, STATE | 1D. ZIP CODE

2. ADDITIONAL DEBTOR (IF ANY) (LAST NAME FIRST—IF AN INDIVIDUAL) | 2A. SOCIAL SECURITY OR FEDERAL TAX NO.

2B. MAILING ADDRESS | 2C. CITY, STATE | 2D. ZIP CODE

3. DEBTOR'S TRADE NAMES OR STYLES (IF ANY) | 3A. FEDERAL TAX NUMBER

4. SECURED PARTY | 4A. SOCIAL SECURITY NO., FEDERAL TAX NO OR BANK TRANSIT AND A.B.A. NO.

NAME

MAILING ADDRESS

CITY   STATE   ZIP CODE

5. ASSIGNEE OF SECURED PARTY (IF ANY) | 5A. SOCIAL SECURITY NO., FEDERAL TAX NO OR BANK TRANSIT AND A.B.A. NO.

NAME

MAILING ADDRESS

CITY   STATE   ZIP CODE

6. This FINANCING STATEMENT covers the following types or items of property **(include description of real property on which located and owner of record when required by instruction 4).**

7. CHECK IF APPLICABLE ☒ | 7A. ☐ PRODUCTS OF COLLATERAL ARE ALSO COVERED | 7B. DEBTOR(S) SIGNATURE NOT REQUIRED IN ACCORDANCE WITH INSTRUCTION 5(a) ITEM: ☐ (1) ☐ (2) ☐ (3) ☐ (4)

8. CHECK IF APPLICABLE ☒ | ☐ DEBTOR IS A "TRANSMITTING UTILITY" IN ACCORDANCE WITH UCC § 9105 (1) (n)

9. DATE:

▶
SIGNATURE(S) OF DEBTOR(S)

TYPE OR PRINT NAME(S) OF DEBTOR(S)

▶
SIGNATURE(S) OF SECURED PARTY(IES)

TYPE OR PRINT NAME(S) OF SECURED PARTY(IES)

CODE 1 2 3 4 5 6 7 8 9 0

10. THIS SPACE FOR USE OF FILING OFFICER (DATE, TIME, FILE NUMBER AND FILING OFFICER)

11. *Return copy to:*

NAME
ADDRESS
CITY
STATE
ZIP CODE

(1) FILING OFFICER COPY   FORM UCC-1 *Approved by the Secretary of State*

STATE OF CALIFORNIA
UNIFORM COMMERCIAL CODE—REQUEST FOR INFORMATION OR COPIES—FORM UCC-3
IMPORTANT—Read instructions on back before completing form

WOLCOTTS FORM UCC-3CA
(price class 13B)

REQUEST FOR INFORMATION OR COPIES. Present in Duplicate to Filing Officer

1. ☐ **INFORMATION REQUEST.** Filing officer please furnish certificate showing whether there is on file any presently effective financing statement naming the Debtor listed below and any statement of assignment thereof, and if there is, giving the date and hour of filing of each such statement and the names and addresses of each secured party named therein.

1A. DEBTOR (LAST NAME FIRST)		1B. SOC. SEC. OR FED. TAX NO.
1C. MAILING ADDRESS	1D. CITY, STATE	1E. ZIP CODE

1F.

Date__________19____ Signature of Requesting Party__________

2. CERTIFICATE:

FILE NUMBER	DATE AND HOUR OF FILING	NAME(S) AND ADDRESS(ES) OF SECURED PARTY(IES) AND ASSIGNEE(S), IF ANY

The undersigned filing officer hereby certifies that the above listing is a record of all presently effective financing statements and statements of assignment which name the above debtor and which are on file in my office as of________19____at____ ___M.

__________19____
(DATE)

____
(FILING OFFICER)

By:__________

3. ☐ **COPY REQUEST.** Filing officer please furnish________copy(ies) of each page of the following statements concerning the debtors listed below ☐ Financing Statement ☐ Amendments ☐ Statements of Assignment ☐ Continuation Statements ☐ Statement of Release ☐ Termination Statement ☐ All Statements on file.

FILE NUMBER	DATE OF FILING	NAME(S) AND MAILING ADDRESS(ES) OF DEBTOR(S)	DEBTORS SOC. SEC. OR FED. TAX NO.

Date__________19____ Signature of Requesting Party__________

4. CERTIFICATE

The undersigned filing officer hereby certifies that the attached copies are true and exact copies of all statements requested above.

__________19____
(DATE)

____
(FILING OFFICER)

By:__________

5. **Mail Information or Copies to**

NAME
MAILING
ADDRESS
CITY AND
STATE

Section IV

Legal Audit Analysis

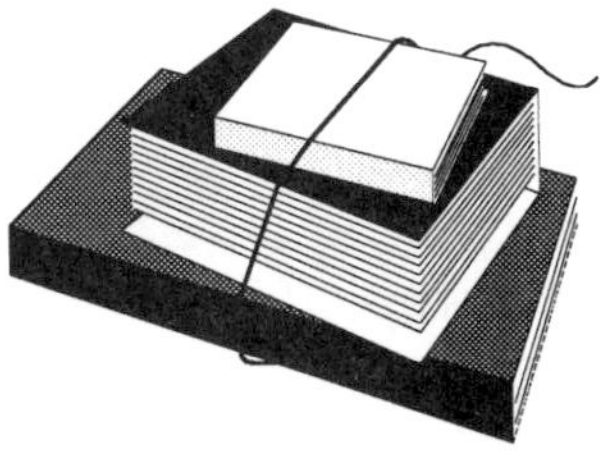

A. Form of Business

1. Sole Proprietorship

a. Has the company applied for a Business License? Regardless of the type of business you are in, your business will be required to get a business license from a county or city agency that handles licensing businesses operating in their territories. Typically, you must obtain this business license within a few days to a couple of weeks of starting or purchasing your business. If you have not obtained this license, do so immediately, because running your business without it may cause the business to incur penalties.

b. Has the company obtained a Resale Permit? With limited exceptions, any business that sells tangible personal property must pay sales or use tax. To determine if your business needs to pay this tax, you must first obtain a seller's permit from the appropriate government agency. Check the government pages in the city where you live to determine which state agency to call and contact that agency to determine which steps to take in order to obtain the seller's permit. Once you acquire a seller's permit, you will generally have the right to purchase property for resale without paying tax. By providing the vendor with a resale certificate (which you acquire at any local stationery store and fill out using your seller's permit number), you will not be required to pay sales tax on tangible personal property you purchase for resale.

c. Has the company filed a Fictitious Business Name Statement in the county where the business is located? If your proprietorship name does not reflect your surname or if it implies additional owners, then you will be required to file a Fictitious Business Name Statement. If your proprietorship is required to file this statement and if you have not already done so, contact your county recorder's office to get instructions on filing this form. (See Form No.8 in Section III for an example of a Fictitious Business Name Statement.)

d. Has the company obtained a Federal Employer Identification Number (FEIN)? Unless you use your social security number for business tax purposes, you must obtain a Federal Employer Identification Number from the IRS. This number is used to identify your business for income tax, payroll, and other federal purposes. The IRS requires that you apply for the number if you or your proprietorship fits one of the following categories: 1) you do not have a FEIN and the business will be or currently is: a) paying wages: b) required to use a FEIN even if the business is not employing anyone; or c) the business is required to withhold taxes on income; or 2) you will become the new owner of an existing business, even if the business does not have employees; or 3) you are incorporating your proprietorship. (See Form No. 9 in Section III for an example of a FEIN application.)

2. Partnership

a. Has the partnership recorded a Notice of Partnership in the county where the partnership is located? No legal filing or recording is necessary to form a general partnership. However, recording a Notice of Partnership provides constructive notice to the world that the partnership exists, who the partners are, and if the partnership owns any real property. Having such a notice could prove beneficial should you have to prove ownership or partnership existence in the future.

b. Have the partners signed a written Partnership Agreement? Although it is not required, it is beneficial to have a written Partnership Agreement, because without one, state law prevails and the agreement created by your state may not be what you had in mind. If you have not already done so, get your agreement in writing. Those who do not will almost always end up in needless litigation. (See Form No. 2 in Section I for an example of a Partnership Agreement.)

c. Has the partnership applied for a Business License? Same as Proprietorship section.

d. Has the partnership obtained a Resale Permit? Same as Proprietorship section.

e. Has the partnership obtained its Federal Employer Identification Number? Partnerships are required to obtain a Federal Employer Identification Number (FEIN). See Proprietorship section above. In addition to the categories listed in the proprietorship section, if you are forming or incorporating your partnership and even if it does not have employees, you will need to obtain a Federal Employer Identification Number. (See Form No. 9 in Section III for an example of a FEIN application.)

f. Has the partnership filed a Fictitious Business Name Statement in the county where the partnership is located? If the partnership name does not reflect the partner's surnames or if it implies additional owners, then most states will require the partnership to file a Fictitious Business Name Statement. If your partnership is required to file this statement and if you have not already done so, contact your county recorder's office to get instructions on filing this form. (See Form No. 8 in Section III for an example of a Fictitious Business Name Statement.)

3. Corporation

a. Is a copy of the Articles of Incorporation in the corporate minute book? The Articles of Incorporation is the initial incorporating document which is filed with the Secretary of State. It sets forth the name of the corporation, the number of shares authorized, the initial agent, and sometimes the name of the first director(s). A copy of the Articles should be placed in the corporate minute book for safe keeping. You will need it to open your corporate bank account, so keep a copy readily available. (See Form No. 5 in Section I for an example of Articles of Incorporation.)

b. Have you checked into the benefits of electing Subchapter S status? Check with your tax accountant or other tax expert to determine if your corporation can qualify for Subchapter S status, and if so, whether it should make that election. The advantage of operating as a Subchapter S Corporation is that the S Corporation is taxed like a partnership and therefore avoids the double taxation disadvantage required when operating as a "C" corporation. (See Form No. 11 in Section III for an example of a federal application for Subchapter S election.)

c. Is a copy of the corporate bylaws included in the corporate minute book? Although the bylaws are somewhat lengthy and complicated, it is important that you review them carefully and keep a copy in the corporate minute book. They provide guidance concerning the handling of the corporation's affairs and they are the rules that the corporation, directors, and officers must abide by. (See Form No. 6 in Section I for an example of corporate bylaws.)

d. Are copies of the incorporating documents in the corporate minute book? These documents contain resolutions regarding actions required to be taken by the Board of Directors and shareholders in connection with the formation of the corporation. They should be fully executed and filed in the corporate minute book. If you have not already done so, prepare such documents, sign where indicated, and file in the corporate minute book. (See Form No. 7 in Section I for an example of the Minutes of the First Meeting of the Directors. The minutes for the First Meeting of the Shareholders are more elementary. They simply ratify the actions taken at the first board of director's meeting.)

e. Are the original shares certificates in the corporate minute book or in a safe place? The share certificates evidence ownership of the corporation's stock. You should file the original share certificates either in the corporate minute book or in another place of safekeeping, such as in a safety deposit box at a bank.

f. Have all the shareholders signed a Shareholders' Agreement? If the corporation has more than one shareholder, a written Shareholders' Agreement should be prepared and executed among all shareholders. Without such a document in place, upon the death of a shareholder, the surviving shareholder(s) may find himself/herself/themselves in business with the late shareholder's spouse or heirs and this may or may not be beneficial to operating the business. (See Form No. 8 in Section I for an example of a Shareholders' Agreement.)

g. Are the corporate annual minutes prepared each year? Under the laws in each state, a corporation is required to conduct annual meetings of directors and shareholders. These meetings and their proper documentation are important for many reasons, including protecting shareholders from personal liability as a result of piercing the corporate veil and protecting corporate directors, officers, and shareholders from personal liability to past, present, and future creditors and tax agencies. If you have not already done so, bring the corporation into compliance with corporate law by preparing such documents, executing them, and placing them in the corporate minute book.

See Form No's. 9 and 10 in Section I for an example of the Annual Written Consent in Lieu of a Directors' Meeting and Annual Written Consent in Lieu of a Shareholders' Meeting. Such written consents are used when the directors and shareholders do not formally hold meetings, but take action having the same effect as holding the annual meetings. These documents can be used only when the corporate bylaws authorize the corporation to use written consents in lieu of holding annual meetings.

h. Are the corporate annual statements filed with the applicable state agency each year? Starting with the year of incorporation, the corporation must file an annual statement with the Secretary of State setting forth the names and addresses of its officers, directors, and other valuable information. Each year thereafter, the annual statement must be filed by the end of the calendar month of the anniversary date of incorporation. If the statement is not filed on a timely basis, the corporation may be suspended and a fine may be imposed.

The corporation generally receives this statement directly from the Secretary of State. All you need to do is fill in the requested information and forward a copy of the statement to the Secretary of State with the required filing fee. If you have not filed the annual statements, start doing so this year and make it a practice to continue to file annually in the future because if the corporation is suspended it will be unable to defend itself if presented with a lawsuit.

i. Has the corporation obtained its Federal Employer Identification Number? Corporations are required to obtain a Federal Employer Identification Number. See Proprietorship section above for details. In addition to the categories listed in the Proprietorship section, if you are forming a corporation, even if it does not have employees, it must obtain a FEIN. (See Form No. 9 in Section III for an example of a FEIN application.)

j. Has the corporation applied for a Business License? Same as Proprietorship section.

k. Has the corporation obtained a Resale Permit? Same as Proprietorship section.

l. Has the corporation filed a Fictitious Business Name Statement in the county where the business is located? If the corporate name does not reflect the name that it will conduct business under, it will be required to file a Fictitious Business Name Statement. If your corporation is required to file this statement and you have not already done so, contact your county recorder's office to get instructions on filing this form. (See Form No. 8 in Section III for an example of a Fictitious Business Name Statement.)

m. If the corporation is doing business in a different state than where incorporated, has it filed for Foreign Registration in the state where it is doing business? Corporations that conduct business in a different state than where incorporated must file to operate their business in that "foreign" jurisdiction. (It is called "foreign" because it is outside the "domestic" jurisdiction, which is the jurisdiction where incorporated. It has nothing to do with being in a foreign country.) Failure to file as a foreign corporation means that the corporation may be exposed to a penalty for non-filing and it risks not being able to defend itself in that jurisdiction if a lawsuit is filed against it. Thus, if your corporation is incorporated in one jurisdiction but doing business in another, it is essential to file as a foreign corporation. Contact your Department of Corporations or Secretary of State and ask for instructions.

4. Prior Business Entities

a. Is the business a continuation of a previous business? If so, were the assets properly transferred to the new business? If not, the new business risks not owning the assets. It is essential that you prepare the documents necessary to transfer the assets to your new entity. Contact an attorney in your area if you need assistance. (See Form No. 4 in Section I for an example of a Transfer of Partnership Assets to a Corporation Agreement.)

B. Employment Considerations

1. Written Agreements, Handbooks, and Manuals

a. Does the company use written employment agreements? Properly drafted employment agreements are essential to reducing risks of wrongful interpretation of the employment relationship. However, one must be careful in drafting such an agreement, because a poorly drafted one could prove to be more of a liability than an asset for your company. If you have not already prepared written agreements to describe the rights and duties of both parties in the employment relationship, do so and have them reviewed by labor counsel to ensure compliance with federal and state labor laws. (See Form No's. 22 and 23 in Section I for examples of two employment agreements.)

b. Are at-will employees informed of their at-will status in a written agreement? It is essential to include at-will language in an at-will employment agreement. If you have not already prepared written agreements to describe the at-will nature of the employment relationship, do so and have it reviewed by labor counsel to ensure compliance with federal and state labor laws.

c. Does the company have a written employee handbook? A written employee handbook is essential in providing answers to questions commonly posed by employees. It is a summary of company personnel policies, benefits, and work rules and how they affect employees. However, as is the case with any written document, the handbook must be properly drafted in order to reduce risks of employment, discrimination, and wrongful termination lawsuits. If you have not already carefully prepared a written employee handbook, do so and have it reviewed by labor counsel to ensure compliance with federal and state labor laws. (See Form No. 24 in Section I for an example of what to put in your employee handbook.)

d. If so, are the terms of the handbook followed consistently on a day-to-day basis? Any written document which is not followed is not only useless, it may be construed against the employer and increase risks of litigation. If you are not following your handbook on a consistent basis, start doing so immediately to reduce risks of litigation against your company.

e. Are employees required to sign a statement acknowledging that they received the handbook? Requiring the signature of employees to indicate that they have received the employee handbook disputes confusion of receipt later on. Also, without such an acknowledgement in an at-will situation, courts have held that the agreement was not "integrated" (complete) and therefore, they allowed oral evidence to dispute the at-will nature of the employment relationship. If you have not already done so, incorporate such a requirement in your procedures.

f. Does the company have a written policies and procedures manual? A written policies and procedures manual is essential to convey to employees how the company should be operated. It is a summary of company policies and procedures and how each affects employees. However, as the case with any written document, the manual must be properly drafted to reduce risks of litigation for the company. If you have not already prepared a written manual, do so and have it reviewed by labor counsel to ensure compliance with federal and state labor laws.

g. If so, are the terms of the policies and procedures manual followed day-by-day? Any written document which is not followed is not only useless, it may be construed against the employer and increase the risks of costly litigation. If you have not already done so, make sure to consistently follow all written terms outlined in the manual.

h. Are employees required to sign a statement acknowledging that they received the manual and agree to its terms? Requiring the signature of employees to indicate that they have received the employee manual disputes confusion of receipt later on. If you are not already doing so, incorporate such a requirement in your procedures.

i. Are employees with access to company trade secrets or confidential information required to sign Confidentiality Agreements? Requiring employees to sign a Confidentiality Agreement assists in preserving the confidentiality of your business. It further provides you with contractual rights if the employee breaches the contract and discloses or uses company information to your company's detriment. If you are not already doing so, start using this type of agreement. (See Form No. 17 in Section I for an example of a Non-Disclosure—Non-Competition—Non-Circumvention Agreement.)

j. Does the company have agreements with employees regarding the ownership of ideas and inventions developed by them in the course of their employment? A company whose industry involves the possible inventions of products and devices, like tools, computer programs, and computer hardware should have an agreement with his/her employees covering ownership of the inventions. This agreement should include an assignment of the rights of the invention to the company. Additionally, the agreement should be prepared and executed at the onset of the employment relationship. Otherwise, the company may incur ownership challenges over those inventions.

Before preparing such an agreement, make sure that the invention should be covered by that arrangement, because sometimes a company is not entitled to ownership of employee inventions. These times are when the employee invention is: 1) created on the employee's own time; 2) with the employee's own equipment and supplies; 3) not incorporating any trade secrets belonging to the company; 4) not a byproduct of the company's business or likely to be invented for the company business; and 5) not a derivative of any work performed by the employee for the company. (See Form No. 16 in Section I for an example of an Employee Confidentiality and Invention Assignment Agreement.

k. Does the company have agreements restricting employees from working for competitors after leaving the company? Many Confidentiality Agreements contain restrictive clauses known as non-compete clauses. These take the form of an employee's promise that he/she will not engage in certain specified competitive activities after the employment relationship ends. Generally, these non-compete clauses are unenforceable unless the company can show that the conduct of the former employee is restrainable under unfair competition laws. A company cannot prevent former employees from using the general skill, experience, and knowledge that they learn on the job. If you require employees to sign non-compete agreement, you should seek the advice of legal counsel to determine if these agreements will survive a legal challenge.

2. Equal Employment Opportunity

a. Does the company have any pending EEO-type complaints? It is essential that the company follow EEOC requirements. If you are not familiar with such federal and state requirements, it is critical that you investigate to determine what they are and take action to follow them precisely.

b. Does the company use standard forms and procedures for interviewing, hiring, and firing? Requiring management to use standard forms and comply with standard procedures in all employment areas reduces the risks of a discrimination, wrongful termination, or other employment related lawsuits later on. If you are not already doing so, implement such procedures immediately.

c. If yes, have the forms and written policies been reviewed by legal counsel? Improperly drafted documents and faulty written policies could hurt a company more than not having any written policies. To prevent your good intentions from becoming a detriment to your business, have all written documents and policies reviewed by legal counsel experienced in such areas.

d. Does the company prepare and keep on file written employee performance reviews? Some attorneys and business owners are in favor of written performance reviews and others are against them. Proponents say that if prepared and used consistently, performance reviews enhance the employee's moral and productivity. Opponents say too many employers are not consistent in their actions regarding performance reviews and, therefore, will be haunted by the written document later on.

e. Does the company prepare and consistently use written employee warnings? Some attorneys and business owners are in favor of written warnings and others are against them. Proponents say that if prepared and used on a consistent basis, written warnings can be an asset in the event of a wrongful termination lawsuit later on. Opponents say too many employers are not consistent in their actions and because such warnings are not used consistently, they will do more damage to the company than if the company did nothing at all.

f. If yes, have such documents and policies been reviewed by legal counsel? This is essential to reducing risks of litigation because of improper drafting.

3. Labor Regulations

a-c. Is the company operating in compliance with the Fair Labor Standards Act provisions for equal pay and hours, the Americans with Disabilities Act, and the Family Leave Act and corresponding state laws? It is essential that the company follow the Fair Labor Standards Act, Americans with Disabilities Act, and Family Leave Act requirements. If you are not familiar with such federal and comparable state requirements, it is critical that you investigate to determine what they are and take the necessary steps to ensure compliance.

d. Do company pension plans comply with Internal Revenue Service and ERISA? It is essential that the company's pension plan comply with IRS and ERISA requirements. Otherwise, the company or company personnel may not qualify for certain benefits. If you are not familiar with such requirements, it is critical that you investigate to determine what they are and take the necessary steps to ensure compliance.

e. Does the company have any potential or outstanding workers' compensation claims? Such claims will cause your company's insurance premiums to be increased. Take action to reduce the possibility of future claims by reviewing your safety policies and by making changes where needed.

4. Employee vs. Independent Contractor

a. Does the company use the services of independent contractors for consulting services or supplemental labor? If the company hires an independent contractor, it will not have to pay social security tax, federal or state unemployment tax, or workers' compensation for that person. The independent contractor will pay his/her own self-employment tax and the employer will be relieved from withholding income and payroll taxes. This is very favorable for most employers, and for this reason the IRS scrutinizes independent contractor relationships very carefully to determine if the relationship should be reclassified as an employer-employee relationship. (To deter misclassifying an employee as an independent contractor, review the IRS factors listed in Form No. 10 in Section III.)

b. If so, are the agreements with contractors in writing? As is the case with any written document, the written word sets forth the terms of the relationship and thus, reduces the chances of misinterpretation later on. However, as with all written agreements, the independent contractor agreement must be properly drafted to reduce risks of litigation. If you have not already prepared a written agreement for your contractors, do so and have it reviewed by legal counsel to reduce the risks of any challenges with the relationship.

c. If the company hires independent contractors, has it checked the Internal Revenue Service factors to make sure they will not be misclassified as employees by the IRS? The IRS uses 20 factors to determine whether a worker is an employee or independent contractor. These factors are listed in Form No. 10 in Section III or they can be obtained from any IRS office. If you are contemplating hiring independent contractors you should peruse this form before doing so. You should also contact your state taxing authority and workers' compensation board because they use factors of their own and you need to consider their factors as well.

C. Goods and Distribution

1. Pricing and General Distribution

a. Does the company sell from a price list? Selling from a price list reduces the chances for insiders to give away or sell company goods and services at a drastically reduced price. If the company does not have such a list, you should take the steps necessary to create one and implement using it immediately.

b. Does the company sell through distributors or independent sales representatives? The benefit of using outside salespersons is that the company will not have to keep them on the payroll and thus will save on employee-related benefits and costs. The downside to hiring outside sales representatives is that the company does not have as much control over them and therefore may not get the company's desired or anticipated results.

c. Does the company have written distribution or sales representative agreements with these individuals? As mentioned, the written word sets forth the terms of the relationship and, thus, reduces the chances of misinterpretation later on. However, as also mentioned, the distribution or sales representative agreements must be properly drafted to reduce risks of litigation and damages to the company. If you have not already prepared written agreements for your distributors and sales representatives, do so and have them reviewed by legal counsel to ensure they are properly drafted.

d. Does the company have any agreements for international distribution? If the company has agreements for international distribution, it must consider the laws in the countries of distribution. Not doing so increases risks of loss of ownership and loss of goods. The company must also assure compliance with customs for importing or exporting materials or products. If you have not taken the steps necessary to protect your international distributions, do so now before you suffer a loss.

e. Have both the domestic and international agreements been reviewed by legal counsel? As mentioned, this is critical to reducing your risks of suffering a loss.

2. Product Safety and Warranties

a. Is someone at the company familiar with product safety and government standards in your industry? If you are not familiar with safety standards in your industry, the company could be blind-sided with a lawsuit regarding the very same issues. It is imperative to educate yourself and bring the company into compliance on these matters.

b. Does the company have written policies and procedures for personnel to voice product safety concerns? It is a good idea to provide an outlet for employees and personnel to voice their safety concerns. Having such a policy reduces the likelihood of litigation against the company for safety violations.

c. Has the company received any product safety complaints or notices from personnel? If the company has been warned about the lack of safety of its products or policies, you have waited too long to change company procedures. Make the necessary changes immediately to reduce your risks of damages or litigation.

d. Does the company offer consumer product warranties? This is a technical area of the law and should be reviewed by legal counsel to reduce the risks of litigation.

3. Confidentiality

a. Has the company taken the steps to assure confidentiality of new products while they are being developed? Company employees and contractors should be required to sign Confidentiality Agreements to reduce the risks of disclosure of information on new products. (See Form No. 16 in Section I for an example of a Confidentiality Agreement.)

b. Have procedures and agreements regarding trade secrets been reviewed by legal counsel? For the same reasons as previously mentioned, this is essential to reducing risks of loss to the company.

4. Copyright, Trademark, Patent, and Trade Secret Protection

a. Have copyright registrations been obtained for company-owned works of authorship? If the company is the author of original works created by its employees, and if these works are eligible for copyright protection, they should be registered with the Copyright Office. Otherwise, the company risks not being able to enforce its rights as the copyright owner and it may even lose some benefits associated with the works. If you have not already done so, take the steps necessary to register all of your copyrightable works. (See Form No's. 1, 2, 3, and 4 in Section III for an example of the most popular categories for copyright registration.)

b. Have trademark registrations been obtained for company names and marks? If the company does not register its trademarks and service marks with the appropriate trademark registry, it cannot avail itself of certain trademark laws and benefits, and it may lose the right to exclusively use those marks in certain areas and to prevent others from infringing on them. If you have not already done so, take the steps necessary to register all of your trademarks and service marks with the appropriate trademark registry. (See Form No's. 5 and 6 in Section III for an example of a U.S. trademark application and Illinois state application.)

c. Have patents been obtained for company owned inventions, design works, and discoveries? If the company owns inventions, discoveries, or designs which are not protected by patents, the company loses its exclusive right to use those inventions, discoveries, and designs and to exclude others from doing the same. If you have not already done so, take the steps necessary to obtain a patent on your invention. (See Form No. 7 in Section III for an example of a U.S. patent application.)

d. Has a trade secret program been put into effect? Companies need to make reasonable efforts to maintain secrecy of their trade secrets. They can do this by using confidentiality agreements, informing employees, contractors, and third persons of the existence of trade secrets, limiting access to such secrets to a need-to-know basis, and controlling access to the business and facilities. If you have not already done so, create a trade secret program and implement it immediately.

e. Have intellectual property and trade secret issues been reviewed by legal counsel? This is essential to reducing the risks of improper or incorrect filings which could mean loss of intellectual property rights.

5. Advertising and Media

a. Have company advertising and copy graphics been reviewed with legal counsel? This is essential to reducing risks of litigation for false advertising, infringement, or related lawsuits.

b. Do company advertisements, marketing brochures, products, etc., prominently display registration indication marks for trademarked™ and copyrighted© materials? If you own any copyrights or trademarks, you should prominently display the respective notices on all materials to reduce risks of a claim of innocent infringement. Such a claim would reduce the amount you could receive if you prove infringement.

c. Are calls from the media regarding the company or company products promptly relayed to legal counsel? If you are not referring calls about your company or products from the media to your legal counsel, you should consider doing so to ensure that only proper disclosures are made.

d. Does the company have a written policy for employees to follow when contacted by members of the press? If you do not have a written policy for your employees to follow when the press contacts them, you could expose your company to needless challenges if an employee misquotes or provides inaccurate information. Make sure to draft and implement such a policy immediately.

D. Contracts and Leases

1. Goods

a-d. Does the company use written purchase orders, sales invoices, bills of lading, and receipts? If the company uses its own forms for the above business transactions, it can place written terms on the respective document, which are beneficial to the company. If the company conducts business without using written documents for the above transactions, it will either not have written proof in the event of a later challenge to the transaction, or it will end up using the other party's forms, which could possibly contain terms that are in the company's detriment. If you don't already use such forms, incorporate them into your systems now.

2. Relationships

a-h. Does the company use written sales, license, royalty, distribution, employment, work-made-for-hire, consultant, contractor, or confidentiality agreements? As mentioned, with all written agreements, the agreements must be properly drafted to reduce risks of litigation. If you have not already prepared written agreements for these business relationships, do so and have them reviewed by legal counsel to ensure that they have been properly drafted.

3. Equipment and Property Leases

a-c. Is the company a party to a lease? If your company is in business for any length of time, chances are it is a party to a lease. Generally, leases are drafted in such a way that they are one-sided in favor of the lessor or landlord. If your company is the lessee or tenant in the leasing situation, be sure to read the terms of the lease very carefully to ensure that you are not obligating your company to live up to onerous terms which cannot be met. If your company has already signed an onerous lease, try to negotiate more favorable terms when the lease period ends.

d. Are the company owners required to sign any personal guarantees in any leasing situation? If the company is operating as a corporation, the owners may be requested to sign a personal guaranty of the lease. If you are asked to do this, this make sure that you agree with its terms before signing, because you are placing your personal assets at risk in the event the corporation cannot live up to its obligations under the terms of the lease. If you must sign, try to negotiate a cap on your liability.

E. Regulatory Compliance

1. Occupational Safety and Health Act (OSHA)

a. Is the company in compliance with OSHA and the applicable state safety requirements? Your company must follow OSHA and your state's safety requirements. If you are not familiar with these requirements, it is critical that you investigate them to determine what steps you need to take to ensure compliance.

2. Environmental Protection Act (EPA)

a. Has the company considered any potential EPA-type or other hazardous materials problems? Your company must follow EPA and hazardous materials requirements. If you are not familiar with these requirements in your area, it is critical that you investigate them to determine what steps you need to take to ensure compliance.

b. If yes, have such matters been reviewed by legal counsel? Check with legal counsel who handle these types of matters to reduce your risks of liability.

3. Permits, Zoning

a. Are the company premises and location in compliance with zoning regulations? If you are operating a home-based business, you may be violating zoning regulations. You should contact your local zoning departments to determine if your business meets your state, county, and city requirements.

b. Have permits to operate your business been obtained? If you have not already done so, you should contact your local municipal departments to determine if you have the necessary permits to operate your business as required by the municipalities.

F. Insurance and Pension

1. Insurance Concerns

a-k. Answers to Insurance Questions. Check with your insurance agent regarding your company's insurance needs. You may want to inquire about the benefits of general and special liability policies, key man insurance, business interruption insurance, board of director's insurance, and disability insurance to name a few.

2. Pension Concerns

a-c. Answers to Pension Questions. Check with your financial planner regarding your IRA, KEOGH, 401(k), or other retirement plans, and stock ownership or deferred compensation plans.

G. Financial and Security Matters

1. Financial Concerns

a. Does the company own any assets which are subject to a security interest? If the company owns assets which are subject to a security interest, it means that the person or company holding the interest has a claim to those assets, and the company is restricted with what it can do with them and it cannot sell them.

b. Has the company recorded UCC statements to protect its ownership in assets? If the company has a security interest in an asset, it should record a UCC statement with the proper state agency to protect its interest in that asset. Otherwise, if someone else obtains an interest in that asset and perfects his/her interest by filing a UCC statement, he/she will have priority over your company regarding that asset. (See Form No's. 12 and 13 in Section III for examples of UCC-1 and UCC-3 statements.)

c. Does the company have pending collection matters? If your company allows its accounts receivable to become more than 45 to 60 days old, it is possible and even probable that you will not collect a good percentage of your receivables. If you fit this category, immediately review your company's collection policies and make changes to ensure earlier collection.

d. Are all company financial transactions recorded on corporate books in accordance with generally accepted accounting principles? Retain an accountant to handle your company's books and records and make sure that he/she follows generally accepted accounting principles in performing all accounting tasks.

2. Securities Concerns

a. Has the company stock been issued in compliance with securities laws or exemptions? Stock is considered a "security." Whenever a transaction involves a security, federal and state securities requirements must be met. When a security is offered or sold, the issuer (which is the corporation) must comply with registration and possible prospectus requirements. Compliance is costly, both in time and fees. However, failure to comply may be more costly in damages assessed against the corporation or in disqualifications from future transactions. In some cases, securities are exempt from the above requirements. If you have not already done so, you need to investigate to determine if the corporation's securities transactions are exempt or need to be registered with the Securities Exchange Commission and/or applicable state securities agencies.

b. Have company securities transactions been reviewed by legal counsel experienced in securities laws? Securities laws are complex and must be strictly adhered to. If you have not already done so, you should check with securities counsel to ensure compliance with all applicable securities laws.

H. Miscellaneous

1. Record Keeping

a. Does the company have a written records retention policy? Your company is required by law to keep certain documents for various lengths of time. If you do not know which documents your company is required to keep, you should seek legal counsel and implement a records retention policy to keep only those documents for the required length of time.

b. If yes, are records maintained by the company in accordance with the policy? A records retention policy cannot be effective if not followed. If you have not already done so, implement such a policy for your company and ensure that it is properly followed by everyone in your company.

c. Are company records in storage kept in an orderly fashion to permit retrieval or destruction in accordance with the records retention policy? To facilitate finding documents that could assist you in the event your company is involved in litigation, it is essential that all documents be listed and organized in an orderly fashion.

2. Litigation

a. Has the company received any threats of lawsuits? If your company has any hints of brewing litigation, it is best to retain litigation counsel as soon as possible to assist in mitigating the possible damages.

b. Is the company currently involved in litigation? If your company is involved in current litigation, it is best to take the affirmative steps necessary to review and amend company policies and procedures which led up to the litigation to prevent or reduce the chances of the same issues occurring in the future.

Appendix

Telephone numbers of 50 State Agencies and the District of Columbia. Contact the agency listed below for incorporating and trademark information and forms for the state in which you plan to do business:

ALABAMA	(334) 242-5324 (Corporations); (334) 242-5325 (Trademarks)
ALASKA	(907) 465-2530 (Corporations & Trademarks)
ARIZONA	(602) 542-3135 (Corporations); (602) 542-6187 (Trademarks)
ARKANSAS	(501) 682-3425 (Corporations); (501) 682-3405 (Trademarks)
CALIFORNIA	(916) 657-5448 (Corporations); (916) 653-4984 (Trademarks)
COLORADO	(303) 894-2251 (Corporations); (303) 894-2200 (Trademarks)
CONNECTICUT	(203) 566-8570 (Corporations); (203) 566-1721 (Trademarks); (203) 556-3216 (Application Form Orders)
DELAWARE	(302) 739-4111 (Secretary of State); (302) 739-3073 (Corporations & Trademarks)
DISTRICT OF COLUMBIA	(202) 727-7278 (Corporations)
FLORIDA	(904) 487-6052 (Corporations); (904) 487-6051 (Trademarks)
GEORGIA	(404) 656-2817 (Corporations & Trademarks)
HAWAII	(808) 586-2727 (General)
IDAHO	(208) 334-2301 (Corporations); (208) 334-2300 (Trademarks)
ILLINOIS	(217) 782-7880 (Corporations); (217) 524-0400 (Trademarks)
INDIANA	(317) 232-6576 (Corporations); (317) 232-6540 (Trademarks)
IOWA	(515) 281-5204 (Secretary of State)
KANSAS	(913) 296-4564 (Corporations); (913) 296-4565 (Trademarks)
KENTUCKY	(502) 564-2848 (Corporations & Trademarks)
LOUISIANA	(504) 922-1000 (Secretary of State); 925-4704 (Corporations & Trademarks)
MAINE	(207) 287-4195 (Corporations & Trademarks)
MARYLAND	(410) 225-1340 or 225-1330 (Corporations); (410) 974-5531 (Trademarks)
MASSACHUSETTS	(617) 727-2850 (Secretary of State); (617) 727-9640 (Corporations); (617) 727-8329 (Trademarks)

MICHIGAN	(517) 322-1166 (Secretary of State); (517) 334-6302 (Corporations); (517) 334-8106 (Trademarks)
MINNESOTA	(612) 296-2803 (Secretary of State)
MISSISSIPPI	(601) 359-1333 (Secretary of State)
MISSOURI	(314) 340-7490 (Corporations and Trademarks)
MONTANA	(406) 444-3665 (Corporations & Trademarks)
NEBRASKA	(402) 471-4079 (Corporations & Trademarks)
NEVADA	(702) 687-5203 (Secretary of State)
NEW HAMPSHIRE	(603) 271-3244 (Corporations & Trademarks)
NEW JERSEY	(609) 984-1900 (Secretary of State); (609) 530-6431 (Corporations); (609) 530-6422 (Trademarks)
NEW MEXICO	(505) 827-4509 (Corporations); (505) 827-3600 (Trademarks)
NEW YORK	(518) 473-2492 (Corporations); (518) 474-4770 (Trademarks)
NORTH CAROLINA	(919) 733-4201 (Corporations); (919) 733-4129 (Trademarks)
NORTH DAKOTA	(701) 328-4284 (Corporations)
OHIO	(614) 466-4980 (Secretary of State); (614) 466-3910 (Corporations); (614) 466-2295 (Trademarks)
OKLAHOMA	(405) 521-3911 (Secretary of State)
OREGON	(503) 986-2200 (Corporations); (503) 986-2228 (Trademarks)
PENNSYLVANIA	(717) 787-1057 (Corporations & Trademarks)
RHODE ISLAND	(401) 277-3040 (Secretary of State); (401) 277-3040 (Corporations); (401) 277-1487 (Trademarks)
SOUTH CAROLINA	Forms sold through Kitco (800) 351-1244; (605) 773-4845 (Corporations); (605) 773-5666 (Trademarks)
SOUTH DAKOTA	(605) 773-4845 (Secretary of State); (605) 773-4845 (Corporations); (605) 773-5666 (Trademarks)
TENNESSEE	(615) 741-0537 (Secretary of State); (615) 741-0531 (Trademarks)
TEXAS	(512) 463-5555 (Corporations); (512) 463-5576 (Trademarks)
UTAH	(801) 530-4849 (Corporations & Trademarks)
VERMONT	(802) 828-2386 (Corporations); (802) 828-2387 (Trademarks)
VIRGINIA	(804) 371-9733 (Corporations & Trademarks)
WASHINGTON	(360) 753-7115 (Corporations); (360) 753-7120 (Trademarks)
WEST VIRGINIA	(304) 558-8000 (Corporations & Trademarks)
WISCONSIN	(608) 266-3590 (Corporations); (608) 266-5653 (Trademarks)
WYOMING	(307) 777-7311 (Corporations & Trademarks)